Christine Burns MBE has campaigned for a quarter of a century for the civil rights of transgender people, and has been involved with the trans community for more than forty years. She has worked as an equalities consultant, helped to put together new employment legislation and the Gender Recognition Act, and wrote the first ever official guidance about trans people for the Department of Health. She lives in Manchester.

Fishing for Birds
Pressing Matters
Making Equality Work (with Shahnaz Ali and Loren Grant)

TRANS BRITAIN
OUR JOURNEY
FROM THE SHADOWS

EDITED BY **CHRISTINE BURNS**

unbound

First published in 2018
This paperback edition first published in 2019

Unbound
6th Floor Mutual House, 70 Conduit Street, London W1S 2GF

www.unbound.com

Text Design by Ellipsis

A CIP record for this book is available from the British Library

ISBN 978-1-78352-844-8 (trade pbk)
ISBN 978-1-78352-471-6 (trade hbk)
ISBN 978-1-78352-470-9 (ebook)
ISBN 978-1-78352-472-3 (limited edition)

Printed and bound in Great Britain by Clays Ltd, Elcograf S.p.A.

5 7 9 8 6 4

To Mermaids

Mermaids is the only charity in Britain specifically focused on supporting whole families with a transgender child. Established in 1995, the organisation has always been parent led, and does vital educational and support work.

This is a book largely about the lives of adult transgender people. But many (if not all) grown-up trans people have a story to tell about their youth – usually involving the fear of expressing who they were and the negative and irreversible bodily changes that they have had to deal with as a result of going through the wrong puberty.

Our hope is for a future where another generation doesn't face that need to hide and suffer in silence, with all the lost opportunity that involves.

Never doubt that a small group of thoughtful, committed citizens can change the world; indeed, it's the only thing that ever has.

Margaret Mead, Anthropologist (1901–78)

CONTENTS

Foreword

Dr Aaron Devor has been studying and teaching about transgender topics for more than thirty-five years and holds the world's only research chair in transgender studies. He was one of the authors of versions six and seven of the World Professional Association for Transgender Health's (WPATH) *Standards of Care* and is overseeing the translation of version seven into world languages. He is a national award-winning teacher, an elected member of the elite International Academy of Sex Research, an elected Fellow of the Society for the Scientific
Study of Sexuality, and has delivered more than twenty keynote addresses to audiences around the world. He is also the author of numerous well-cited scholarly articles, and the widely acclaimed books *FTM: Female-to-Male Transsexuals in Society* (2016, 1997), Lambda Literary Awards finalist *The Transgender Archives: Foundations for the Future* (2014), and *Gender Blending: Confronting the Limits of Duality* (1989). Dr Devor, an out trans man, is the founder and academic director of the world's largest transgender archives, a former dean of graduate studies (2002–12) and a professor of sociology at the University of Victoria in British Columbia, Canada.

As Christine Burns has so aptly pointed out in this book, with all the media attention these days, it would be easy to be fooled into thinking that trans and non-binary people just appeared on the scene in the past few years. After all, it is almost impossible to look at any kind of media today and not see stories about trans and non-binary lives. Increasingly, commentators are working hard to be fair and accurate – even as there is still a long way to go – and more and more of them are trans and non-binary people themselves. However, as Christine illustrates in her introduction, the reality is that people who we would today think of as trans or gender non-binary have been around as long as we have been human (and probably even before that).

As the world's only holder of a chair in transgender studies, the founder and academic director of the world's largest transgender archives at the University of Victoria in British Columbia, Canada, and someone who has been around trans communities for more than thirty-five years, I know a very different reality. I know it from my own experiences as a gender nonconforming youth and adult, from countless hours spent with other trans people learning their stories from them, as a trans man, and from the history held in the extensive holdings of the Transgender Archives.

I'm old enough to remember when it was illegal to be LGBT, and queer was still a word that people spat at you because they either knew that you were gay, or they thought you were queer because of the way you spoke, dressed or acted. Back then, there were transvestites, drag queens (drag kings were unknown even to most gay people) and transsexuals – everything was very binary. As is so eloquently told by the narrators in part one, this was a time when everyone who was not straight (sexually or genderwise) lived in fear and, when they had the courage and the resources to seek out likeminded souls, gathered together in dark, hidden, out of the way places.

For trans and non-binary people of this era, locating others like themselves was fraught with possibilities for public disgrace and punishment. The overwhelming reality for trans and non-binary people, until the Internet changed it all, was profound isolation, secrecy, silence and shame. As you will read in the first-person accounts in this volume, pretty much every trans person over a certain age went through years, if not decades, of feeling that they were the only ones in the whole world who felt the way that they did; that they were unimaginable freaks for whom there were no respectable words or names. When they were unable, or unwilling, to hide their differences, the consequences were often dire: rejection by family and friends; loss of employment and housing; rejection by religious communities, social services and medical providers; incarceration in jails and mental hospitals; forced medication and electroshock; rapes; beatings; murder. There were no legal protections. There were no social support networks to speak of until the first pioneers started to band together into support groups in the late 1960s and early 1970s.

Winning legal rights and social recognition required people to come together for more than individual support; they needed to build on the help they received from their peers, and the occasional cisgender (non-trans) allies, and create common cause for change. That activism, spearheaded by groups like Press for Change, took incredible courage, perseverance and just plain hard work in pre-Internet and pre-mobile phone days, when communications were much slower and more costly than they are today. At less than 1 per cent of the population, trans and non-binary people are few in number. This is compounded by the fact that many of us are unrecognisable as trans or non-binary unless we say something to identify ourselves as such. In the days before the Internet, this combined with immense social stigma, harsh laws, physical dangers and limited communications options meant that we had enormous obstacles to finding one another. Networking could only be done through face-to-face meetings, postal mail or telephone communications. However, travel was beyond many trans people's budgets, and telephone communications were much more cumbersome, less private and more expensive than today. Radio and television broadcasts, print newspapers and magazines, and film were the main forms of public media; printing your own materials was costly and required specialised equipment. The media was in the hands of a few powerful agencies. Trans and non-binary people's platforms for speaking for themselves were extremely limited.

Nonetheless, trans people did what needed to be done, as is so vividly recounted by the voices in part two, 'Activism'. Multiple organisations worked together to change laws and open up social possibilities that a generation before were almost unimaginable. Letters and broadsides were written and distributed. Meetings were held with key decision-makers. Much lobbying was done. Demonstrations were held. Songs were sung. Documentaries were made. People told their stories and became real in the eyes of the public. Small steps in the 1970s built into significant momentum in the 1980s and 1990s. Milestone advances were won with the passage of the Sex Discrimination (Gender Reassignment) Regulations (1999) and the Gender Recognition Act (2004).

Laws, although essential, are not enough. Policies also need(ed) to be adjusted. Social attitudes and beliefs need(ed) to be brought into the twenty-first century. The Internet has been a great boon to the new generation who have taken up the cause as the pioneers are ageing and in need of successors. In the final section of *Trans Britain* we hear from some of the young people who came of age during a time when almost everything you needed to know about being trans or non-binary was a few clicks away, when anyone with access to the Internet could find others like them easily. Spared from extended periods of ignorance and isolation, they are ready and eager to do what it takes to claim lives of dignity for trans and non-binary people. As they do so, we will see the gender spectrum continue to diversify away from a forced binary into a more natural (statistically) 'normal' distribution (better known as a bell curve).

Trans Britain is, in many ways, a breathtaking story of courage and determination. It is told largely through the authentic voices of the people who were there, risking so very much, so that the rest of us could live safely and with some modicum of dignity and pride. It is a specific set of stories, told by a carefully selected group of people, representing a particular time and place. However, the arc of change described here is universal. Individuals finding and supporting each other, community building, activism for change, a new generation rising to new challenges: if you have ever worked to repair your world, you will see your own story here too. These are stories that need to be told, that need to be remembered. We need them to know who we are, where we came from. We need them to know where to go next. And we need them so that we can say *thank you* to the people who gave so much so that we can just be ourselves.

Aaron H. Devor, Ph.D., FSSS, FSTLHE
Chair in Transgender Studies
Founder and Academic Director, the Transgender Archives
Professor, Sociology Department
University of Victoria, Canada

July 2017

A Beginner's Glossary

Trans / transgender: The preferred current-day adjectives used to describe anyone whose gender identity and/or presentation does not align stereotypically with the gender assigned to them at birth. These are broad 'umbrella' terms which encompass all more specific words for gender non-conformity including (but not limited to) transsexual people, non-binary or genderqueer people and those who cross-dress. The word 'trans' was introduced in Britain during the second half of the nineties and was promoted by activists at that time to replace words such as 'transsexual', which were seen as more problematic. 'Transgender' has a longer history and the meaning attached to it has become less specific since being coined in the 1960s.

Cross-dresser / transvestite: 'Cross-dresser' is nowadays considered a more polite way of referring to people who episodically adopt the dress of the opposite sex for relaxation or pleasure. People who cross-dress normally identify with the gender assigned to them at birth and have no desire to change more permanently. In the 1970s and earlier, the only two terms (besides 'drag') in common use were 'transvestite' (TV) and 'transsexual' (TS) – clearly distinguished by the permanency of the role change and how the person involved saw themselves. The origin of the term 'transvestite' is attributed to the Berlin-based clinician Magnus Hirschfeld, who first used it as a clinical descriptor in 1910.

Transsexual: 'Transsexual' is a clinical term used to describe people who specifically seek to change their gender on a permanent basis from that which was assigned to them at birth. It is partly attributed to Magnus Hirschfeld ('transsexualismus' – 1923) but credit is also due to American surgeon David Caldwell, who created the anglicised form in 1950. It was then popularised by the psychiatrist Harry Benjamin, regarded as the father of modern clinical treatment for trans people. Some people reject the term because of its medical origin but it is the most unambiguous way of describing people on the grounds of the permanence of their transition. Transsexual people may or may not seek hormonal treatment and/or 'gender reassignment' or 'gender affirming' surgeries. People who dislike the term will generally use trans or transgender as a synonym. Historically 'transsexual' was used by clinicians and commentators as a noun; however that usage is strongly deprecated by trans people, who prefer it to be used as an adjective. The arguments are similar to the reason 'black' is deprecated as a noun.

Introduction

The Visible Tipping Point

The year 2015 was described by American *Vogue* magazine as 'the year of trans visibility'. Around the world a tiny minority, whose media coverage had been historically confined to tabloid tales of shock and titillation, seemed to have gone seriously mainstream.

In the United States every age group appeared to be included. At one extreme sixty-seven-year-old Caitlyn Jenner's 'coming out' as trans was a global news story. Jenner, famous as an Olympic gold-winning decathlete and the head of the Kardashian family, was the highest profile person known to have changed gender in America in popular memory – at least since former GI Christine Jorgensen was revealed to the world. The *New York Daily News* had broken *that* landmark story in December 1952, under the front-page headline 'Ex-GI Becomes Blonde Bombshell'. During the intervening sixty years there had been stories of others, of course, but none so big, so global.

At the other end of the age spectrum, trans teenager Jazz Jennings – with a 2011 documentary and children's book already to her credit – won a deal in March 2015 to appear in a series of commercials promoting a facial cleanser for pharmaceuticals giant Johnson and Johnson. Cable TV channel TLC also began screening her reality show *I Am Jazz*. That a big corporate advertiser should use Jennings as an ambassador for their product spoke volumes.

The same year Laverne Cox, co-starring in the popular Netflix series *Orange Is the New Black*, was named one of the world's most beautiful women by *People* magazine. Amazon,

1

meanwhile, was heavily promoting Golden Globe and Emmy award-winning comedy-drama *Transparent*, starring non-trans actor Jeffrey Tambor as an elderly patriarch beginning the change from man to woman surrounded by their family. As is the norm these days, such cultural events weren't confined to North America. These shows were watched and discussed in many countries with satellite TV or streaming video services.

The surge didn't actually start in 2015. *Orange Is the New Black* first streamed to viewers worldwide back in July 2013 and, by May 2014, *Time* magazine was featuring Cox on their cover, the editors declaring all this visibility to represent a 'trans tipping point'.

It also wasn't just about television. American magazine editor Janet Mock's 2014 autobiography *Redefining Realness* was a bestseller after she revealed herself to be trans, and her book helped create the conversations which brought more American trans people to public notice. Mock's controversial televised interviews about being trans, with high-profile interviewers such as Katie Couric and Oprah Winfrey, created what were dubbed by Couric as 'teachable moments' from inappropriate questioning, whilst a subsequent car-crash interview with Piers Morgan hammered those lessons home, as he stubbornly failed to acknowledge the points being made. From Hollywood, meanwhile, there was *The Danish Girl* starring Eddie Redmayne – a period piece about one of the trans community's key historical figures, Lily Elbe – feeding a growing public debate about whether the parts of trans people should be played by trans actors.

Fashion and modelling had a part to play too. In May 2015 Yugoslavian trans model Andreja Pejić became the first openly transgender model profiled by *Vogue*, following in the footsteps of previous generations of beautiful transgender women like Britons Caroline Cossey and April Ashley. However, whereas Cossey and Ashley's modelling careers were destroyed twenty years apart by salacious tabloid revelations of their trans backgrounds in the *News of the World* (Cossey, 1981) and the *Sunday People* (Ashley, 1961), Pejić and others were positively in demand for their exotic appeal and versatility. That year *Allure* magazine profiled 'Eight Transgender Models You Need to Know', including (alongside Pejić) Geena Rocero, Carmen Carrera, Lea T (raised in Italy), Hari Nef, Isis King and Ines Rau (from France). Aydian Dowling, also on that list of eight, became the first trans man to be featured on the cover of *Men's Health* magazine, underscoring the point that people cross the gender divide in both directions. Hari Nef later became the first trans woman to grace the cover of *Elle* in the UK.

Visibility begets more visibility. By 2017 Nepalese transgender model Anjali Lama was the talk of the Indian catwalk shows and the *New York Times* was reporting on a new wave of agencies specialising in transgender models. Yet whilst media and fashion celebrity are important cultural forces, helping to determine what constitutes the zeitgeist, the majority of trans people pursue more sedate careers and are thus less likely to be seen. Nevertheless, the wave of international interest was opening up interest in some of them too.

In Australia, former senior army officer Cate McGregor was establishing herself as a very articulate voice; she was named Queenslander of the Year and became a finalist for 2016 Australian of the Year. New Zealand had even had the world's first transgender Member of Parliament, Georgina Beyer, between 1999 and her retirement in 2007. Everywhere you looked there were beautiful, successful and articulate trans people in the public eye, putting forward the case for transgender equality. Yet a backlash was perhaps inevitable, with fundamentalist Christian think tanks and law firms in the United States advancing state-by-state attempts to make it difficult for trans adults and youth to go about their lives safely. The focus of these actions was to try and make it illegal for transgender people to use the public toilets in which they would be safest – so-called 'bathroom bills' – on the pretext of protecting cisgender (non-trans) people from a non-existent peril. If you can't use public toilets safely then your freedom of movement in society is seriously affected. The backlash is very much ongoing as this book goes to press.

Britain had a part to play too during this dramatic upsurge in visibility. As in the rest of the world it began on television and in the print media – both areas that had hitherto been relative no-go areas for trans people speaking for themselves. But we can also trace the development back further.

In 2010 the *Guardian* was the first national newspaper in the UK to feature a series written by a trans person about trans issues. 'A Transgender Journey', in the paper's online 'Life and Style' section, was a high-profile series by writer and historian Juliet Jacques, writing philosophically and practically about the issues surrounding her transition to womanhood. The series progressively taught readers about the realities of a complex process only previously tackled in confessional or scandalous exposé formats by the country's tabloid newspapers. A vigorous cultural debate raged among readers 'below the line' after each new instalment was published. The following year broadcaster Channel 4 signed a memorandum of understanding with campaign group Trans Media Watch, formally marking the beginning of a turn within British media organisations towards thinking actively about how they represent trans people. One of the fruits of that was the groundbreaking fly-on-the-wall documentary *My Transsexual Summer*. Fox Fisher, one of those featured in the series, writes in chapter 18 about the work that grew out of that exposure.

In 2013 the *Independent on Sunday*'s annual 'Pink List' of the country's leading LGBT figures placed trans journalist Paris

Lees in the top spot, along with a hugely increased number of trans people across the other ninety-nine positions. Two years previously there had been very few trans figures in the list – that was how fast things were moving. Lees was suddenly guesting on the BBC's flagship political debate show *Question Time* and later *Newsnight*. New writing and broadcasting opportunities soon followed.

Next came trans people from other high-profile walks of life. In 2014 the boxing promoter Francis 'Frank' Maloney (under threat of being outed by the tabloids) went ahead and announced publicly that they would henceforth be a woman, Kellie. That same year a nationally successful independent radio DJ revealed on BBC 5 Live that they intended to transition and become Stephanie. What would once have been a career-ending move became now just a minor career break, with a reborn Stephanie Hirst soon returning to host popular shows on BBC local radio. Fittingly, Stephanie rounds off the contributions to this book in chapter 19.

In TV drama, British producers took their cue from the United States, persuaded and helped by new and effective lobby groups and outreach projects like All About Trans, which focused on improving British media representation of trans people. The long running soap *Coronation Street* had featured a trans character, Hayley Cropper, since 1997 – played by cisgender (non-trans) actress Julie Hesmondhalgh. That character had a fictional death in 2014, bowing out just as a new wave of trans actors were seeing their first opportunity to play trans characters themselves.

Hollyoaks and *EastEnders* picked up where *Coronation Street* had left off, the latter by putting a trans man, Riley Carter Millington, on screen at the end of 2015. ('Trans man' refers to someone who was assigned female at birth but later 'transitions' to live as a man.) *Hollyoaks*, meanwhile, took on established trans actress Annie Wallace for a permanent role. In chapter 10 Annie examines the phenomenon of trans people in the media in more detail.

The following year trans performers moved into comedy too, with the debut of BBC Two's specially commissioned series *Boy Meets Girl*, starring Rebecca Root. Even quiz shows got the transgender touch: Kellie Maloney and Rebecca Root both had recent appearances on celebrity editions of BBC's *Mastermind*, whilst others began competing on shows such as *Pointless* and *University Challenge*.

And then there was politics. In 1994 trans activist Mark Rees (see chapter 7) appeared to have been the first 'out' trans man to be elected as a local councillor, representing the Liberal Democrats in Kent. But later we learned that Mark was not the first elected trans candidate. Militant Tendency activist Rachael Webb, who became a councillor in Lambeth during the early eighties, may be the one to hold that title – at least until another is unearthed. By the noughties, however, trans local council candidates were almost routine, with fourteen unbroken years of at least one electoral success for an increasing number of candidates between 2000 and 2014. The bigger prize to aim for by then was a seat in the Westminster elections. Liberal Democrat activist and candidate Zoe O'Connell, who tracks these things, reported four trans parliamentary candidates in 2015: Charlie Kiss and Stella Gardiner (both Green), Emily Brothers (contesting Sutton and Cheam for Labour) and Zoe herself as the Liberal Democrat candidate in Maldon. None of these candidates won a Westminster seat that year, but O'Connell took a seat on Cambridge City Council instead.

By the time of Theresa May's snap general election in 2017 there were no fewer than nine trans parliamentary candidates: Helen Belcher, Charley Hasted and Zoe O'Connell (Liberal Democrat); Sophie Cook and Heather Peto (Labour); and

Aimee Challenor, Andrew Creak, Dom Horsman and Lee-Anne Lawrance (Green). Nobody won a seat but three of the candidates achieved very respectable second places, showing that their trans status didn't worry the electorate or the parties selecting them.

We must also not forget the trans candidates who may not have chosen to be 'out' when running or serving – and it can happen. The trans background of UKIP MEP Nikki Sinclaire, who served in Brussels from 2009 to 2014, was never mentioned when in office, but she was outed after standing down. All of this makes it increasingly likely that Britain will eventually elect an 'out' trans candidate to Parliament, joining New Zealand (Georgina Beyer), Italy (Vladimir Luxuria) and Poland (Anna Grodzka) as countries to have achieved that trans emancipation milestone.

With all of this exposure it was perhaps inevitable that some commentators would decide that the apparently sudden visibility of trans people everywhere was evidence of some kind of 'fad'. Such an assertion is risible of course – less of a mere misapprehension, more a case of studied ignorance. If trans people in Britain were some sort of 'overnight phenomenon' then it was a long night, lasting generations. A fad would have disappeared by now; fads have a short half-life in our novelty-obsessed media. Fads have shallow roots, like fancy flowers that bloom once spectacularly and then die back completely. The roots of trans people's journey into public consciousness were sown long ago. They reach deep and they have been growing for decades. That is what this book is about.

> 2015 shouldn't be remembered as the year that trans people caught up in the race for media attention – it was the year the media caught up to the work that trans people have been doing for decades.
>
> Kaite Welsh, *Daily Telegraph*, 31 December 2015

It Was a Long Night

It is difficult to say with any certainty where to pin the start of trans history. Labelling figures from antiquity with modern terms such as 'transgender' is a dangerous thing. People living hundreds of years ago couldn't have 'identified' with such a term because it didn't exist. We rely on the co-evolution of identities and the words available to describe them in order to provide the script for how to interpret our feelings and possibilities – the things we can be and embrace. What we can look for, however, are behaviours identified by ancient documents and historical analyses which provide the evidence for people living life in ways that apparently departed from a simple binary man-woman model of life. Those exist throughout recorded history and across cultures.

In his 1979 book *Dressing Up*, journalist Peter Ackroyd charts the evidence from anthropologists and social historians involving ancient cultures from around the world. He quotes the sociologist Edvard Westermarck (1862–1939), who declared in 1917 that, 'In nearly every part of North America there seem to have been, since ancient times, men dressing themselves in the clothes and performing the functions of women.'

These phenomena are not limited to one part of the world – they appear seemingly everywhere. The Indian subcontinent has an ancient tradition of the *hijra* caste and Pakistan *khawaja sira*. Samoa has the *fa'afafine*, Thailand *kathoey*, Brazil *cudinas*, Hawaii *mahu* and Tahiti *mahoos*. The Inuit people have the third sex category of *itijjuaq*. Indeed, third and multiple gender categories are quite commonplace outside of the West. The idea of gender being strictly binary – restricted to just men and women as very separate categories – seems to be a peculiar exception that grew up in Western Christian culture in the last two thousand years, rather than the universal truth it is commonly supposed to be.

Russian-born anthropologist Vladimir Bogoraz (1865–1936) lived among the Chukchi people of Siberia from 1890 to 1908 and describes no fewer than seven gender categories besides 'man' and 'woman'. In comparison, the modern Western concept of non-binary identity (see chapter 15) seems rather late to the party.

You don't have to go that far to find cultural evidence of humanity's far-from-binary gender history. Rabbi Elliot Kukla lists no fewer than six gender categories in classical Jewish texts such as the Torah: *zachar* (male), *nekeva* (female), *androgynos* (having both male and female characteristics), *tumtum* (a person whose sexual characteristics are indeterminate), *ay'lonit* and *saris* (people who are identified one way at birth but who develop the characteristics of the opposite sex later). Admittedly, this sounds more like a detailed understanding of what we nowadays call intersex conditions rather than transgender identities, but it puts to shame our own culture's attempts to erase intersex people from contemporary visibility and shows that 'ancient' is not 'unsophisticated'.

Closer to the present time we see more specific instances of gender variance even within British and European culture. Charles-Geneviève-Louis-Auguste-André-Timothée d'Éon de Beaumont (1728–1810) – commonly known as the Chevalier d'Éon – is perhaps the most widely known gender transgressor in modern history. D'Éon lived publicly as a man and pursued masculine occupations for his first forty-nine years, although an androgynous appearance greatly facilitated a 1756 spying mission where he successfully infiltrated the court of the Empress Elizabeth of Russia as a woman. For the latter thirty-three years of life d'Éon lived permanently as a woman – the classic definition of what we would now term trans or transgender – and claimed that she had been assigned this way at birth but had needed to present formerly as a man for reasons of inheritance. Inevitably the 'true' nature of the Chevalier's sex became a hotly debated topic in British society. Large bets were placed on one possibility or the other in her later years. A cutting from the *Chester Chronicle* documents the mission to settle all bets with an autopsy after she died.

Intersex is a modern clinical term used for a whole range of naturally occurring differences in sexual characteristics that occur in humans and other mammals. Some of these differences are immediately visible, leading to accounts of so-called 'hermaphrodites' in many ancient societies. The classic idea of a hermaphrodite as someone possessing a full set of both male and female genitalia is relatively rare, but there are many other ways in which people's genitals, internal sexual organs, chromosomes and biochemistry can differ from the two commonly expected patterns for male and female, resulting in dozens of different ways to be human. Add together those individually rare ways for people to be different and you end up with an overall phenomenon that accounts for more than 1 per cent of the population. Intersex conditions are therefore quite common, but the reason you might not have heard about them is the actions typically taken by doctors to 'normalise' babies and young children. It is those actions which give rise to an increasingly vocal lobby of intersex campaigners, angry about things done without their consent and the lies told to them as children. The history of intersex people is separate from that of trans people and there are different issues driving their activism. Nevertheless there are interests in common too. Some trans people have physical intersex traits. Some intersex people wanting to reverse the sex assignment imposed on them as babies find themselves going through the same medical transition process as other trans people. It's a complex area with overlaps and shades of grey.

CHEVALIER D'EON.

The *Gazette de Sante*, or Gazette of Health, published in Paris by a society of Physicians, contains, on the Chevalier D'Eon, some curious particulars.—The Paris Physicians—after very properly premising, that to ascertain the identity of the individual beyond the possibility of a doubt, is was necessary that the Physician who generously attended D'Eon, as a *woman*, during his last years, should ascertain at his death that the very same individual was a man—pay high and deserved compliments to Pere Elizée, who was the only Gentleman of the faculty in that situation ; and who called for a meeting of Surgeons to inspect and open the body. After stating, from their own knowledge, the respectability of that Gentleman, who was known to them in Paris as being at the head of the *Hospice de la Charité*, and successor to the celebrated *Frère Come;* they proceed to state the report of Mr. Copeland, who performed the operation in his presence, and in that of several illustrious and professional characters. They add afterwards the following particulars :—

" It is singular enough that while all Europe was making a woman of that dubious character, there existed in Paris many unimpeachable witnesses who would have vouched for his manhood long before it was put in question. We have had the following details from M. le Baron de Cleybrocke, who has authorised us to publish them.

British Newspaper Archive

From the *Chester Chronicle*, 2 November 1810. Doctors set out to answer through a post mortem whether the Chevalier d'Éon was genitally male or female.

The case of the Chevalier d'Éon (who inspired the naming of the transgender Beaumont Society in 1966) was not an isolated instance. Some of the richest sources of evidence from the Victorian era are newspaper, police and court records. It was a period when all forms of cross-dressing were somewhat frowned upon. As-yet-unpublished research by writer and historian Juliet Jacques includes an 1859 inquest on fifty-year-old labourer Harry Stokes, who had married a woman and worked for thirty to forty years as a bricklayer. The autopsy revealed he had female genitals. In a similar and better-known case in 1865 the surgeon James Barry was found, after death, to have been female-bodied. In cases like this there is sometimes dispute over whether the individual should be claimed as a feminist icon (switching gender to access professions and benefits closed to women) or a lesbian heroine (switching to legitimise a same-sex relationship) or indeed a transgender pioneer. In truth we can never be entirely sure – the best guide is to see how people like this lived the totality of their lives, beyond mere appearances. The point here is not to claim one person or another as a trans historical figure but to underline that gender crossing has a lengthy history, even in Britain.

Moving into the early twentieth century there was a much clearer and more documented effort to investigate and understand gender-crossers. In 1910 Berlin-based clinician Magnus Hirschfeld published *Transvestites: The Erotic Drive to Cross-Dress*, thus coining the term long used for people who episodically cross-dress. Hirschfeld's Institute for Sexual Science, founded in 1919, was very much a centre for research in this field. It was where pioneering surgical techniques were devised which would help trans people of that time achieve physical transition from one gender to the other. This is what led to the famous surgical reassignment of Danish painter Lili Elbe in 1931, although her surgery was not actually the first. That credit appears to go to Alan Hart (1890–1962), an Oregon physician and trans man, who underwent hysterectomy and gonadectomy in the United States in 1917 to facilitate living for the rest of his life as a man. Hart incidentally went on to pioneer the use of X-rays in diagnosing tuberculosis, thereby saving thousands of lives.

Magnus Hirschfeld's *Institut für Sexualwissenschaft* was pillaged by the Nazis in 1933. The photograph of books being burned on a huge pyre is iconic; few realise, however, that much of that work going up in flames was the first systematic research into helping trans people and other sexual minorities. Genderqueer activist, musician and writer CN Lester, in their book *Trans Like Me* says, 'The destruction ... set the emerging LGBT rights movement back by decades ... the drives – legal, social, scientific – towards investigation, knowledge and compassionate acceptance were erased.'

Public domain

Nazis burn Magnus Hirschfeld's work in 1933.

There are many more documented cases, besides those of Lili Elbe and Alan Hart, during the first half of the twentieth century. In 1932 Colonel Sir Victor Barker's Brighton marriage to Elfrida Howard was annulled upon discovery that he was born female. That same year the *News of the World* reported an 'amazing change of sex' involving a person from Sussex who apparently went from Margery to Maurice.

On 11 September 1933, the *Dundee Evening Telegraph* reported the case of Mark Woods (born Mary), who claimed to have spontaneously begun to change sex at the age of eighteen. In fact truly spontaneous changes of sex don't happen in humans. The phenomenon occurs in some other species like fish but, in humans, alleged cases are more likely linked to one or other of the myriad physical intersex conditions with which people can be born. Even that isn't certain as an explanation, however: as we'll see shortly, a couple of documented cases underline that claims of an intersex diagnosis were sometimes employed to justify carrying out early gender reassignment surgeries when these were still medically frowned upon.

WOMAN'S PHYSICAL TRANSFORMATION

Starting Life Afresh as a Man

A remarkable case of physical transformation in a woman has been revealed. Madeline Mary Woods, daughter of a Gosport naval hospital worker, who for 28 years lived as a woman is now starting life afresh as Mark Woods, a man.

At Thornton Heath, where he is staying with friends, Mark Woods related to a reporter last night the story of his amazing change of sex. "I first noticed the change in my sex," he said, "ten years ago when I was a girl of 18, working as a nurse.

Eventually a specialist advised me to change into man's attire. I opened a small cake business in Wokingham. A man promised me financial support which did not materialise. I had only a capital of twopence, and I was arrested for debt and sent to Holloway prison for a month.

"The prison medical authorities said I could not go on living as a woman. Ten days after I came out of prison in January I changed into men's clothes.

"Since I have changed I have found life much easier," Madge Woods added. "My whole outlook is entirely masculine."

D.C. Thompson & Co Ltd

The matter-of-fact reporting of Mark Woods changing gender in 1933.

In 1936, the *Portsmouth Evening News* reported another case: that of Mark Weston of Plymouth who, unlike Colonel Barker, went on to marry a childhood friend, Miss Alberta Bray, apparently without legal incident. What is so interesting about this period in British history is that so many cases involved people going from female to male and that, by and large, the press were curious but not scandalised. That attitude was to change twenty years later. Journalist Jane Fae discusses the evolving role of the press in chapter 9. But, certainly during the thirties and forties, gender changing in Britain seemed to be fairly unremarkable, albeit quite rare.

MAN, ONCE GIRL, WEDS FRIEND

HE WAS FORMERLY WOMAN ATHLETE

Mr. Mark Weston, of Oreston, near Plymouth, formerly a woman athlete, who changed her sex from woman to man recently, has secretly married a girl friend.

Mr. Weston was formerly Miss Mary Edith Louise Weston. His bride is Miss Alberta Bray.

He says, "She is a girl in a million. Through all the anxious years of my change from 1928 to the actual operations in May this year Miss Bray was a real friend. We were friends as girls."

The wedding took place at Plymouth Registry Office. The new Mrs. Weston is in her early twenties.

Johnston Press Plc

Mark Weston reported by the *Portsmouth Evening News* in August 1936.

The next interesting case began in the same era and involved the daughter of the heir to the baronetcy of Lismullen. The story of Michael Dillon (1915–62), who transitioned to male in 1942, has been especially well documented by the journalist and writer Liz Hodgkinson in her book *From a Girl to a Man*, based on Dillon's own unpublished autobiography and (in the 2015 edition) a treasure trove of letters and documents donated by another trans pioneer, Roberta Cowell. It is through this work that we obtain a detailed picture of the effort required by people in that era to find a surgeon willing to help them. We also discover the white lies that were necessary to avoid the surgeon's censure by the General Medical Council.

Dillon, who underwent a complete bilateral mastectomy in 1942 and then a series of genital transformation surgeries by pioneering plastic surgeon Sir Harold Gillies in 1945, used the pretext of a supposed intersex condition to protect Gillies. He also managed to get his birth certificate altered in 1942 –

a practice that subsequently became closed to trans people for thirty-five years after an infamous legal case in 1970. What's more, he even got his degree records at Oxford changed in order to avoid the embarrassment of having attended an all-women college (St Anne's). Again, it was amazing how accommodating administrators and officials could be in that era – especially if you had the right class background.

Just to underline that issue of class, there is also the case of Ewan Forbes-Sempill, another child of Britain's titled aristocracy. On 22 September 1952, *Time* magazine reported on a paid advertisement in the previous week's *Aberdeen Press and Journal*, announcing that 'Dr E. Forbes-Sempill, Brux Lodge, Alford wishes to intimate that in future he will be known as Dr Ewan Forbes-Sempill. All legal formalities have been completed.' But what the advertisement hadn't made clear, and which *Time*'s British stringers had spotted, was that the good doctor's former name had been the Hon. *Elizabeth* Forbes-Sempill, second daughter of the 18th Baron Sempill. The story didn't appear to spread in the UK – no doubt helped by the sealing of all the records by Scotland's officials. Discussion of the case was even prohibited by the judge hearing the 1969 divorce case of April Ashley, greatly disappointing her legal team, who wanted to point to it as an example of precedent for official recognition of gender change. It's clear that you could achieve a lot in terms of changing official status in the forties and fifties if you had the right background. Indeed, if changing status from female to male you could even put yourself in line to inherit hereditary titles.

Being an aristocrat also had a downside, though, as Michael Dillon was to discover. Whilst updating his own records he had been careless. He assumed that, after successfully requesting a discreet change to his details in *Debrett's*, the rival *Burke's Peerage* would automatically follow suit. They didn't, however.

And it was the disparity between those two entries that led to him being outed by the *Sunday Express* in 1958, whilst he was travelling the world as a ship's physician. The trauma of his outing drove Michael to seek a new life as the first Western man to be ordained as a Tibetan monk. He died not long afterwards, in 1962.

Hodgkinson's research also reveals the hitherto unappreciated relationship between Dillon and another British trans pioneer, Roberta Cowell (1918–2011). Dillon was for a time romantically obsessed by Cowell (she spurned his advances) and he even had a hand in carrying out a highly dubious kitchen-table surgery on Cowell to help build the case to persuade Sir Harold Gillies to complete the rest for her in 1951.

Roberta Cowell is generally recognised as the first of the modern-era British male to female transsexual women, but her fame was somewhat eclipsed by the much bigger international story of a former American GI, Christine Jorgensen (1926–89), whose physical transformation was carried out by surgeons in Denmark at about the same time. Roberta's story was further eclipsed when Michael Dillon was outed in 1958 and the *Sunday People* exposed another of their contemporaries, April Ashley, in November 1961 under the headline 'The Extraordinary Case of Top Model April Ashley – Her Secret Is Out'. These outings of Ashley and Dillon were to create the mould for how British trans people were to be treated by the press for another fifty years. The fear of being outed drove the pursuit of legal protection for privacy later in the nineties.

And so the story of pioneers, document changes and press exposures brings us to the mission of this book.

The thing that unites every one of the cases described in these last few pages, going back a century, was that trans people in those days were out on their own. There was no easy way to find information or role models. The lucky ones – for we only usually hear their stories – somehow found a way to obtain help with their passionate desire to change their gender. Adrienne Nash, in chapter 1, recounts her personal story of what it was like if your background was more ordinary than (say) Dillon, Cowell or Forbes-Sempill's. The determined few would seek out surgeons – whether in Harley Street or Casablanca – get fixed and then try to settle down and disappear. Indeed, the cooperation of pioneering surgeons like Gillies was contingent on that assumption: that the patients would melt back into society. We know that during the sixties people changing their birth registration were marrying and settling down – the case of Georgina Somerset (1923–2013, neé George Edwin Turtle) being a classic example.

So how did things come to evolve? There must be something that accounts for the change between then – when solitary individuals sought out help for themselves, often in secret – and now, as a visible, organised, networked community of people have 'suddenly' become a global phenomenon.

That 'something' was the emergence, during the 1960s, of the concept of community between trans people – the formation of support organisations and safe meeting spaces where people could get together, realise they weren't alone, discover what they had in common, and learn to help each other. It is from that watershed advance that everything else in the last fifty years has flowed.

First support, later activism: that is where the real story of 'Trans Britain' lies, and where our long journey from darkness, isolation and fear truly began.

ROBERTA
COWELL'S
OWN STORY

1947 *Bob Cowell, ex-R.A.F. fighter pilot and well-known racing driver, husband and father* **1954** *Roberta Cowell, now a modern young woman and a potential wife*

ONLY Roberta Cowell herself, now a young woman of 35, can tell the story of what it felt like to be Robert Cowell, the 23-year-old Spitfire pilot—and to be Bob Cowell, the well-known racing motorist who "seemed to disappear" in 1948.

The extraordinary truth is that, three years after Bob Cowell disappeared, Roberta Cowell appeared. Bob, the young man who had been a husband and the father of two children, became Roberta, a sensitive young woman — and a potential wife.

This was a change so complete and total that it is considered unique in human history.

Only Roberta Cowell herself can tell the story.

Only in PICTURE POST can you read Roberta Cowell's own story.

only in—

OUT TODAY 4d

Johnson Press Plc cx BNA

The serialised story of Roberta Cowell in the *Picture Post*, as advertised in the *Yorkshire Post* and *Leeds Intelligencer* in March 1954.

Christine Burns

The National Transgender Remembrance Memorial is located in a shaded corner of Sackville Gardens in the Canal Street district of Manchester. Carved from a single piece of sycamore, the monument stands twelve feet tall. Originally planned as simply a trans memorial for Manchester, it soon became evident that this was going to be the first such monument nationally in the UK and therefore, by default, the National Transgender Remembrance Memorial. As a community facing escalating global violence, including hundreds of unsolved murders, trans people around the world remember their dead at ceremonies held on 20 November every year.

Part One
Survival

My childhood was spent every evening praying that God would put right this terrible mistake and that the following morning I would wake up a proper girl.

Carol Steele, chapter 3

Is There Anyone Else Like Me?

The sixties began in much the same way as the fifties had ended as far as trans people were concerned. It was a time when the chances are that a person feeling like Michael Dillon or Roberta Cowell might not even know there were other people like themselves.

There was no Internet. There was nowhere to find out information, unless you had access to a medical library. What you found in such a library would not be very encouraging. Biographies about trans people were many years away. *Conundrum*, the first British mainstream trans autobiography, by historian and writer Jan Morris, would not appear until 1974. The most likely way for a newcomer to hear about trans people before that was through the salacious revelations that were becoming the stock-in-trade of the popular Sunday newspapers. The outing of Michael Dillon in 1958 had been pursued without any regard to the effect that it might have upon him, or anyone like him. The same was true when April Ashley's story was splashed across a front page in 1961.

Not every newspaper story in those days was an 'outing'. It is said that Roberta Cowell sold her story to the *Picture Post* in March 1954 to derive some income for herself – perhaps noting how Christine Jorgensen was monetising her status over in the United States. That is far from the norm, however. 'Outing' is more commonplace, and if the choice is between being splashed without consent or agreeing to cooperate, exert a little influence over the copy and be paid, most people would probably cut their losses. What we do know is that such stories were not one-offs. In what looks like a 'me too' story, the *Sunday People* were advertising in January 1955 a confessional feature about someone called Liz Wind.

32 years a male—25 years a female

MY LIFE AS MAN *and* WOMAN

For 25 years, Elizabeth (ex Adolf) Wind has kept a terrible secret—the most astounding case of sex-change fully authenticated by doctors.

But at last the story of the only human being who has lived for more than a quarter of a century as a man, and a quarter of a century as a woman, can be told.

It is an amazing tale—for Wind, when a man, married and became a father! What happened when the change took place is one of the strangest, most intriguing true-life stories of all time.

LYNDOE

urges you to meet the **CHALLENGE OF THE STARS**

The world's greatest astrologer brings you new light on the role of the stars in your life—learns behind popular astrology's "do's" and "don'ts"—and shows you how to take positive decisive action—to mould your own destiny for the better!

A New PEOPLE Series

READ IT ALL—EXCLUSIVELY IN

THE PEOPLE

ON SUNDAY

Johnson Press Plc ex BNA

'Me too' for the *Sunday People*? An advertisement from January 1955 for a newspaper feature bearing a strong resemblance to the *Picture Post*'s story about Roberta Cowell.

If you harboured trans feelings in the fifties and early sixties, this was the most accessible way you could possibly find out that there was anyone else remotely similar. And it wasn't high-quality information. Roberta Cowell had constructed a fiction about her background – the claim that she had been born with a physical intersex condition – in order to enable Sir Harold Gillies to operate on her without censure. The claim also played a part in her bid to have her birth certificate altered. Michael Dillon's clinical history was portrayed in a similar way. Those transitions reported in the 1930s – Mark Weston and Mark Woods, for instance – were reported as magically spontaneous natural changes of sex. And if you clung on to every breathless word about April Ashley in the Sunday papers then you would have been led to believe that in order to pursue gender reassignment surgery without the supposed hand of God then you would have to get a plane ticket to Casablanca. Even a decade later, in Jan Morris's 1974 autobiography, that was the clear implication.

This was also a world where homosexuality was still completely illegal, and trans people – whether occasional cross-dressers or those who fitted the clinical definition of transsexual – were seen as a sort of subcategory.

The Sexual Offences Act was passed in 1967 after lengthy and tortuous public and parliamentary debate. The act legalised homosexual contact between two men over the age of twenty-one in private, although Stonewall co-founder Lord Michael Cashman CBE has pointed out how, in practice, the early years after that act was passed saw anyone perceived as gay being harassed *more* rather than less. James Anderton, who served as chief constable of Greater Manchester from 1976 to 1991, was notorious for policies that seemed to target the city's sexual minorities – cross-dressers and transsexual people included. In the 1980s he famously accused homosexuals, drug addicts and prostitutes – all part of the HIV/AIDS epidemic – of 'swirling in a human cesspit of their own making'. The words were not directly aimed at cross-dressers or transsexuals, but the general perception that such people were gay or otherwise seeking men for paid sex meant that trans people throughout that era perceived that the threat applied to them too. A common assumption about transsexual women at that time was that they transitioned just in order to access sex with men. Even some gay men bought into that narrative in those days, deciding that trans women were simply gay men who had gone too far or were looking to make their desire for men more acceptable.

Incidentally, the lumping together of transvestites (episodic cross-dressers) and transsexual people (permanent transitioners) may offend some trans readers. Many transsexual people have spent their lives trying to explain to strangers that these two like-sounding terms for superficially similar people mean a world of difference – even though trans people of all stripes would at one time casually use the expression 'transvestites and transsexuals' (TV/TS in the vernacular) as though it were a single concept.

An American medical textbook from 1960. A note on the rear cover apparently instructs that this was 'only to be sold to members of the medical profession'. The book is ostensibly about cross-dressing but the author casually labels many obviously transsexual women as 'Professional Female Impersonators' and reduces discussion of transsexualism as a distinct phenomenon to a seven-page chapter.

This book is mostly about the people who change permanently, but we have to talk about cross-dressers too – not only because they are part of the 'trans umbrella' but also because the two were deeply co-dependent for a while. Also, some transsexual people pass through a period of experimentation to find who they really are. Trying out the possibility that you might be happy just cross-dressing now and then sounds a whole lot less frightening than acknowledging the need to permanently transition. It's only through experimentation in that way that some people may arrive at the conclusion that there really is no alternative to transitioning permanently.

The main point about the early sixties was that trans people had nowhere of their own to go; nothing of theirs to belong to. If they wanted somewhere safe – transvestite or transsexual – then the only places available were those where the gays and lesbians and drag queens hung out. Some people were happy with that, some were not.

Dr Tracie O'Keefe is a lesbian transsexual woman who remembers that period well. She would later go on to marry her cisgender (non-trans) female partner Katrina in 1998 – an officially sanctioned same-sex marriage – because, even though she had transitioned almost thirty years earlier in 1970, the law at that time still regarded her as a man. In the sixties she liked to party:

> In the late sixties we used to go to a pub in Peckham that had drag shows. I remember going there on the back of my boyfriend's Lambretta at fourteen years old with my feather cut hair do and my Parka coat thinking I was way cool. We would also go to the Black Cap pub in Camden town. With enough make-up I could pass for older. They had the funniest drag in London, with Jean Fredricks and Mrs Shufflewick.

However it was always tricky being trans and going into gay pubs and clubs because you knew the staff might ask you to leave at any time, telling you trans people were not allowed. In Chelsea it was safe to go to the Queen's Head – or was it the King's Head? – anyway it was full of queens. Ron Storm used to hold balls in East London in the seventies and Andrew Logan ran the Alternative Miss World too. Trans people who were part of the fashion and music set would also socialise in clubs like the Sombrero where I would go with my friend Ossie Clarke the designer in Kensington High Street. Sometimes Amanda Lear would come down. In the seventies you could go to the Vauxhall Tavern, run by a fabulous woman called Peggy who was the salt of the earth and welcomed everyone.

Partying is all very well, but sometimes people needed support and information. As we've seen, in the early sixties the only public information about trans people seemed to be in the tabloids – conveying the impression that trans people were rare, shocking and needed to go to North Africa to get their 'freakish' changes.

The first big milestone in British trans history – the spark that arguably set in motion the chain of events that led to today's very different world of confident, diverse, well-informed and articulate trans people – was when a scattered handful of pioneers came across one another and founded the first ever organisation to support and help people like themselves. And the inspiration for that came from across the Atlantic...

In the late 1950s a US pharmacist called Dr Virginia Prince (1912–2009) began a correspondence-based network for (primarily) transvestites. The organisation she set up had the trappings of a college sorority. The name Phi Pi Epsilon was the

Greek-lettered acronym for Full Personality Expression (FPE) and it was organised into geographic 'chapters'. Members of the group received a periodic magazine called *Transvestia*, first published in 1960 by Prince's own Chevalier Publications.

Prince had radical views (for the time) about her identity. She carved an alternative path between the classic understanding of transvestism and transsexualism, arguing that a person could transition permanently – live all the time as a woman, maybe even using hormones to develop breasts and curves – and yet do so without resort to genital reassignment surgery. It is not agreed whether she coined the term, but she undoubtedly popularised the word 'transgender' and it became initially attached to the idea of her middle-ground, non-operative way of transitioning. These days 'transgender' has acquired a much broader meaning and it is stressed to people seeking medical help that reassignment surgery is an option, not compulsory. The rise of a culture of non-binary expression in recent years only serves to reinforce the idea of options. Yet in the early sixties, Prince's views were not universally welcomed.

Nevertheless, it was through international distribution of Prince's magazine *Transvestia* that Phi Pi Epsilon indirectly encouraged the creation of the first support organisation for cross-dressers and transsexuals in Britain – the Beaumont Society – and, with it, sowed the seeds for a trans community where none had existed before.

Transvestia was stocked by some fringe outlets, such as London's Soho bookshops. This is how Britons came to know about it and join FPE. Four European FPE members – Alga Campbell, Alice Purnell, Sylvia Carter and someone called Giselle – met through FPE's contact system and set up a European Chapter of the American parent organisation. Later they went a step further, arranging to create a separate group, which they called the Beaumont Society (after the Chevalier d'Éon de Beaumont). They figured that this would sound innocuous to outsiders but carry meaning for those they wanted to reach.

The stated objectives of the new society, set up in 1966, were:

1. To provide information and education to the general public, the medical and legal professions on transvestism and to encourage research aimed at fuller understanding.
2. To provide transvestites with an opportunity for a social life together.

Note that these aims were couched in terms of transvestism and not transsexualism. Nevertheless, beggars can't be choosers. Transsexual people on their own were (at least initially) too small in number to support a dedicated organisation. Transvestites were much more commonplace. Besides, in practice the Beaumont Society didn't set out to turn transsexual people away – the founders seem to have been simply more afraid of frightening the wives and girlfriends of the transvestite majority. Transvestites would commonly be at pains to assure partners that their 'hobby' of dressing up didn't mean they desired or were contemplating a 'sex change'. And yet co-founder Alice Purnell was a transsexual woman, and one of the trans community's other founding figures, Stephen Whittle (a trans man, who used to babysit Purnell's children in Brighton), was very much involved alongside her in the organisation, helping to produce the group's newsletter in the seventies.

Aside from the superficial appearance of being focused on cross-dressers, the most controversial aspect of the Beaumont Society was its official attitude towards homosexuality. In a 2010 history of the Beaumont Society, Alice Purnell explains it thus: 'although we were never anti-gay, we had to exclude any hint of being a homosexual society by stating and insisting, as the membership application form demanded and sponsorship insisted, that no hint of overt gayness would be tolerated.'

Everything about the Beaumont Society was steeped in caution and paranoia, befitting the age in which it was established. To be identified as gay was to invite the attention of the authorities, before and even after the 1967 act that partially decriminalised homosexuality. And to be identified as transvestite or transsexual was to be lumped into the same basket – at least to the extent of losing your job and perhaps your family. So, everything about the young Beaumont Society was grounded in vigilance and a degree of secrecy. New faces had to be vetted and sponsored by an existing member before being invited to any face-to-face meetings. Like FPE, the organisation operated through a correspondence address: BM3084. 'BM' box addresses operated by British Monomarks were to become a staple of trans organising right up until the mid-noughties, when the Internet and social media like Facebook seemed to sweep away trans people's fears of exposure almost overnight.

The Beaumont Society rapidly grew in membership and also spun off associated groups and organisations: the Women of the Beaumont Society (WOBS) provided a focus for wives, girlfriends and other female relations of members. Then, in 1975, a separate charity was formed – the Beaumont Trust – to complement the membership organisation and support the needs of trans people and their families. The purpose of the charity (the first trans support charity in Britain) was 'to provide a caring and supportive response for the complex issues that [trans] people face'. The Trust set out to help people cope with isolation and emotional difficulties, confusion, the effects of discrimination or violence, medical and counselling needs. Recognising the sensitivity of these issues, the leadership team of the Trust was made up of physicians, nurses and Samaritan helpline volunteers, which remains a key feature of the charity even today.

This was just the beginning. The sense of community fostered by the existence of the Beaumont Society and its regional groups, coupled with the exchange of knowledge through a key conference organised in Leeds in 1974, helped to trigger more regional initiatives. In chapter 3 Carol Steele describes two of the principal meeting places of the seventies: one in Manchester and the other in London.

The 'Manchester TV/TS Group', as the name suggests, still recognised the need for cross-dressing men and transsexual women and men to work together. Set up in 1974, it met initially in the back room of a Victorian house on Camp Street in Higher Broughton, Salford, close to the Manchester city boundary. Sadly nothing remains of the house today – it was bulldozed a few years ago for major redevelopment of the area. Later, as the group grew, it moved to the modern redbrick setting of St Peter's Chaplaincy on Oxford Road in Manchester, in the middle of the city's university campus. Later still, in the second half of the eighties, the group moved to the Rembrandt Hotel on Canal Street, where in 1987 it transformed into the social and self-help group known as the Northern Concord, still in existence today.

The Rembrandt Hotel on Canal Street, Manchester, pictured in 2011 from the National Transgender Remembrance Memorial in Sackville Gardens. From the late eighties the Northern Concord group met in the first-floor function room and bar most Wednesday evenings.

Christine Burns

274 Upper Street, Islington as it is today. The 'TV/TS Support Group' which met here at weekends in the early seventies later moved to a dedicated venue at 2-4 French Place in Shoreditch.

In London, meanwhile, there was the 'TV/TS Support Group', established in 1972, which met several times a week on the premises of London Friend, at 274 Upper Street in Islington. The group, run by a charismatic and opinionated cross-dresser, Yvonne Sinclair (1934–2013), was if anything more transvestite-dominated than its Manchester counterpart. Dawn Wyvern, a regular visitor in the seventies, recalls:

London Friend was a community support venue that Yvonne Sinclair had secured for use by the TV/TS group to use on weekend nights. It had a vibrant membership and saw itself as a breakaway from the Beaumont Society, as it was not TV-heterosexual-only and accepted anyone who wished to attend. There were drag queens, TVs, TSs and 'professional boys' who posed as 'ladies of the night', admirers and supportive family members. I was quickly taken under the wing of some of the members and introduced to the full alternative London scene. This

33

was at the start of the 'New Romantic' explosion as the punk era had reached its peak, and I was just twenty-three years old. Very quickly I became part of the 'in' crowd of alternative London, receiving invites to balls at the Porchester and Tudor Lodge, attending Ron Storme's parties, clubbing at Heaven, Stallions and all the other trendy night clubs of the day, rubbing shoulders with rock stars, those on the up, DJs of the day, politicians, and people you could see in the newspaper gossip columns.

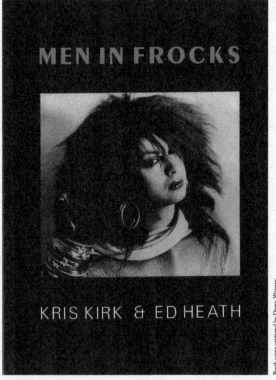

Although primarily concerned with the London drag scene, the book *Men in Frocks* (Gay Men's Publishing, 1984) didn't draw distinct lines and includes the story of the TV/TS Group in Islington and its overlap with contemporary happenings.

By the mid-seventies there were therefore several sources of support in Britain where, a decade previously, there had been none. Various regional groups of the Beaumont Society met in other towns and cities, and groups akin to the Manchester and London ones met in places like Leeds, Nottingham and Derby. As these groups reached out and were listed by the Samaritans and the early lesbian and gay help lines, it became easier for trans people to find help and community. In the seventies it was likely to be the case that a trans person would first meet someone like themselves via one of these groups.

The year 1974 saw the first National Transvestite and Transsexual Conference in Leeds, organised by the Beaumont Society. This was significant in bringing people together to learn about themselves, the law and the state of medicine in a world which didn't have the Internet.

This was also the year that saw the publication of the autobiography *Conundrum* by historian and journalist Jan Morris. It is hard to convey nowadays the importance of that book to so many people. Information about how one would set about transitioning was scarce. If you attended one of the groups mentioned above then you could learn the essentials from another transsexual person, but *Conundrum* reached out further – to the unseen population of transsexual people who had not even got that far.

Conundrum reinforced some ideas about how difficult transition would be for anyone at that time. Morris's own transformation began as a low-key affair in 1964 and reached its climax with a trip to Casablanca for surgery in 1972. But again, as with the pioneers of the forties and fifties, it is very much the tale of someone with privileges (albeit not a baronetcy in Morris's case). It was quite possible to think back then (and this writer speaks from personal experience) that transition – typified by visible role models such as April Ashley and Jan Morris – was a thing undertaken by a different and more exotic kind of person. Even the rich and poetic language of Morris's account underlines that this was maybe not something for more common mortals.

As Adrienne Nash and Stuart Lorimer explain from their different perspectives in chapters 1 and 2, treatment closer to home was already a possibility from the mid-1960s, when the psychiatrist John Randell established a clinic at the Charing Cross Hospital in London – the beginning of a service still known as 'Charing Cross' today. But, as many contributors to this book attest, Randell's approach was not everyone's cup of tea. He either liked and supported you, or he didn't. And

George and Julia (New English Library, 1980) was the book tie-in to the BBC series *A Change of Sex*, charting the transition of Julia Grant (1954–2019). As with the TV series, the book became an essential 'how-to' manual for transsexual people to plan and achieve their transition without being constrained by the NHS route. Many discovered the surgeon Michael Royle and his clinic in Hove, East Sussex, this way.

woe betide any trans person who dared assert that it was their transition and not his. To read different people's recollections you would think that John Randell was two very different men, not one.

So instead it was really a television documentary in 1979 that showed the way forward for many. As Stuart Lorimer describes in chapter 2, the BBC series *A Change of Sex* broke a wall by showing an ordinary trans person seeking – and finding – the way to achieve

The Avenue private clinic, featured in the BBC documentary *A Change of Sex*.

a transition on their own terms.

It is no accident that most of the chapters in this part of the book relate to the achievement of transition at a time when it was hard to see a way to accomplish it. Along with the establishment of a network of support groups, and a charity in the form of the Beaumont Trust, finding the ways and means to change their gender – under the NHS or via alternative routes – was an absolute priority for those driven to do so. It was all about support, both medical and social. This is also a theme illustrated by Margaret Griffiths in chapter 4, although in her case it was the later development of support for the families of trans children through the charity Mermaids.

No account of this period – from the sixties through to the late eighties and early nineties – would be complete without consideration of the soundtrack. The more you dig into the lyrics of rock and pop music, the more you are reminded that gender crossing is not the sole preserve of trans people. The public may think it is only trans people who think about gender and ambiguity, but our wider culture is steeped in it. In the 1960s female impersonator Danny La Rue was a variety star with top billing. Theatre and comedy lean heavily on gender crossing and confusion for plot lines. From Stanley Baxter and Dick Emery to the *Two Ronnies*, our national television served a regular diet of cross-dressing, albeit in a safe form, as this was 'entertainment'. But it was rock music that really pushed the envelope. So it felt appropriate to invite a trans rock musician, Kate Hutchinson, to reflect in chapter 5 on how those lyrics affected her and the rest of us.

And, finally, it's important to know that whilst many trans people have quite similar accounts for how they came to transition, they don't all follow the same script. That's why this section is rounded off by the slightly different account of a trans vicar, the Rev. Christina Beardsley, in chapter 6.

In the second part of this book we focus on what the support generation gave rise to next – the birth of trans activism – but for activism to succeed there needed to be a long period of community, support and network building first.

1

The Doctor Won't
See You Now

ADRIENNE NASH

Adrienne was born in Surrey at the beginning
of World War Two. For most of her working
life she was a civil servant. Having transitioned
in 1977, she says that the civil service was
unusually prepared to employ a trans woman
when most organisations would not. Since
retiring she has turned to writing novels – many
with trans-related themes. Besides the events
described in this chapter, Adrienne also fought
for trans women's pension rights against the
Department for Work and Pensions for thirteen years, achieving a degree of
success against a department which (in spite of the Gender Recognition Act
(2004)) seemed implacably opposed to changing its policies and compensating
trans women of her generation unable to claim their pension at the socially
expected age of sixty.

I was born in 1939 into a world at war and, after four or so
years, found myself at war with my world. I remember dreaming
before I started school that my mum's best friend, Wyn, had cut
off my penis, and feeling so pleased. Of course, in those days the
idea of a 'sex change' was unknown.

At five I went to school and found girls there. I had never
met a girl until that day and yet I identified with them rather
than the boys. I returned home and asked for a pinafore
dress. I didn't know what it was called and mother asked
me to describe it. I did. 'Only girls wear them,' she said. I

didn't realise I was a boy. I did realise that I had in some way offended.

I used to play dress-up. My favourite was a dress that mum had discarded as too small for her – a silky affair in white, black and green stripes. I kept it in my bedroom. It disappeared and I found it in what we called the rag bag, cut to pieces. I asked why but received no answer. I knew that in some way I had transgressed – that I had committed some unspeakable crime. From that time I became a secretive child, afraid to display my true feelings.

I was not a rough and tumble boy. I hated boys' ebullience in the playground: the punching, kicking and leaping upon each other and the seeming delight in hurting that they displayed.

My parents sent me to boarding school at twelve years old to toughen me up. I was completely lost, bereft. Somehow I managed to survive without overmuch bullying, but I was very unhappy and unable to concentrate. I plucked my eyebrows and stole lipsticks from shop displays. Although I dressed as a boy, grown-ups often responded to me as if I were a girl. Those occasions made my heart soar for a few minutes.

1952. Thirteen years old.

Roberta Cowell was in the newspapers in 1952, the first British transsexual to attract the ongoing attention of the press, as she used her story to derive an income. I was of course fascinated. I discussed her change with my mum. She said it was fascinating but I dared take the conversation no further. Was I like that? I hoped but didn't risk saying. Funnily enough, had my parents not thought I needed boarding school to make me tougher, I would have gone to Whitgift School in Croydon, the same establishment Roberta had attended.

I read avidly all I could. The school took, for the benefit of us boarders, the *Daily Mail* and the *Express*. They both stated that Roberta Cowell was intersex. I went to Cambridge Central

Library and looked up intersex. It was quite a long hunt. Eventually I found a definition that I seem to remember said 'having the attributes of both sexes'. I examined myself. I was no different to the other nude boys in the communal showers. I wasn't intersex.

1953. Fourteen years old.

My breasts swelled. I began to believe that maybe I *was* intersex. My breasts swelled more and were painful. I wondered: was this the deliverance I had prayed for every day in morning assembly and at every Sunday church service? I was confirmed into the Church of England and the Bishop of Ely laid his hand upon my head, but God double-crossed me. My breasts came to a halt and then retreated to nothing. I became an atheist, not because of that but for reasons of logic. I became a 'thing', an automaton almost, acting out a part. I self-harmed in the toilets or the privacy of the gardener's potting shed. I cross-dressed in clothes kept in two large cake tins that I hid under potato sacks, and then punished myself for doing so. I smoked and burnt my arms with the cigarette, and pushed needles through my skin, particularly my genitalia.

1956. Sixteen years old.

I saw my GP and told him I wanted to be a girl. I confessed to cross-dressing and said I had been out in public. He warned me that I could be arrested. He had no knowledge of what we now call transgenderism or transsexuality and could offer me nothing, but then he wouldn't have, would he? Changing sex was almost unknown at that time. The warning he gave was real. There were cases in the newspapers of men, in the vernacular of the time, 'posing as women'. These people were derided and punished by the courts, while no one cared if a woman posed as a man. I speculated why that double standard might exist.

1958. Eighteen years old.

I left school and joined the Bank of West Africa. I was still in severe anguish, training in the City of London prior to work in West Africa. Under my first business suit, I wore women's underwear. I knew it was risky but at least it made me feel slightly feminine. I loved working with girls in the office, my first real contact with women for ten years, but I wanted to be in their gang. I smiled at people a lot. I was stopped on the stairs one day and this tough-looking London boy threatened to 'fill me in' if I didn't stop smiling and talking to 'his' girls. I didn't know I was doing anything wrong; I was just reacting normally for me. Now I realise that girls smile far more than boys and hold a smile for longer. That was my natural behaviour. I saw my GP again. I requested to be referred to a psychiatrist, to someone dealing with 'sex changes'. I was referred to St Bartholomew's and walked there from my office in Gracechurch Street, in the heart of the City of London. The psychiatric department was in a sort of outhouse. I met the psychiatrist coming out. He had his cycle clips on ready to go home for lunch. He had forgotten my appointment, or maybe he considered he had no knowledge and nothing to offer me. We spoke in the open air, while he gestured with his bicycle pump. He offered group therapy. Would there be more like me? I asked. 'No, a variety of different problems,' he said. I didn't attend. What would have been the point of exchanging my shame with people possessed by entirely different devils?

1960. Twenty years old.

I attended a medical for National Service. I was in the last month of intake before National Service finished. I pointed out to the doctor as he felt my genitalia that I had always considered I was the wrong sex and I cross-dressed. He replied that lots of people do that and it was no reason to escape National Service. I said I wanted to change sex. He said it was impossible. I was terrified that, living in a barrack block, others would discover the real me and I would end up a victim of bullying or worse. At the same time I wondered what he wore under that white coat. After an appeal, I was found unfit. Meanwhile, my employers had sent me to West Africa to escape National Service. They had trained me for two years and wanted the use of their investment. I was twenty-one years and one week old when I flew to Freetown, Sierra Leone.

1961. Head Office, Freetown. Twenty-one years old.

In Freetown, my colleagues led an extreme bachelor life. They played hard and they drank hard and above all, they worked hard. I could not manage to drink more than two bottles of beer before being very ill. I had poor health in this part of Africa that used to be called the white man's grave. I was anaemic. My nose bled all one day. I pleaded to see the doctor. I had pills for anaemia, iron that gave me severe stomach cramps.

While at the army cinema watching *On the Beach*, a Stanley Kramer film, I started to shiver in the twenty-five-degree evening warmth. The boys more or less carried me to the car and tucked me up in bed on the veranda that overlooked Freetown Bay. I had dengue fever, for which there is no protection. I was nine stone but descended to seven and a half in three days. It was Independence Day for Sierra Leone. I staggered to the kitchen and found we had three American guests, naval lieutenants from a visiting American destroyer. One asked whether I was a refugee from Belsen. I was allowed four days off but the sickness left me with terrible depression. The boys got me out of it.

Management decided it was sink or swim for me. I was posted to Port Loko as the local branch manager. After three months they sent me to Pendembu. In both places I lived alone.

My staff were all African. At least I had privacy in the evening. I mail-ordered clothes from Selfridges and cross-dressed in the evening in the light provided by hissing, pressurised paraffin lamps. I cut patterns designed by me and sewed my own clothes by hand. I self-harmed again.

1962. On leave in the UK. Twenty-two years old.

I lived in four and five star hotels as a woman. I was never challenged. I spent days in London as a twenty-two-year-old girl, at the theatre or shopping. My GP referred me to a Harley Street psychiatrist. He said if I ever presented as a woman he would have me arrested. He charged £25 – roughly twice the average weekly wage. It was a complete and utter waste of time and money.

1964. On leave in the UK. Twenty-five years old.

I lived my dual life as before. I resigned from the bank due to ill health. They offered Nigeria instead. I declined. I began work as a sales rep. I still cross-dressed. I talked to my GP, a Dr O.J. Curl (deceased). He said that 'sex change' was impossible. Moreover, as a lay preacher he said it was against God's law. He quoted the Bible, Leviticus 19:28, Corinthians 6:19–20 and Deuteronomy 23:1: 'No one whose testicles are crushed or whose male organ is cut off shall enter the assembly of the Lord.'

I quoted Matthew 18:9: 'If thine eye offend thee pluck it out.' I said that all these biblical rules were open to interpretation and, in any case, what had they to do with medicine? I asked whether it was possible under his rules to amputate if one has a bad infection? He said that was different. Really? Gangrene could kill someone. This thing between my legs could kill me and it was slowly doing so.

I alternated between periods of cross-dressing and periods when I was determined to resist these illegal impulses. In the periods of denial I fell into depression until I found an opportunity to cross-dress and be my other self.

1966. Dr Curl again. Twenty-seven years old.
I was given another referral to a psychiatrist in the backwoods of Norfolk. This one suggested amateur dramatics – as though the very occasional dressing as a maid or playing the lead in *Charley's Aunt* could satisfy the demon in my soul. It merely demonstrated his lack of knowledge and understanding. I left considering suicide. I planned to drive at full speed into the brickwork of a disused railway bridge. While contemplating that and other alternatives, I sat by the shore on a cold winter's day at Weybourne and listened to the waves beating relentlessly against the shingle bank. The cold drove me to seek warmth. I went to my parents and chatted as though nothing had happened. I told Curl how I felt. He didn't take it seriously. He admitted that he and the psychiatrist had decided what to say before the consultation.

1968. Dr Curl again. Twenty-nine years old.
I felt my life was just drifting pointlessly away. Curl suggested the solution put to him by Norfolk Mental Health: that they put me to sleep for three months to 'rebalance' my mind and see whether I would 'wake up right'. They might also use ECT. Luckily I had the sense to decline. I recognised experimental treatment, even if those supposedly clever people didn't. Was there no depth psychiatry would not stoop to in the name of experimentation, I wondered?

1971. Dr Curl again. Thirty-two years old.
Curl referred me to a London psychiatrist working in Harley Street and at Charing Cross Hospital. I met Dr John Randell – soon to become a figure of fear and disdain for a generation

of transsexuals – in an unused washroom. Charing Cross was at that time opposite the eponymous railway station, just prior to the hospital's move to Fulham. Ten students sat in a semicircle. The site of my interrogation, in this white-tiled room, seemed an added threat. I imagined myself being tortured, the blood being hosed away. I told them my problem. The students laughed. Dr Randell (who died in 1982) reprimanded them. He offered his new cure, aversion therapy: showing photos of me as a woman and applying electric shocks and an emetic. I would have to supply photos of myself dressed this way. I took the photos. They told me they were very nice. I imagined them chuckling. They phoned to say they wanted more, this time of me dressed as a man. By chance I read a *Times* article that rubbished aversion therapy. I declined to attend.

I had also been referred to the care of the social services. I was shown a report written by Dr O. J. Curl. He said what I intended was against God's will and teaching. He called me 'a marine: neither soldier nor sailor; neither fish nor fowl'.

They sent me for an interview with another psychiatrist. The interview was, he admitted, a farcical waste of time. He had no experience, had read nothing and knew no one. If anything was decided by this interview, I never heard about it.

1975. Dr Curl again. Thirty-six years old.
I was near collapse. I saw my life drifting away and the future in my present state looked grey, uninviting. I was self-harming more than ever, burning myself with a cigarette and using my needle. I was referred back to Dr Randell. He was regarded by now as the guru of sex change (really the only clinician operating in a field of one).

He said, 'I offered you treatment for your obsession four years ago. You didn't take it.'

According to a paper presented by Drs Dave King and Richard Ekins at the University of Ulster Gendys conference in 2002, John Bulmer Randell was born in 1918 and trained at the Welsh National School of Medicine, from where he qualified in 1941. He was the Physician for Psychological Medicine at Charing Cross from 1950 until his sudden death from a heart attack in 1982, aged sixty-three. Figures from Randell himself indicate that he had seen 2,438 trans patients by 1980 – making him, in effect, even more experienced than the famous Harry Benjamin in New York. King and Ekins note that Randell was not at first in favour of the use of surgery for transsexual people but came around to the idea, having seen the happy outcomes for patients who had taken their own decision to go abroad. Still, surgeries were limited: in a July 1969 paper for the First International Symposium on Gender Identity in London, Randell reported a total of fifty-two surgeries by his preferred surgeon, Peter Phillip, at Charing Cross Hospital. Numbers increased during the 1970s; again Randell is himself quoted as saying there were by then over thirty a year but he also makes clear that the volume of surgeries was still but a fraction of the number of patients seen (about one-fifth).

I replied, 'Your treatment didn't work.' The students were interested and smiled. They were with me.

'That is not entirely true,' he said defensively.

'Yes it is, that's why the treatment has been discontinued.'

The students giggled. This was much better.

He sulked. He was a very sulky man. He agreed to treat me. He was lugubrious and also enjoyed his power. He always emphasised that he could continue or refuse treatment to us. His conditions and those of the NHS were demanding. I had to work as a woman and support myself. I must also remain lawful: no assaults or importuning. I must be single, so had I been married I would have had to divorce. If I complied with these conditions for at least two years I could have surgery. He wished me to see him again in three months but, by that time, I would have to fulfil the conditions and live as a woman full time. He gave me a card that said I was receiving treatment. It meant that I could avoid prosecution for 'posing'.

Today, and since 1999, demanding that I divorce as a condition of treatment would be against the Human Rights Act, but even then such a demand was against the terms of the European Convention on Human Rights signed in Rome in 1950. It breached Article 8: the Right to Family Life, but also Article 10: Freedom of Expression.

Back at the GP's I did what I should have done a long time ago. I moved to a new young doctor within the practice.

I worked to get my affairs in order. My company told me to resign, although I had just been awarded the prize for the greatest increase in turnover among 130 sales staff. By Christmas 1976 I was out of work but had begun to live full time as a woman. I was already taking the female hormone oestrogen to begin feminising my body.

1977. Thirty-seven years old.

At the end of the year I was placed on the surgical list, at number 186. At that time they were doing about one operation per week, so that was nearly four years to wait. Randell had become a disciple of 'the change' but he still believed in nurture and blamed a dominant mother. He put this theory to me, saying that he knew it to be true. 'Then why is my very masculine brother not trans?' I asked. He had no answer except to be disagreeably morose.

Randell had the idea that we transitioners from male to female should be Stepford wives, and wear only skirts, not trousers. We should acquire a boyfriend. Adele, another patient who usually saw Randell for appointments before me, had a furious row with him because she had come in a very feminine trouser suit. She refused to be browbeaten by him. I heard every word from my seat in the corridor.

Adrienne Nash on holiday in Portugal in 1995.

I started work as the lowest form of civil servant, a clerical assistant, but I was lucky to be employed at all. I was what they called 'unestablished', that is, I could be dismissed on a month's notice for any absence, such as for ill health. In civil service parlance I was considered a 'health risk' employee. Nevertheless, after two years, I became established and was promoted to clerical officer and then executive officer and, finally, higher executive officer. I suffered nineteen years of discrimination at work – the whispers and the sniggers persisting because one person from my former life had recognised me and started gossip. I was made redundant in 1996 prior to the privatisation of my agency, and haven't worked since.

2017. Seventy-eight years old.

I am a woman going on eighty. I love being 'a girl', as I told my GP today. I sincerely believe that had Dr Randell not changed horses and become a 'changer' I would not be here. Life is not ideal but I love it. I enjoy being a woman, free to express my real persona, and my psyche is at peace.

The struggle to free transsexuality from the rather lascivious coverage it receives on TV goes on, as does the fight against outmoded psychiatric theories about what causes it. The reasons for this syndrome are only partly discovered, and we need more science-based research instead of the cockeyed theories of some in the psychiatric profession. That profession has, over the twentieth century, committed many crimes, exercised dubious cures and experimented to the detriment of its patients. I feel lucky to have escaped its excesses.

2

1966 and All That: The History of Charing Cross Gender Identity Clinic

DR STUART LORIMER

Dr Stuart Lorimer graduated from the University of Aberdeen Medical School in 1993, with a distinction in psychiatry. He subsequently gained membership of the Royal College of Psychiatrists and further qualifications in both general adult and liaison psychiatry. He first began working at the Charing Cross Gender Identity Clinic in 2002 and became a full-time consultant there in 2007. He estimates that he has seen around 4,000 individual gender variant people. In 2015, he was included in the *Independent on Sunday*'s 'Rainbow List' of the most influential LGBTI people in the UK. He loves his work. His preferred pronouns are he/him/his.

25 June 1979, a comfortable house in an inner suburb of Aberdeen, and I'd suffered the indignity of being put to bed at the same time as my younger siblings. Something was up and – a more than averagely inquisitive nine-year-old – I decided that if adults wanted it kept secret, it must be a secret worth knowing.

From the stair landing, I could hear the television, volume lowered but snatches of voiceover just audible: 'sex change'. The specifics eluded me but not the accompanying whiff of taboo.

The object of my parents' hushed fascination was, I later learned, Julia Grant in BBC Two's groundbreaking documentary, *A Change of Sex*.

It's impossible to overstate the significance of *A Change of Sex* within any history of trans awareness in Britain. Jan Morris's *Conundrum* came before (1974) and April Ashley's biography after (1982) but both of these texts bore a degree of exoticism – surgery in far-off Casablanca seemed beyond the reach of ordinary mortals – whereas Julia was immediately relatable.

Certain scenes from the documentary have become notorious. In one, the psychiatrist Dr John Randell, in the style of a frosty Captain Mainwaring, interrogates Julia on the subjectivity of gender ('what does it feel like to be female?'); in another, he makes clear his displeasure that she has undergone breast surgery without his express permission.

Even allowing for the climate of seventies medicine, Randell comes across as paternalistic and petulant. Although there do exist more benign accounts – Caroline 'Tula' Cossey's experience of him was a little warmer – his onscreen brusqueness has become legendary.

When, in 2014, I had the privilege of meeting (and being rendered somewhat starstruck by) Julia herself, I wondered whether Randell had been put off by the presence of the television crew. It seemed not: she told me that, off-camera, he was even worse.

She remembered him as arrogant and all-powerful, 'like God'. On her twenty-first birthday, train delays meant Julia was fifteen minutes late for her first appointment. When she finally entered his office, Randell reacted with fury, seeming to view her lateness as a personal affront and telling her to come back 'in two or three years'. When she did return, three years later, she brought the BBC.

Following the documentaries – there were three in total, regularly repeated over the next two decades – Julia was inundated with sympathetic letters ('it was really the first time people understood our plight') and gender referrals surged.

Randell is remembered much less fondly, having struck a negative chord in the British psyche. His old-school manner was ripe for parody: as recently as 2002, *The League of Gentlemen* writers cribbed several of his lines, word-for-word, for one of their grotesques, a 'despotic GP' who forced other characters to play party games in exchange for medical remedies. Almost too close to the bone for comedy.

Crustily reactionary as he seems today, Randell was nonetheless a trailblazer, the originator, in 1966, of one of the largest and oldest trans treatment centres in the world: the NHS gender identity clinic (GIC) at Charing Cross Hospital. Rejecting the then-fashionable psychoanalytical approach as ineffective, he preferred physical treatments – hormones such as Diethylstilboestrol, an oestrogen used to treat prostate cancer, and referral (of a small minority) for surgery.

Randell's focus on the physical prefigured a more general shift in psychiatry through the seventies, a moving away from The Asylum (real and notional) and towards general medicine. He investigated his growing cohort – fifty per year in the sixties, 200 per year in the seventies – for chromosomal abnormalities, finding no one 'cause'.

Intersex conditions – where sexual or reproductive anatomy doesn't fit typical definitions of male or female – were (and are) distinct from issues related to gender identity, albeit with some degree of overlap: some of Randell's patients with gender dysphoria had coincidental intersex conditions; also, unhappily, some intersex people sought to correct surgery wrongly carried out on them as babies.

The First International Symposium on Gender Identity took place over the weekend of 25–27 July 1969 at the Piccadilly Hotel in London, just days after Apollo 11 landed on the Moon. Entry was £8. Chaired by Professor C. J. Dewhurst (Chair of Obstetrics at Queen Charlotte's Hospital), the event was apparently the first to bring together clinicians from both sides of the Atlantic to exchange knowledge about treating both transvestism and transsexualism, as they were then known. Those presenting papers included Dr Peter Scott (a consultant physician at the Maudsley Hospital), Dr John Randell (from Charing Cross Hospital), Mrs Margaret Branch (senior psychiatric social worker, Guy's Hospital) Dr Paul Fogh-Andersen (a surgeon from Denmark with first-hand experience of the Christine Jorgensen case) and, from the United States, Dr Fred Oremland (a private physician from Los Angeles), Dr Richard Green (University of California) and Dr John Money (John Hopkins Hospital, Baltimore). Attendees also included Dr Harry Benjamin, Reed Erickson and Dr Virginia Prince (the latter two being seemingly the only trans people present). The event was subtitled 'Aims, Functions and Clinical Problems of a Gender Identity Unit' and it is clear from the proceedings that one of the goals was to discuss setting up a more formal clinic in London – an idea that was opposed by Dr Scott and others. Other topics, besides the purely clinical, included the legal status of patients before and after surgery and the corresponding (still uncertain) status of clinicians treating them. The symposium took place at around the time that the April Ashley divorce case was being heard in court, so these questions were very germane. The event was sponsored jointly by the Erickson Educational Foundation (set up by millionaire American philanthropist Reed L. Erickson (1917–1992), a trans man himself) and the UK-based Albany Trust, which had (in 1967) extended its focus from homosexual welfare to include trans people.

The chromosome tests performed by Randell are no longer routine in GICs because they don't fundamentally change the plan of treatment: these days, there's a more pragmatic focus on 'What does this person need?' rather than 'What's the underlying cause?'

In 1973, the GIC took up residence in the new Charing Cross Hospital, Fulham, ushering in decades of geographical confusion. Gender conditions were then ensconced in the 'disorders of adult personality and behaviour' section of the International Classification of Diseases – arguably, a similarly confused location.

Smaller clinics came and went, in Leeds, Croydon, Manchester and Scotland, run on a part-time basis by psychiatrists, tending to peter out when those psychiatrists died, retired or were overwhelmed by work.

Charing Cross GIC continued under Randell until his unexpected death in 1982. After a brief period of limbo, it was taken over by another psychiatrist, Dr Ashley Robin, working part-time. Following Robin's death in the mid-nineties, leadership shifted to Dr Donald Montgomery, an analytically trained New Zealander who pushed to expand the service. A host of new doctors joined the clinic: Charles Mate-Kole, Alfred Hohberger, David Dalrymple (psychiatrist and brother of James Dalrymple, a surgeon who entered the field along with urological specialist Michael Royle), Russell Reid and James Barrett.

Barrett, now lead clinician of Charing Cross GIC, recalls being drawn to gender work by 'the patients… they weren't very psychiatric but needed medical things doing'. He remembers the moment when he met a former patient in the supermarket and was introduced to her partner; he was struck by the ordinariness of her circumstances ('they were basically a nice young couple') but also how completely transition had transformed her life.

Encounters with medical colleagues were less sanguine. According to Barrett, the most common assumption made of him was 'you'll be gay, then?' and he remembers medics laughing then straightening their faces and saying, 'of course, it's perfectly serious'. Among those mistakenly referred to the GIC were seemingly endless numbers of people with sexual dysfunction or gay and bisexual individuals quite happy with their sexuality.

Through the eighties, the mainstays of treatment were the oestrogen Ethinyloestradiol and the androgen Sustanon but there was no routine monitoring of blood levels or complications in general. Mental illness or learning disability often precluded referral but not always treatment. Barrett speculates that many of those diagnosed with learning disability might now be viewed as being on the autistic spectrum.

The nineties also saw the arrival of Professor Richard Green, a New Yorker with a proven record in research, a protégé of the maverick US sexologist who pioneered the whole shebang: Harry Benjamin.

German by birth, Benjamin started out renting (and sleeping in) a Manhattan consulting room in 1915. He treated – with Premarin, an oestrogen extracted from pregnant mare urine, hence the name – his first trans person in 1948. Distinguishing his patients from transvestites (a term not coined until Benjamin was twenty-five), he opened the doors of his first proper clinic in 1966, the same year as Randell's GIC at Charing Cross.

Benjamin worked with trans people throughout his life, seeing his final patient in 1986, at age 101.

On both sides of the Atlantic, the field continued to expand, referral numbers rising through the nineties. Under Major's government in the UK, the NHS was divided into regions in which local providers (the old district general hospitals) were expected to compete with each other for funds provided by another part of the NHS, the commissioners. It cost those commissioners much more to treat patients out of their own region, so many set up local gatekeeping arrangements. Some refused treatment altogether.

Although prescription fees are capped (and in some cases free) for NHS patients in Britain, the cost has to be accounted for at some point within the system. This has led to the general convention that whilst a specialist clinic or hospital consultant may be needed to make the recommendation for starting a particular medication, the patient's own general practitioner (GP) is tasked with writing out the actual prescription and monitoring the patient's health. In the case of prescribing cross-sex hormones for trans patients, however, GPs have sometimes resisted this convention, arguing that this is a specialist area of medicine for which they have no training. Their argument is bolstered by the fact that such prescribing is often 'off-label' – a term denoting that the medication concerned is not specifically licensed for use in treating a particular condition. Off-label prescribing is actually commonplace. Using drugs to treat children is essentially off-label for instance and GPs are given protocols for how to cooperate with specialist consultants so that they are supported to do so safely. For these reasons there is some scepticism surrounding the insistence by some local GPs and their NHS managers that prescribing and monitoring for trans patients should be carried out by the gender identity clinics, who would then of course bear the cost. Life-long prescribing and monitoring by gender identity clinics would also have enormous impacts for patients, who would have to travel (sometimes very long distances) to renew prescriptions and obtain blood tests that their GP could easily do close to home.

Inevitably, an increasingly organised group of trans people took legal action, and blanket bans on funding were deemed unlawful. In response, commissioners introduced 'criteria' for funding of treatment, insisting on local residency for improbable lengths of time.

The region containing Charing Cross GIC became reluctant, understandably, to fund prescribing for those living in other parts of the UK, so GP prescribing was to become the norm – in theory, anyway.

As the end of the millennium approached, leadership of Charing Cross GIC shifted from Ashley Robin via David Dalrymple to Richard Green, and the clinic's physical base moved from the hospital itself to a smaller building, the Claybrook Centre. There, it became seen as part of community psychiatry, an awkward fit for staff and patients alike, who felt less and less 'psychiatric'. There persisted at this time a perception in the wider health care Trust that the GIC was 'small', although it dealt with greater numbers than any community psychiatry team.

The year 2000 passed in a blaze of anti-climax. Treatments continued to evolve in safety and sophistication. Hormone regimes became more nuanced. Surgical teams expanded. Speech therapy was delivered in house.

In 2002, I joined Charing Cross GIC, almost by accident. At that time, one could only attend a gender clinic after seeing a general psychiatrist (these days, the GP can refer directly). As a jobbing general psych, I assessed a succession of trans people en route to the GIC. Like Barrett, I was struck by how different they seemed from my usual patients, how 'non-psychiatric'. They were essentially ordinary people caught up in extraordinary circumstances.

Intrigued, I phoned the GIC, spoke to Barrett and, before long, had my own weekly clinic there.

The start of the new millennium saw the gender field in a curious stage of development. The early pioneers – Benjamin, Randell – had practised 'off the map', according to their own individual theories and observations. But psychiatry, and medicine generally, had evolved away from such adventurism and towards standardisation.

Gender didn't (and still doesn't) fit easily into one single category but had moved, almost through a quirk of history, from being a mostly endocrine entity to becoming the province of psychiatrists. How did psychs 'steal' the field? Shifting the clinic location to Charing Cross Hospital likely played a part and the outcome of the April Ashley case in 1969–70 also arguably elevated the importance of psychiatry, as a result of the weight accorded to psychiatric evidence by the judge.

Some of this was reflected in the way conditions were classified internationally. In the US, the Diagnostic and Statistical Manual of Mental Disorders (DSM), having dropped its sexual orientation category, adopted a slew of trans-related categories instead. Suddenly, there were labels to apply and treatment pathways to follow. In practice, many of these labels and pathways mimicked the previous, abandoned approach to homosexuality in tending to pathologise that which made mainstream 'straight' society uncomfortable.

Resistance was inevitable. In 2002, only a matter of months into my new role, I attended an event at the Royal Society of Medicine: UK practitioners were attempting to define their own standards of care for treating gender dysphoria (the US had had standards of care for many years, produced by the Harry Benjamin International Gender Dysphoria Association, or HBIGDA – now known as the World Professional Association for Transgender Health, or WPATH). A protest by trans activists had ensued, in and outside the building, with several influential clinicians withdrawing their support when the proposals were explained to them by activists. The protesters' argument was that, aside from any lack of consultation with them over the guidelines, the proposals on the table were more regressive than the American standards they were intended to replace. In the end it took until 2013 for the Royal College of Psychiatrists, consulting widely, to come up with guidance which everyone – Royal Colleges and patient activists – could agree upon.

For a rookie gender psych, the event was bewildering. Trans people mingled with clinicians, and a series of spikily articulate activists asked pointed questions about patriarchy, exclusion and 'the Foucauldian concept of the clinic'. (Years later, I was befriended by the most notable interrogatrix, Claire McNab, formerly of the trans lobby group Press for Change. I can only hope we never fall out.)

I'd encountered nothing quite like this in psychiatry, nothing with this level of organisation, energy or sheer intellect. It was unfamiliar, intimidating and invigorating all at once.

Fast-forward five years to 2007 and I was in the spotlight myself, representing Charing Cross GIC in a panel discussion of trans health care, part of London's LGBT History Month events. As the (then) 'Only Gay in the GIC', I'd agreed to take part, but was secretly terrified. The chair, Dr Justin Varney, reassured me the audience would be gentle and he was right – no one asked me about Foucault. People seemed gratified by my presence, but some of their questions took me by surprise: did one have to wear a skirt to be taken seriously by the GIC? Did one have to be heterosexual? Was genital surgery compulsory? And I encountered the term 'genderqueer' for the first time. Who knew what was to grow from *that* seed!

After the LGBT History Month panel, doors began to open. Christine Burns invited me to join her rather convivial Sexual Orientation and Gender Identity Advisory Group (or, less mouth-twistingly, SOGIAG) policy workstream at the Department of Health and the less outward-looking Parliamentary Forum (see chapters 7 and 8). I travelled to Manchester to co-present a workshop as part of the 2007 LGBT

Health Summit and, as anxious keynote speaker in 2010, talked for far too long.

One of the odder events was hosted by the LGBT organisation Pink Therapy: an evening reception honouring the celebrated US gender theorist, family therapist and writer Arlene (Ari) Istar Lev. Introduced to one half of the veteran lobbying group GIRES (the Gender Identity Research and Education Society), I found myself steered bodily around the room to meet a private gender GP, Dr Richard Curtis (who seemed as nervous as myself), and a young man described to me, with ceremony, as 'trans... and *gay*', as if this were a novelty I had not encountered in my half-dozen years as a gender clinician.

Lobby groups and charities are discussed in part two of the book. The Gender Identity Research and Education Society (GIRES) was originally created in 1997 by the trans lobby organisation Press for Change as a charitable offshoot, intended to access the kinds of funding that were not available to a political activist organisation like itself. GIRES has been led, since its inception, by the non-trans husband and wife couple Bernard and Terry Reed – both awarded OBEs for their work in 2010. After more than twenty years the charity is now one of the longest-standing trans-focused organisations in Britain. The couple are pictured here at Exeter College, Oxford in 2004, along with activist Mark Rees (L).

Christine Burns

Dr Russell Reid photographed in 2004.

Finally, I was introduced to the other half of GIRES, who asked if I approved of gatekeeping hormones and surgery. I mumbled something about public sector resources being finite, meaning there would always be a need for at least some preliminary assessment, at least in the NHS. Wrong answer.

Gatekeeping – controlling and limiting access to – gender treatment is a perennially thorny topic, but it was especially so in 2007. The year before had marked the start of a General Medical Council (GMC) investigation into ex-Charing Cross psychiatrist Dr Russell Reid following allegations by his former colleagues of inappropriate prescribing in his private-sector practice. Reid was a polarising figure, popular with his patients partly because his manner was a million miles from Randell's chilly imperiousness and partly because his threshold for recommending hormones was seen as far lower than that of his NHS contemporaries.

While the specifics of his practice set him at odds with some of his professional fellows, Reid's approachability and flexibility around gatekeeping were already being echoed in a general, if gradual, softening of strictures at the GIC – a new user-friendliness. The landscape was evolving, the gap between NHS and private sector approaches narrowing.

Other trans groups were, I found, easier to get on with than GIRES. I formed friendly connections with Trans London, FTM London, Spectrum London and the Gender Trust; later, Gendered Intelligence (chapter 14), Transpire, MORF, TMSA UK (Transmasculine Support and Advice) and Sparkle.

Charing Cross GIC also underwent further sea changes. Green and Montgomery retired within a couple of years of each other. Barrett, the youngest when I joined the clinic in 2002, was suddenly the oldest. A newer tranche of clinicians – whom I liked to think of as my generation – set out to do things differently. Dr Penny Lenihan, a consultant psychologist, wasted no time in developing a proper psychology service. Dr Leighton Seal, an endocrinologist and workaholic, revolutionised hormone management, grounding the clinic in safe, scientific principles, a reassuringly solid evidence base. Crossing over with Green and Montgomery, we were joined by Dr Christina Richards, psychologist, psychotherapist, writer, academic and the first 'out' trans clinician at an NHS gender clinic. With satisfying circularity, she inherited Green's desk when he left. The year 2009 saw the return of another dynamic and much-loved figure, experienced surgical and endocrine supernurse, known to all with affection as 'Saint' Iffy Middleton.

As a group, we worked to change the somewhat 'ivory tower' perception of the GIC and to challenge the widespread myths that had grown up about the service and its ways of working over the years. Green, Montgomery and others had been well known in research and policy-making circles, but we wanted to engage at a more grass-roots level. We built on the connections I had made, visiting trans groups, such as those mentioned above, answering questions and soliciting feedback.

Referral numbers continued to rise, accelerated by the developing Internet and the advent of accessible information on transition. Other gender clinics had sprung up to meet the demand: Nottingham, Newcastle, Exeter, Leeds, Sheffield and Northamptonshire. Scotland and Ireland followed suit.

With proliferation came internal politics, small-p and big-P, some of it toxic. At times, it seemed that those of us with the most clinical experience (and the highest caseload) exerted the least influence. This was mirrored, sometimes, in the tendency for other organisations to pursue policies that weren't necessarily in the best interests of trans people, while purporting to represent them. An increasingly irrelevant Parliamentary Forum played favourites, courting some and excluding others.

As a group, the Charing Cross gender clinicians were late to the international party. I emerged, blinking, into the sunlight of my first World Professional Association for Trans Health conference in Bangkok, in 2014, a couple of years after their *Standards of Care* had shed its sixth skin to reveal the shiny new version seven. Version seven represented a significant shaking loose of many of the previous protocols, allowing for yet more flexibility in treatment. As a rule, the day-to-day work of gender care changes by evolution rather than revolution, but Dr Chris McIntosh of Toronto's adult gender service, presenting at that Bangkok event, gave a particularly inspiring account of how his clinic had overhauled itself in a handful of months.

In November of the following year, I found myself at another gathering of the great and good: a party thrown by the *Independent on Sunday* to celebrate its Rainbow List of 'the 101 most influential lesbian, gay, bisexual, transgender and intersex people in Britain'. I wasn't the only doctor on the list – a certain anaesthetist and television cake supremo also featured – but I was the only psychiatrist and certainly the only gender specialist. It felt like recognition, not only of me but of gender practitioners in general, a very welcome counter to the low-level disdain with which we are more familiar. Dr Samuel Hall, a friend and fellow medic, himself trans, theorises that clinicians who work with trans people are stigmatised in association and parallel with those we treat.

The World Professional Association for Transgender Health (WPATH), formerly known as the Harry Benjamin International Gender Dysphoria Association (HBIGDA), is an interdisciplinary professional and educational organisation devoted to transgender health. Their vision is to bring together diverse professionals dedicated to developing best practices and supportive policies worldwide that promote health, research, education, respect, dignity and equality for transgender, transsexual and gender-variant people in all cultural settings. The organisation's main publication is the *Standards of Care* (SoC), which it first published in 1979 and has periodically updated ever since (in 1980, 1981, 1990, 1998, 2001 and 2012). The eighth edition is currently under development at the time of writing. According to the organisation, the aim of the guidelines is to provide safe and effective pathways for the health of transsexual, transgender and gender nonconforming people. The stated goal of psychotherapeutic, endocrine or surgical therapy for gender transitioning clients is lasting personal comfort with their gendered selves, to maximise overall psychological well-being and self-fulfilment.

The Rainbow List party also brought home the degree to which trans has become thoroughly mainstream. I clinked glasses with the glamorous, ferociously intelligent writer and journalist Paris Lees, and introduced myself to the young but preternaturally cool Riley Carter Millington, a trans actor playing a trans character in *EastEnders* (I had to fight down my inner doctor, who wanted to nag him about smoking). Hobnobbing with the trans glitterati, I felt an eternity away from the nine-year-old being put to bed early while his parents tuned in to *A Change of Sex*.

My Rainbow List placing was also notable in that the characteristically muted response of the GIC's then host organisation, West London Mental Health Trust (WLMHT), proved another nail in the coffin of the Trust/GIC relationship. Never having known quite what to do with this strange little service on its periphery, WLMHT had, historically, left Charing Cross GIC to its own devices. With the passing of years, however, it became increasingly obvious that gender, as a speciality, was not especially 'psychiatric' in nature – while WLMHT, taking its cue from the forensic psych services at Broadmoor, was overwhelmingly so.

In his 2016 presidential address to the British Association of Gender Identity Specialists (BAGIS), Barrett had likened the gender field to the discovery of the platypus by eighteenth-century naturalists – with vexed arguments as to whether it was a bird, a mammal or a mixture of both. Like the platypus, gender medicine is its own creature, distinct and different. As relations with WLMHT grew more strained, Barrett extended the metaphor: the GIC was a platypus egg placed, decades ago, in a duck's nest. Having hatched and grown, it became more and more apparent that the clinic needed to be... elsewhere.

The GIC's departure from WLMHT was eerily akin to ending an unbalanced relationship – we were told it was impossible for us to leave, we'd have no prospects, no one else would ever love us – but persistence prevailed. As of April 2017, we find ourselves nestled in the bosom of the Tavistock and Portman, the Trust responsible for providing child and adolescent gender services throughout the UK. It's too early to say how the seismic shift in management culture will pan out but initial impressions are good. There's a pleasing symmetry to the timing, with Charing Cross GIC starting its second half-century in an optimistic new home.

There's symmetry of sorts to my own circumstances also, in

that I recently agreed to have some of my patient consultations filmed as part of an upcoming television documentary. Now I'm the middle-aged man in a suit, flustered by the cameras and trying not to appear preposterous. It's harder than it looks.

I have Julia Grant's phone number and call her to discuss *A Change of Sex*. She's quietly proud of the way it changed the entire landscape for trans people: 'It's going to happen two ways: sensationalised or true to life. I came over as a genuine person, they got the good with the bad.' She reflects on how 'terrified' the BBC was to be involved in something so apparently controversial but praises the television crew for supporting her. The British press, too, 'got really behind it'.

On Randell, she hasn't mellowed – 'I can look back with anger' – but she notes that his refusal to recommend her for genital surgery led, paradoxically, to kinder meetings with more sympathetic medics, including the surgeon who went on develop vaginoplasty techniques still in use today.

Despite myself, I feel just a tiny bit more sympathetic towards old Randell, monstrous as he undoubtedly could be. None of us can know how history will judge us.

Not even Foucault.

3

The Formative Years

CAROL STEELE

Born in 1945, Carol realised that she identified as female by the time she was five, but these things were hidden from society back then. She initially tried to transition in 1962 at the age of seventeen but failed. It was only after two unsuccessful suicide attempts that she acquired the strength to start her transition in the early 1970s. An early campaigner for trans rights, she went into so-called 'stealth mode' (keeping her trans background private) to protect her businesses. On retirement she restarted her activism for transgender rights, creating another support group and working with the police and NHS to raise awareness.

Although the formative years of transgender groups starting to appear in the UK was during the early to middle seventies, my own personal history and how I became involved in the struggle for the recognition of transgender people began in 1950, when I was just five years old. It was at that age that I started to feel troubled and uneasy at being recognised as a boy. Then, at the age of six and a half, I was sent away to a children's convalescent home (Dr Garrett's Home for Sick Children, in Conwy, North Wales) for six months because of an eating disorder (I just wouldn't eat). It was during my time there that I found I would settle and eat when I was allowed to be with the other girls, but went off my food again when I was forced into the boys' groups. At that time, nothing was diagnosed from my behaviour, but

I should imagine that these days further investigations would happen with the increased knowledge that paediatricians have regarding gender identity issues.

A year later, in December of 1952, I was lying on the floor reading a comic. My father read out a story from the *News of the World* to my mother, and suddenly it all became clear to me. The story was, of course, about Christine Jorgensen, the first transgender person to receive worldwide publicity about her gender confirmation surgery. I recognised myself in that story. This was who I was too. I also remember, in chilling detail, the words my father said after he had finished reading that story: 'Perverts like that need locking away in a loony-bin and the key throwing away.' That was the beginning of the shame that haunted me for a further twenty years and resulted in two attempts at suicide.

From that point on, my childhood was spent every evening praying that God would put right this terrible mistake and that the following morning I would wake up a proper girl. At primary school, I used to be teased and called a sissy and the boys started calling me Stella. Oddly enough, even though I knew this was meant to be bullying, it gave me a sense of peace and confirmation that my peers recognised me for who I actually was.

I sat and passed my eleven-plus exam at the age of ten and, back in the 1950s, schools were segregated by sex, so it was an all boys' school that I attended: Manchester Central Grammar School for Boys. I realised that I would have to toughen up, as the bullying would shift from being just name calling to physical abuse. By the time I was in the second year at that school the express train called 'puberty' was hurtling down the track towards me. I was terrified of the changes that were about to happen and I read in a magazine (maybe *Reader's Digest*) of the *castrati* – Italian boys who were castrated to preserve their soprano voices. The castration meant they also didn't grow facial hair and they remained small and more feminine in stature. I made plans to run away to Italy, but on pocket money of just 6d (2½ pence) a week I quickly realised that I wouldn't make it much further south than Stockport, never mind Italy. If I tried to hitchhike I would be brought home to face the consequences. Still haunted by my father's words, I thought maybe I would be locked away in a mental institution for life. It was just after puberty hit me that I realised that, somewhat strangely, I was beginning to be attracted to boys. All through my primary school I had mainly other girls as friends. This new attraction to boys freaked me out even more. What sort of a travesty of a human being was I?

I initially did well at school – I even managed to pass four O-Levels at the age of fourteen, but the following year was a disaster. My gender dysphoria was beginning to hit hard and the turmoil going on in my head was so distracting that I failed all the other seven subjects that I sat. It had been exacerbated by the fact that my father had said that no matter how many O-Levels I passed, I had to leave school and could not go on to the sixth form to study for my A-Levels and then university.

I left school in 1961 to start work at the Clayton Aniline Company in Manchester as a laboratory assistant. They allowed me one day off each week to study, initially for my ONC and then HNC in Chemistry. I also did an HNC in maths because I enjoyed it and I was finding that studying was helping to keep the gender dysphoria in check somewhat. However, I did leave home in 1962 and set myself up in a bedsit in Chorlton-cum-Hardy with the intention of starting to go out as a woman. This was doomed to failure though, as I did not have the courage to buy clothing, wigs, make-up, etc. and there were no support groups around back then. Home computers, the Internet and search engines hadn't even been dreamt of.

Then came my first lucky break. The company I worked for asked me if I would like to do a sandwich course for my B.Sc. at Salford University. I jumped at the chance because, to me, more study meant keeping the growing gender dysphoria in check. Indeed it worked to a large extent, as I obtained an upper second in organic chemistry, just missing out on a first class degree by a couple of percentage points. After returning to the company, I was pleasantly surprised when they asked me if I would like to go back to Salford University to study for a Ph.D. I again jumped at this chance and started back under the tutelage of Professor Hans Suschitzky.

It was during my first year back at Salford in 1972 that the gender dysphoria returned with a vengeance. I realised that there was no further escape from the thoughts that constantly plagued me when my studies ended. It was during this period when I started drinking heavily to numb down the torment that was going on in my head. It was at this point that I made my first suicide attempt, because I could not see any way forward. I was trapped. I hated myself. I was so deeply ashamed for feeling the way I did. When I awoke the following morning, I realised that I didn't want to die, I just wanted to be 'me' and be accepted by the world as that person: a woman.

I then had my second lucky break. A student helpline had just started in Manchester called Nightline and I carried an information sheet around with me for weeks before I picked up enough courage to ring them. I was lucky to get through to a young woman and I simply poured out my heart to her – the hurt I had been feeling for all those years, the suicide attempt, the shame, the self-hatred. She listened and I cried and she listened some more and she empathised with me. She told me that she knew somebody who might be able to help me and to phone back the following evening, which I did. That phone call saved my life and put me on the road to who I am today.

The Nightline volunteer put me in contact with a counsellor called Jack and his lovely understanding wife. After an initial spell of counselling he introduced me to another person who was treading the same road as me, a young transgender woman called Linda B. Oddly enough I found out that she lived less than a mile from where I once lived.

Unfortunately, over the years Linda and I have lost touch and therefore I have anonymised her name, and various other people in this chapter, as I do not wish to out them without their consent. For some people who might be living in what we call 'stealth mode', it could be dangerous to do so.

Together Linda and myself joined the Beaumont Society, but the nearest meetings were held in Leeds, at the home of their local representative called June W. Although this was a relief at first, it quickly turned into a nightmare as the Beaumont Society didn't support transsexual women who were attracted to men. This ultimately led to us leaving and starting our own group, the Manchester TV/TS Group, which catered for everybody who identified as what we now call transgender, by which I mean people who cross-dressed and people who were transsexual. Non-binary people (chapter 15) were still very much unknown in Western society back then.

It was during this time that I went to see my GP, who referred me to my local hospital and my first psychiatrist, at Ashton-under-Lyne General Hospital. He was an elderly man, who no doubt learned his psychiatry in the 1930s, as the first thing he tried to do was undertake electro-convulsive shock therapy on me. When I adamantly refused this, he tried to persuade me to go on a course of testosterone therapy as it would 'make a man out of me'. This was the furthest thing from my mind, so I again refused. It was then that I had another lucky break. A specialist gender clinic had recently opened in Withington Hospital in Manchester, so I asked if he would refer me there. I think he was simply glad to get rid of me and gave me a referral without a moment's hesitation. At the same time I started having electrolysis to get rid of my facial hair. I had my first appointment at the gender identity clinic at Withington, which consisted of three hours doing puzzles, Rorschach tests and other psychological tests. I went back to see them a few weeks later and they told me that they had diagnosed gender dysphoria and, after some discussion, started me on oestrogen therapy. I find it difficult to describe my elation and joy at that point. I was so happy; my dreams from my childhood were actually starting to come to life.

I went back to see Jack to tell him about the results and we also discussed the new group that Linda and I were planning. I explained that we needed somewhere to meet and he put me in contact with a friend called Piers and his partner Nesta, who kindly offered us the use of their home. And so, in late 1973, the Manchester TV/TS Group was born. The meeting place was an old, soot-and-smog-blackened Victorian house in Camp Street in Salford, just around the corner from Salford University, which I was attending at the time. The changing facilities were in the basement. You had to crouch down to get in, as the headroom was only around five feet. But, for us, it was adequate. The membership slowly started to grow. People were spreading the news of our existence via the Beaumont Society and other groups were starting to spring into life around the country. Another friend, Caroline R., who was a student at Leeds University, started one in Leeds. Another one sprang into being, founded by a transgender woman called Pat S., that met in the Archway Road area of London. Another one, which was more activist, was called TAG (Transsexual Action Group). There was an explosion of groups beginning to form in the mid-seventies, which catered for all transgender people instead of the restricted membership of the Beaumont Society.

Christine Burns

During the second half of the 1970s and the first part of the 1980s the Manchester TV/TS group would meet on Wednesday evenings at St Peter's Chaplaincy on Oxford Road, at the heart of the Manchester University campus. The building, completed in 1972, had much nicer facilities than Camp Street. People attending meetings could change in safety in a room set aside for the purpose if they needed to do so.

By early 1975 we had outgrown the Camp Street venue. By then Stephen Whittle had joined the group and it was because of his involvement with Manchester University that we were able to move to the campus's recently built St Peter's Chaplaincy on Oxford Road, which was altogether far nicer.

After gaining my Ph.D. from Salford University in 1974, I returned to my employers, the Clayton Aniline Company, to work in their research laboratories. Eight months later I was told that they required me to undertake a medical examination in order to join their pension scheme. I was examined by the works doctor. By then my body had, of course, started changing under the influence of the cross-sex hormones which I was taking. The doctor raised his eyebrows and asked me whether anything had been done about my breast growth, so I explained to him what was happening. He just nodded and carried on with the examination and I breathed a sigh of relief, thinking that everything was OK. Two days later I received a phone call from the director of research and, not thinking anything amiss as it was normal practice to talk to him once or twice a week about the current direction of research, I went up to see him in his office. When I got there, I noticed that the atmosphere was icy. He didn't invite me to sit down as per usual and then just stated that he had received information from my medical about my impeding change of gender and that nothing of that sort would be tolerated by the company. According to him, I could either work my one month's notice or he would fire me on the spot. I was absolutely devastated and mumbled that I would work my month's notice. Then I was out of his office. I later discovered that in the small print of the forms I signed after the medical was the clause that the doctor could disclose any information to the company of any 'illness or medical condition' which had been discovered.

Although I had intended to finish my electrolysis (to permanently remove my facial hair) before I started living my life full-time as a woman, the stress of living this dual existence was finally catching up with me. If I took another job I did not want the humiliation of being sacked again once my electrolysis was finished and I was ready to start living permanently in my correct gender. I therefore decided to transition as soon as I had finished working my one month's notice. It was quite by co-incidence that I finished at Clayton Aniline on 31 October 1975 – Halloween. I often jokingly refer to this as 'the night the witch was born'.

There followed a period of unemployment and, although I was getting plenty of interviews from up and down the country, I never seemed to make it past the shortlist. Finally, I discovered the reason why this was happening. In frustration, after yet another rejection, I phoned the personnel manager who had been one of the interviewers at my last interview in an attempt to find out where I was going wrong. What she told me chilled me to the bone and explained many things. Apparently, when they took up my references, my previous place of employment had been telling prospective employers of my past and that, when I had worked there, I had done so as a man. I was devastated. This company had promised to give me a good reference and I had trusted it to do so.

Just as I was reeling from this shock, the dark clouds that hovered over my head turned into a brilliant silver lining. About two weeks after this terrible revelation, my old professor at Salford University wrote to me about my thesis. Hans Suschitzky was a really lovely, kindly man. He had apparently made sure my degrees were re-issued in my new name as he was the head of senate at the time and this had never happened at Salford University before. The professor wanted my thoughts on some new research which had come out after my own. After we had met up and discussed the research, we went for lunch and the talk turned to my transition and how things were going. I explained to the professor what had happened with my previous referee. He told me to forget about them and to use his name instead. He added that if I was still having trouble then he would arrange for a post-doctoral research post at the university for me. I did as instructed in my next job application and, unsurprisingly, I was offered the position – at a small pharmaceutical company called Biorex Laboratories, situated in the Canonbury area of Islington in London.

It was during my year's period of unemployment that I became quite active in working for a better life for transgender people. In the spring of 1976 Caroline R. from the Leeds group, Linda B. from our group and myself decided to go and heckle at the annual meeting of the Royal College of Psychiatrists which was being held in Harrogate that year. Our little protest was heard in stunned silence by the meeting until the security guards intervened and ejected us from the meeting. Then, later that year, we heard of a psychiatrist who was practising at the local psychiatric hospital in Inverness: a certain Dr Whittet, who was willing to help transgender people both with cross-sex hormone prescriptions and also with referrals for surgeries. A road trip was quickly organised and a group of us, including Stephen Whittle, travelled up to Scotland to meet him. The hospital was in an isolated location outside Inverness and was approached via a long driveway – a dark and foreboding building made from Inverness granite. We were escorted down long dark corridors into an equally dark but charmingly olde worlde office, where we had tea and biscuits. Dr Whittet himself was, as I remember, a smallish man, utterly charming and polite. He appeared willing to help. But, as I had been on hormones for a couple of years by then, and his surgical team had not actually carried out any surgeries at that time, I decided that maybe this was not for me. Later that year he stopped offering any services as somebody had betrayed his trust and gone to the press about what he was doing. The revelation resulted in him being terribly maligned in the papers. In addition to the humiliation of his patients, the press inferred that Dr Whittet should be admitted into his own institution for pandering to the 'fantasies of his patients'.

So, in December of 1976, I left Manchester and the group I had formed there and moved to start a completely new life in London. It was exciting and exhilarating and, after a couple of months, I had a new circle of friends. I managed to get a mortgage on a small two-bedroomed maisonette in Finchley (after a lot of trouble with lenders as many, even in the mid-seventies, would not give mortgages to women – even women with Ph.D.s). I really loved this new life where I was gaining far more confidence and complete acceptance as myself. I had met

Yvonne Sinclair pictured on a website that she created before her death.

and become friends with Dudley Cave and his partner Bernard. Dudley was co-founder of the London Gay Switchboard and a very active member of the Campaign for Homosexual Equality (CHE). He was also the founder of the Gay Bereavement Project. I went to many of the services at the church he attended, Golders Green Unitarian Church, where the minister, the Rev. Keith Gilley was one of the first of the Christian clergy to fully accept me as a woman.

In the summer of 1977 I heard about a new group that had been set up for transgender people in Upper Street, Islington. It was hosted by London Friend, a befriending offshoot of CHE, which was just around the corner from where I worked in Canonbury Villas. I went along one evening to one of their meetings. The group was run by a much-larger-than-life character called Yvonne Sinclair, who was a gay man who cross-dressed. He was a somewhat complex character in that, although he loved his cross-dressing, he tended to look down on people who were transsexual and tried to persuade many of us that it was wrong. I attended the group on and off for around six months before deciding it was the wrong environment for me to grow, as I was determined to go through with gender confirmation surgery.

When I had moved down to London I switched from the gender identity clinic at Withington Hospital in Manchester to the renowned Charing Cross Gender Identity Clinic, which was based in Hammersmith Hospital in Fulham Palace Road. This meant I came under the care of the wonderful Dr John Randell. People tell horror stories about Dr Randell, but I always found him to be caring and with a quite wicked sense of humour. When I went to see him initially he told me that I could not count my time at Withington GIC towards my Real Life Experience (RLE) and that I would have to do four years of RLE under his care. He insisted that I also needed to be working for at least three out of the four years of the RLE and that he would see me every four months to make sure that I was adjusting and coping well. This seemed to be forever, as I had already been living for over a year as my true self. So, after my first visit, I decided to speed things up a little. After each appointment he would tell me to go and make an appointment to see him in four months and I would go to reception and tell them that Dr Randell wanted to see me in two months' time. After my twelve appointments were up (in two years instead of the four) I asked when he would refer me for surgery as I had completed my twelve appointments. He looked at my records, hummed and hawed a little and told me that he might do it on my next visit – which, to his credit, he did. I was referred to the surgeon Mr Peter Phillip.

Despite what other people have said about Dr Randell being cold, brusque and demeaning, I think a little anecdote of what happened to me after my surgery will reveal the true nature of the man. After surgery, when people were starting to become mobile again, it was customary to make an appointment to see him whilst still in hospital. I did this and, when I walked in and gingerly sat down on his chair (which was like a whoopee cushion), I thanked him for his care and compassion. I was in tears (of joy and happiness) and he very softly and gently said, 'That's OK, I think you deserved this.' I swear that his eyes were glistening when he said it.

The Real Life Test was a fundamental part of the clinical protocol for treating transsexual people and persists to this day, albeit in a toned-down form. Candidates needed to show evidence of successfully living permanently in their target gender, including having an appropriate job (being a carer or volunteer didn't qualify), maintaining stable living arrangements and avoiding trouble. The process was later renamed Real Life Experience to defuse the idea that it was an endurance test the patient needed to survive, as opposed to being a learning and observing opportunity for both patient and doctor. Subjects were expected to live this ordeal for an extended time even before hormones would be prescribed, meaning that they were effectively required to survive at their most visible. In recent years the requirements have been toned down but the core principle remains a staple of treatment through the NHS.

Shortly before my surgery I had decided to leave my job at Biorex Laboratories because I was finding it increasingly difficult to accept the animal testing which was carried out there. I had already started learning a new trade as an electrologist and, after my recovery, set up a new business in London doing this. Unfortunately other things were also happening in my life. I was being stalked sexually and I had my flat broken into on three occasions. I was mugged and then finally a boyfriend decided to physically assault me because of me being transsexual. I resolved to move to Torquay for a new start. At the same time I decided that, in order for my new business to flourish, I would have to live in what transgender people call 'stealth mode'. This is when someone lives as though they are a cisgender person, without disclosing their trans background to anyone. I bought an existing hair salon in Torquay and expanded it into a hair and beauty business. I sold this business after around ten years and started another business as a photographer, specialising in wedding and children's photography.

In 2005 I successfully applied for my gender recognition certificate, becoming one of the first people to obtain one. When it arrived, I filed it away without really thinking about it. However, it was a totally different story when my new birth certificate arrived about two weeks later. I took the unopened envelope upstairs to similarly file it away but, on opening it, and upon seeing in the column marked 'gender' the word 'girl', I was simply overcome with emotion. I sat on the edge of my bed and sobbed quietly for about half an hour. I had not realised the impact which that one single word would have on me.

These days I have started another support group for transgender people of all ages in Torquay and I work closely with the Devon and Cornwall Police, being on several of their committees dealing with hate crimes and training. I also work with our local hospital on their protocols for how transgender patients and staff are treated and give talks to various other organisations about transgender people and the issues that we face. I was recently awarded a Citizens in Policing award and was also shortlisted out of thousands in the National Diversity Awards. But the work goes on until all transgender people are accepted in society without fear and prejudice.

4

Where Do the Mermaids Stand?

MARGARET GRIFFITHS

Margaret (a pen name) is a Londoner, grammar school educated, who enjoyed a career doing clerical and admin work, mainly with computer firms and the civil service, until enhancing her family with two children. Having volunteered with various local education establishments as the children grew, and having also run a
group supporting new mothers, she was very keen to help start the Mermaids support group when the opportunity arose. She resigned from the committee in 2015 and is still helping in a small way, but, as she says, she is now over seventy years old, and 'it may be time to complete my retirement soon'. Ever modest, Margaret stresses: 'My story is just one of those that could be told by any other of the people who came together to start Mermaids.'

Some expectant mothers will tell you that they somehow knew the gender of their child whilst they were in the womb. That would be a romantic spin on how I came to have a beautiful trans daughter and to become, as a result, an advocate for the parents and families of other trans children. It would be romantic, but it couldn't be further from the truth.

Roy and I had been married for about nine years already, and I was thirty-one, when we eventually decided to start a family. Like many couples – especially during the seventies – we were in no rush to tie ourselves down, so it was 1978 when my first child arrived, and two years later when the second came.

Did I want a boy or a girl on either occasion? People sometimes expect me to say I wanted a girl. They're almost willing me to say that. It would fit the amateur psychological theories that parents of trans children are somehow fulfilling their gender preferences through the transition of their children. But they'd be wrong. I really wasn't at all concerned about which sex my children were going to be. Indeed, if you really pressed me in those days, then I would have expressed a preference to have a boy. Growing up, I'd had a brother ten years younger than me and I was used to having a small boy around. And, of course, that's exactly what I thought we'd got when the first arrived.

With the arrival of our second child Meg in 1980 we were a pretty happy family – one boy, one girl – with nothing to hint at the challenges that lay ahead. The children were free to play however they wished and make a mess everywhere. They got on well with each other and yet, as they developed, there was an indefinable sense that Lisa had something missing in her life. It would be years before we understood the root cause. Gender dysphoria is honestly the last thing you think of. But, even at primary school, our eldest was a magnet for bullying – in fact both children were. In our part of Oxfordshire being a bright child at school (they both were) made you stand out like a sore thumb.

It wasn't as though Lisa came across as notably effeminate. She hid her problem very well. Her interests were the sort that people would be more likely to associate with tomboys. We just saw her as a gentle boy who didn't like rough-and-tumble games. She also liked playing with Meg, and other boys and girls. Trans children, I later learned, aren't always obvious. Some are, of course – some parents will tell you that their child was vocal about their cross-gender identification from as soon as they could talk. But not Lisa. That's why it took us so long to find out.

The crunch eventually came, however, when Lisa was about fourteen and she started refusing to go to school. To make matters worse, her younger sister Meg (who was still in primary school at this time) also stopped wanting to go. That's when we knew there was a real problem of some kind. The schools were as worried as we were. I took both children to our doctor and all sorts of tests followed – medical and behavioural. They even interviewed the children privately to see whether there was any funny business going on. Nothing was off the table as everyone searched for explanations.

After a year, we finally worked out that Meg was not happy with the way the teachers at her school were ignoring her. We put her in another school and her own problem disappeared overnight. But that wasn't the explanation for Lisa's behaviour. Was it the school environment? We arranged a period of home schooling, but that changed nothing. And then I started running through every possibility I could think of: was she being bullied? No, that wasn't it. Was she gay? No. Taking drugs? No. It was like Twenty Questions, but every idea I tried drew a blank. Lisa protested that she was OK, but it was very clear from her inability to go to school that she wasn't.

Time passed and I was running out of ideas to pursue but, as luck would have it, Lisa and I both watched a programme on TV about the model Caroline Cossey (aka 'Tula'). Caroline was a trans woman. She had lost her modelling career and her fiancé when she was outed by a tabloid in 1981. She couldn't marry a man legally – the law regarded her as male, and this was a whole lifetime before equal marriage. The government's unwillingness to correct her birth certificate meant she would forever be vulnerable to exposure as the press had already demonstrated. She had taken her case all the way to the European Court of Human Rights, which was why she was being featured on television. I remember saying at the time, 'That poor woman.

Fancy having to go through all the things she has just to be the person she is.'

I still had no clue at the time that that's what was bothering Lisa, and she gave nothing away. But eventually it came into my head that I ought to ask her this. I'd exhausted every other idea. I said, 'Are you entirely happy being a boy?'

'No,' she answered. My reaction was roughly: 'Look, I don't care if you're male or female or whatever. You're my kid and I'm still your mum. Now that we've found out what the problem is, we can find a way of sorting it out.'

So, I set about finding someone who could advise us and help. In those days I used to read a magazine called *Family Circle* and in the back I found the details for the London Lesbian and Gay Switchboard. This was around 1992. The World Wide Web hadn't yet arrived for people like us. Where else would you begin? They were extremely reassuring, as it happened. The switchboard said they couldn't help directly, but they gave me a list of numbers to try. I went through them all and got the same response every time: 'We can't help you ourselves but try these numbers.' These days it is so much easier for worried parents like us to find reliable advice, but this is really what it was like just twenty-five years ago.

Eventually I came across a support group for transgender adults called the Gender Dysphoria Trust International (GDTI), set up by a therapist named Fran Springfield. I called the number and spoke to a very helpful trans woman named Helen. She was the first trans person I had ever knowingly spoken to. I remember she had a very deep voice and that shocked me a little at first, but I realised there were a lot of things I was going to have to learn if I was going to get the help my child needed.

Helen's advice was to go back to my doctor. His response was, 'Ah, now we know what's going on.' He, in turn, referred us to the Oxfordshire Child and Adolescent Mental Health Service (CAMHS), although I also kept in touch with the GDTI too – just as well, as it happened.

Fran Springfield told us about the relatively new Gender Identity Development Service (GIDS) which was based in London. However, she actually wanted to refer us directly to a private clinician with whom she worked quite closely: Dr Russell Reid. We weren't keen though. As we put it, 'You're not qualified to make a diagnosis and referral. Your experience is with adults. Our child is still only fifteen. We'd rather go through the right channels.' So we went to see the CAMHS team, although I made a mental note of Dr Reid as well. It underlines how parents in those days were really out on their own – reliant on their instincts.

As it turned out, the CAMHS team in Oxford were of only limited help. Lisa's needs were beyond their training. The staff eventually said, 'There's no sign of depression in your child, therefore we suggest just half an hour a week with the school counsellor.' And, with that, they signed us off.

It was so frustrating. Every time we went to see the CAMHS team Lisa was on a high. She imagined that that was going to be the occasion when the doctors would see the light and she could start making progress towards her goal of reassignment. The rest of the time she was depressed. The CAMHS team were missing the whole point about Lisa's needs.

Our GP was furious. He referred us back to CAMHS with a demand that they do better, but the staff were bewildered. 'We don't know what to do for you. What would you *like* us to do?' I demanded that they refer us to the GIDS clinic, which was led by a Dr Domenico Di Ceglie at St George's Hospital in Tooting; thankfully, they did.

Domenico Di Ceglie was a delight once we'd beaten this

path to his door. He was a kindly, quiet-spoken man who radiated calm. He used to see Lisa, my husband and myself all together once a month, along with a social worker, Mary, who worked with him. On one occasion they saw Meg too, as they liked to see other members of the family unit regarding possible family dynamics or other issues. It was through these visits that the clinic's endocrinologist first prescribed Lisa a hormone-blocking drug, Buserelin acetate, administered as a nasal spray. I don't know if Lisa was actually the first child in the UK to be put on blocking medication, but she was certainly one of the first.

People often confuse these so-called 'blockers' with cross-sex hormones, and that inevitably sets them off in a panic about the idea of prescribing supposedly irreversible hormone treatment to children. But that couldn't be further from the truth. Blockers are nothing new. Their main clinical use is in even younger children to treat a serious condition known as precocious puberty. This is where children as young as five years old begin to go through the stages of puberty long before their body is ready. Drugs like Buserelin acetate were developed to prevent this (and all the negative effects it can bring). Another such drug is Leuprorelin acetate, which is often used to treat a range of conditions including enlarged prostate in men and endometriosis in women and girls.

The use of these kinds of drugs for treating precocious puberty means that doctors have decades of experience with them. They know they are safe. They know the effects are fully reversible. Prescribed for a trans child like Lisa, the drugs merely buy time for more in-depth evaluation. They prevent the irreversible effects of natural puberty – like the voice breaking or male pattern skeletal development, and are a diagnostic tool for both the therapist and the child. If Lisa had changed her mind the Buserelin could have been discontinued and her male puberty would have kicked back in. But if she was going to persist and insist upon seeking ultimate gender reassignment then the blocking treatment was going to preserve her options and assure her of more chance of fitting in as a young woman. When you understand what blocking treatment is about then it really is a no-brainer. It is the safe, conservative course. By contrast, doing nothing is not a neutral course of action. It amounts to knowingly submitting a child to a course of development that may mark them out for life with physical features that cannot be undone.

It was while seeing us every month as a family that Dr Di Ceglie said that he would like to set up a series of half a dozen parents' evenings. This was to enable him and his team to give us more information about the treatment protocol and transsexuality in general, but it was also to enable us all to feed back to him as well. Up to that point, we had had no interaction with other parents in the same boat as us. It was from these initial evening meetings that the idea of a support group arose.

We realised from meeting and talking to other parents how much we all could benefit from some kind of mutual support. We were a diverse bunch – this phenomenon knows no social or economic boundaries – but we shared similar experiences in so many ways. None of us would ever have wished this on our child or our families but, faced with the reality of it happening, we had all fought to find help in a medical system that was largely uninformed and unprepared. We had all had struggles of some kind with partners, parents, siblings, neighbours, schools and doctors – confrontations with denial or outright hostility. Compared to some, my family had accepted Lisa's transition better than most. My husband was like me – we wanted whatever was going to help Lisa. Our families and friends were very supportive as they knew Lisa had been so unhappy, but some were unsupportive initially and took a little more time than others to accept the situation. Seeing how much her transition had helped her let them see that this was right for her.

Domenico Di Ceglie's Gender Identity Development Service (GIDS) had only limited resources at the time. When we first met him and Mary at St George's in Tooting I got the impression that they were running the clinic on a limited budget with the help of volunteers. I think it only operated a couple of afternoons a week, and that the consulting rooms were borrowed – perhaps it was seen as an experimental service to see if there was a real need. I believe there were just the two paid clinicians. Domenico and the staff could see there was an unmet need for families like ours with a frightening problem which nobody was officially set up to deal with. After a few years the clinic found an official home at the Portman Clinic – eventually part of the Tavistock and Portman NHS Trust – but in those early days the team needed our help almost as much as we needed theirs. That's why it was suggested that the parents should set up a support group – not only for families to help each other with information and reassurance, but also to field growing enquiries from a media that was getting wind of our cases.

Our support group was a collective effort from the start. Not all parents wanted to be involved at first – it took a while to find enough to set it up – but eventually there were sufficient numbers to form a committee which took all the important decisions in a way that everyone could be happy about. The main aim was to help more families like our own. All the people who were on the committee have been pivotal in not only founding Mermaids, but also in giving their own time and experiences to help others – the group would not have thrived without them. We also had immense help from grown-up trans people like Pamela Crossland (who set up our first website) and Krystyna Haywood, who later lent her professional expertise as a social worker. The involvement of the trans adults helped a lot of parents, who naturally wondered whether their trans child could have a happy and fulfilled life ahead. That's easier for people to see nowadays, with so much information online and so many good role models in the media, but it's hard to convey how desperately we needed such assurance back then in the mid-nineties, when all of this was full of unknowns.

One of the first tasks for the group was to find a name. The young son of one of our members, W, had once asked her, 'Would you still love me if I was a mermaid?' In other words, no matter how different he was, would he still be loved? Domenico thought *Mermaids* was very apt because, according to him, male to female children quite often expressed a fascination with them. There was also a moving story from the 1988 book *All I Really Need To Know I Learned in Kindergarten* by American author and Unitarian Universalist minister Robert Fulghum. In one chapter the writer describes organising a kindergarten game of giants, wizards and dwarfs. But one little girl did not identify with any of the game's categories, which the children were all expected to choose. Within the game's universe of possibilities, this child saw herself as a Mermaid. Fulghum writes: 'She intended to participate, wherever Mermaids fit into the scheme of things. Without giving up dignity or identity. She took it for granted that there was a place for Mermaids and that I would know just where.' Fulghum goes on to ask: 'Where *do* the Mermaids stand? All the "Mermaids" – all those who are different, who do not fit the norm and who do not accept the available boxes and pigeonholes.' Such a good analogy for our trans children.

I don't want to overplay my own part in the development of the group. It's true that because I was a stay-at-home mum and was sometimes more available than other committee members I often ended up dealing with enquiries from journalists and people seeking help. But, as I say, it was always very democratic and inclusive. Nobody was in it for glory. Parents were involved because of how it helped them to help their own families better, and you just pay it forward.

In the years since that beginning in 1994 Mermaids has grown significantly though. It has been helped immeasurably by so many people. I've mentioned Pamela and Krystyna already. The Beaumont Society was immensely helpful with donations and Press for Change provided legal advice when needed. Awareness of the group's existence (and, importantly for us, my own education) was also expanded by involvement with online forums such as TG Folk UK. Later the group received a huge boost thanks to musician and *Celebrity Big Brother* star Pete Burns, whose generous personal donation helped start a series of residential weekends for families and to improve the services offered. And, with the increased visibility of transgender issues in the media, the charity's services are in higher demand than ever.

Our family meanwhile has grown up and both my children have independent lives of their own. My husband and I are now both retired. Lisa continued the transition she began at the age of sixteen, left school, and went to college. We are immensely proud of both our children. None of us in our family has ever regretted her transition – and that includes her of course. If she hadn't transitioned then I know for certain that we wouldn't have her now. She's not completely without problems (well, no one is!) but, as I tell people, transitioning will only solve *one* of your problems – the gender dysphoria that's so big and all-consuming that you may not even be able to see what else there is. You may still have other things to deal with but, with the gender issues out of the way, you'll be better able to cope with them.

5

Sex, Gender and Rock 'N' Roll

KATE HUTCHINSON
Kate Hutchinson is a woman with a passion for equality for the LGBT+ community. Over the last four years she has been involved with a number of organisations such as Wipe Out Transphobia, All About Trans and the Transgender Equality Legal Initiative. She quite proudly describes herself as a trans activist with a big mouth. When not trying to save the world, she enjoys playing bass guitar in both rock  and jazz bands. She works for Diversity Role Models, a charity that aims to prevent homophobic, biphobic and transphobic bullying in schools.

The first tingling of awareness regarding my transness came to me at the age of five or six. It was during break time in the playground at school. I recall standing on my own, looking for friends to play with. I looked over to a group of boys playing football, then over to a group of girls playing hopscotch. This was the mid-seventies; the playground was a very gendered place. But hopscotch won. That's when I was told by a teacher to 'leave the girls alone. Go and play with the other boys.'

My childhood marched on into adolescence. My feelings of disconnection with my birth-assigned gender grew. I began to see tabloid news articles about trans people – articles that made fun of the person featured – but all I saw was someone like me. The red-top headlines were full of sensationalist, attention-grabbing humiliation. 'SEX SWAP SHOCKER', 'She's my DAD', and similar.

Then, sometime in the early eighties, I saw something that both raised hopes and terrified me at the same time. The BBC *Inside Story* documentary *A Change of Sex* chronicled the transition of trans woman, Julia Grant.

This show switched on the lightbulb in a big way for a lot of trans people in the closet trying to find themselves. Here we saw a walking, talking, trans woman. A person that we could identify with completely, in full colour on our TV screens. Somebody like us. Julia was somebody who showed that it was possible to embrace your true self and live your truth. But the scenes showing Julia attending Charing Cross Gender Identity Clinic with clinician John Randell terrified me. What came across was his constant denial of her identity and his outrage at the breast augmentation she had organised for herself. It raised feelings of doubt and shame, pushing me further into the closet despite the positive visibility of Julia. I'm sure that Randell's negativity had a huge negative impact on a lot of trans people who were watching that documentary.

Tabloid press articles and Julia's documentary were as far as early eighties trans visibility went for me. I secretly videotaped the programme. I cut press articles out of the papers and hid them away in my bedroom. That sort of visibility was so precious at the time, even if it was negative. It gave people in the trans community some sort of connection or validation in how they felt. Those clippings and that recording were so valuable when there was so little other information available.

The only other media around at this time that mentioned transition was in the form of out-of-reach medical journals or memoirs such as Jan Morris's *Conundrum* and the autobiography of the American Christine Jorgensen. Just the act of trying to obtain these books could cause a lot of anxiety about outing yourself. They were not easy to acquire and could often throw up awkward questions: 'Why would you want to read about this?'

I was still in high school in the eighties. For anyone struggling with their gender identity back then, there really was nowhere obvious to turn for help or advice. No Internet, no Facebook with all its secret online peer support groups. No one within my school environment with whom I felt comfortable enough to confide. Thinking back to how alone and desperate I felt in those days highlights why it's important for LGB and trans inclusion to be part of the curriculum today. Things have improved greatly, but we still have so far to go.

The press articles and the television documentaries were the only *mainstream* visibility of trans folks. Nevertheless, there were other avenues through which society's accepted boundaries of gender were beginning to be pushed.

Within the music business there were several bands and artists appearing that blurred those gender boundaries. Rock and pop music has long been a catalyst for social change, a haven for the misfits, the misunderstood, the rebels – a medium and form for expression and thought.

The one shining beacon that lit my way during the eighties with some positivity was music. Discovering rock music and artists within pop and rock who were out there, queer and authentic, was a complete inspiration to a struggling and confused teenager.

A moment of realisation came when, as an eleven-year-old, I was sitting in the front room of my parents' house in the north-west of England on a Thursday night engaging in our weekly televisual ritual. The television was tuned to BBC One, the screen displayed the rotating globe of the BBC logo of the day, and then there was the announcer's voice: 'It's Thursday night. It's seven o'clock. It's *Top of the Pops!*'

Top of the Pops was a weekly BBC television show that showcased the best of the music charts at the time. Apparently, that night, Shakin' Stevens couldn't make it and, instead, they had a new band called Culture Club. Within five seconds of their lead singer Boy George appearing on the screen, one of my parents asked: 'Is that a boy or a girl?'

For an eleven-year-old child who was experiencing a lot of inner turmoil over their gender identity at the time, this made a huge impact.

Here was somebody who was colourful and expressive. There were ribbons in his hair and he wore make-up and clothing that was so individual. Here was a person that people couldn't initially place into one of those binary gender boxes that society loves so much.

Boy George doesn't identify as a trans person, but as a young, music-loving, gender-questioning person. To see someone blurring those lines of gender through their outward expression gave me so much to think about.

Here was someone who was unashamedly being themselves. To see him projecting that through his clothes, make-up and music lit a fire of hope in my heart, that maybe someday I could show my true self to the world.

For that young kid watching *Top of the Pops*, it was everything.

Rock and pop music has long been a force that has grabbed people's attention – rocked, shocked, astounded. But often that shock and awe have had a deeper impact in changing attitudes.

The simple visibility of people breaking the supposed conventions of gender expression – even if it was just part of a performance – planted the seeds of hope for gender-questioning folks. It could even provide a camouflage of sorts for some to experiment with expressing their own gender identity, as it did for me.

The seventies and eighties saw a deluge of artists whose gender presentation didn't fit into the boxes that society expected. It brought them into the living rooms of the nation via television shows like *Top of the Pops* and through the media platform of the rock music video.

Glam rock and punk had grown out of a New York art rock scene, with Andy Warhol and the Velvet Underground at its centre. When Lou Reed wrote 'Walk on the Wild Side', a song that mentioned three trans women who were known as Warhol's superstars, he created a song that sang out to trans people all around the world, that helped keep a flame burning, or for some stoked the embers of authenticity within them. One of the people who produced that record was David Bowie.

When David Bowie wore a dress on the cover of his third album *The Man Who Sold the World*, he made a bold statement about gender and expression. It was a statement that his American record label Mercury couldn't handle, as they declined the cover and went with an alternative one. Bowie was a musician who meant so much to a generation of trans folks. He was a person who never fitted neatly into the categories of gender or sexuality that society expected, and he's been described variously as changeling, chameleon, visionary and innovator. He was a role model.

In a 1999 interview with Jeremy Paxman, Bowie said he was attracted to becoming a musician because it was rebellious and because he thought 'it could bring change to a form'. Bowie showed how identity can be fluid. He took expression, gender and sexuality and shaped it into something that was uniquely his, constantly shifting with his identity, not constrained by society's rigid opinions on how people should look, sound or love. He demonstrated this with his words, too. In 'Rebel Rebel', for instance, he wrote:

You've got your mother in a whirl
She's not sure if you're a boy or a girl

Bowie was far from the only musician publicly pushing the boundaries of gender and identity. Jayne County, a trans woman originally from Atlanta, found her way to the UK and put together a punk band, the Electric Chairs. Jayne was completely unapologetic and to the point with both her expression and lyrics.

> I got a transsexual feeling
> It's hard to be true to the one that's really you
> I got a scandalous feeling
> It's hard to be true when they point and stare at you
> Conditioned to portraying the mask of masculinity
> Another blend of different shading
> I am what I am
> I don't give a damn

Jayne's empowerment was inspirational to many a trans music fan who still sat in the closet. Her image as well as her lyrics was bold and out there. This was positive trans visibility (and audibility!) in the mid-eighties.

When I first started hearing these tales of trans folks in songs – 'Walk on the Wild Side', or 'Lola' by the Kinks – they had an impact. When I started hearing about Jayne County standing up proudly and singing about being 'Man Enough to Be a Woman', I heard lyrics that gave me validation and something to hang onto.

These were musicians who didn't want your pity. They were empowered. They were being true to themselves. Whether trans or not, they didn't give a damn about what you thought about their clothing or expression. They were rock 'n' roll embodied.

In the UK, the early eighties gave us the New Romantics. This music scene presented acts like Boy George and Culture Club, Steve Strange and Visage, who both changed the wider public's perceptions of gender. David Bowie used Strange and other people who were Blitz club regulars in his 'Ashes to Ashes' music video. The Blitz was a nightclub which kickstarted the whole New Romantic scene. It was yet another music scene where I know that several friends found a haven for their gender expression before coming out as trans.

The usualising of people appearing in media with atypical gender expression was slowly but surely taking place. It was sinking into the nation's brains through the TV and shows like *Top of the Pops* with the rise of the music video.

As the eighties moved on, other musical subgenres appeared with differing expression, such as the goth subculture, where a lot of the community overlapped with, or also identified as, queer and pagan. A lot of men in the goth culture were expressing their identity in androgynous or feminine clothing and make-up. Women in that scene were quite independent and feminine in expression. The music was from bands such as Bauhaus, Siouxsie and the Banshees, the Mission, Sisters of Mercy, the Cure and Christian Death.

An evolution of glam rock came along – referred to these days as hair metal – where artists took on an image of big backcombed long hair, lots of make-up and very feminine expression in clothing. It was almost a complete opposite to the sometimes very misogynistic lyrics of their songs.

It was within the music scene that I and a number of other trans people found a place to explore our identities. It was through eighties hair metal that, as a teenager, I found a way to start exploring my own gender and how to express it. From trying to fit into the 'boy' mould – being an army cadet, playing rugby – I went to trying to find a better fit for myself.

I grew my hair long, spent many hours learning my trade as a musician, sat in my room playing guitar. I started playing in bands, and with that came an excuse and camouflage for me to explore my identity. As well as the long hair, I started wearing jewellery, got my ears pierced and began wearing make-up. To the world, I was just an extravagant glam rocker, but to me it was wonderful to be able to freely express my femininity in that outward, but also strangely stealthy, way. Hiding in plain sight.

Music, as with many forms of entertainment, goes through phases. The scene in which I found shelter for my identity issues eventually came to an end. I went back to trying to blend in to society. The only place that I felt safe dressing in the way I felt comfortable was back within the confines of my own home. My struggles with depression increased.

In the mid- to late-nineties more trans visibility started to make its way on to our screens through the rising popularity of reality television and the arrival of the first trans character in a British soap opera. In *Coronation Street* we saw the arrival of Hayley Cropper (née Patterson) and, in the fly-on-the-wall documentary *Paddington Green*, we followed the life of Jackie McAuliffe, a trans woman sex worker trying to move her life forward.

What was different about these shows and their trans characters and subjects? They both built up a lot of empathy for the character. They showed a person. They were no longer an object of ridicule. Jackie McAuliffe was the person whose visibility triggered my own coming out to close friends and family and my first attempt at transition in the late nineties.

A positive change in attitudes towards transgender people and the way we were portrayed in mainstream media was occurring. Meanwhile, over in the music business, some bands and acts were tackling trans issues in their songs in a more thoughtful way than had been done previously.

On their 1998 album *This Is My Truth Tell Me Yours* the Manic Street Preachers recorded a song with the title 'Born a Girl':

The censorship of my skin
Is screaming inside and from within
There's no room in this world for a girl like me
No place around there where I fit in

These lyrics, while not altogether positive and inspirational, gave comfort that you were not the only one who felt like this. They showed a level of understanding and empathy that hadn't been seen before in lyrics about trans people.

The change in attitudes towards trans people's stories and struggles was starting to sink in to our culture. Acceptance and understanding was creeping into the minds of the wider public. We were no longer just objects of pity or the punch line for comedy sketch shows.

These pieces of increasing visibility and public understanding also had the effect of giving people who had not yet come out as trans, or were thinking about transition, confidence in some cases to make that leap.

Eventually, after an abortive attempt at the end of the nineties, I made my move towards a successful transition in 2012. This was shortly after I had seen another positive piece of media in Channel 4's *My Transsexual Summer*. This was a show that put a group of trans people into a house together to share and explore parts of their lives and identities.

Ironically, when I got to the point in my life where I decided to transition, I was playing in a band that I had been in for five years and loved. I decided I needed to quit playing. I decided the thing that had helped me get through all those years would now become a hindrance. I made a pre-judgement of my bandmates: that they wouldn't accept me. I got it into my head that people would laugh, point, shout at me. It really hit me hard. But it was a sacrifice I needed to make at that time. I felt like a part of me had died.

It turned out I was wrong, but I had already made my decision and quit the band.

A few months later music returned to empower and help me through transition. A friend from another local band asked me why I wasn't making music anymore. I was still scared of reactions, but I pushed against my own fear and accepted an invitation to join her band. These days I play more music than I ever have in my life, with two different bands. I have never loved it as much, being up there on stage as my authentic self.

Today there are so many people in rock music out and proud to be trans. People who will open their hearts to the world in their lyrics and music and express what it is to be like us – artists like Jordan Gray and Anohni, who incidentally was nominated for a Brit award for 'Best British Female Artist' after being nominated for 'Best British Male' before transitioning. Anohni is very possibly the first person to pull off that double.

We now have bands like Against Me! with frontwoman Laura Jane Grace, a singer who is trans and proud. She's a woman who, through her onstage presence and performance, gave me the confidence to use my natural voice when singing on stage, and to own it. Songs like 'Transgender Dysphoria Blues' give voice to feelings that were hidden for so long:

Your tells are so obvious,
Shoulders too broad for a girl.
It keeps you reminded,
Helps you remember where you come from.

The power of art, poetry, music, the written word and visible role models should never be underestimated. Everybody needs inspiration; music is mine. Find your inspirations and use them to help realise your dreams, rock your authentic self, and you might inspire someone to live their truth too.

6

A Vicar's Story

REV. CHRISTINA BEARDSLEY
The Rev. Dr Christina Beardsley, a Church of England priest for thirty-eight years, recently retired as Head of Multi-faith Chaplaincy at Chelsea and Westminster Hospital, London where she remains engaged in research. Tina co-founded the Clare Project, a transgender support group in Brighton and Hove, in 2000. A member of the Sibyls, a Christian spirituality group for trans people, she is

Photo by Christa Holka, 2015 @Twilight

a writer and activist for trans inclusion in the Church. The co-editor (with Michelle O'Brien) of *This is My Body: Hearing the Theology of Transgender Christians*, she is currently writing a transgender pastoral care manual with the Rev. Dr Chris Dowd.

I began to seriously address my gender identity in 1997, aged forty-six, and transitioned four years later, in 2001. In 1979, aged twenty-eight, I had been ordained as a Church of England priest – then, and until 1993, an exclusively male calling. Becoming a vicar complicated my coming to terms with being trans. Another factor was that, prior to an amendment to the law in 1999, employment protection for trans people who transitioned had been non-existent. The Church still remains exempt from such legislation.

Since 1972 I have also been with the same male partner, Rob. He supported me on the journey to live as my true self. Looking back to the start of our relationship I would now say that I first sorted out my sexuality – I am attracted to men. Only later was I able to fully express my feminine gender identity. I would have preferred to have transitioned when young, as children can sometimes do these days. However, growing up when I did and with the religious beliefs I held then, that seemed impossible. Let me explain further by describing my early life...

Life's a drag

Much to my father's disappointment, I was a feminine boy. As a young child I was happy being myself, largely unaware that I was 'different', but once I reached puberty that changed. I hated it when my legs began to sprout hair, for instance. I tried, reluctantly, to conform to my family's expectations of masculinity, but this was the sixties and I began to hear about homosexuals. I was attracted to other boys. Did this mean I was gay? I also heard about people who had undergone a 'sex change'. Already a secret cross-dresser, I wondered if I should do that too.

In 1967, aged sixteen, a friend's sister lent me Geoff Brown's groundbreaking novel about gender transition, *I Want What I Want*. I hoped to discover the way forward in its pages, but the book made me fearful of expressing my female gender identity as it opens in a mental hospital where the protagonist, Roy/Wendy, has been sent for stealing women's clothes. At this time a boy from my school was arrested in Leeds for cross-dressing. To fully become who I was seemed fraught with danger.

This novel, as I've recently discovered, re-reading it fifty years later, also instilled in me the notion that transition perhaps had to be done by way of theatre. That's the advice of Wendy's fictional clinician, which she firmly rejects; however, I assumed it was correct. The idea rang true because of the extensive publicity at the time about April Ashley, formerly a cabaret artiste in Paris, who underwent gender reassignment surgery in Casablanca in 1960. Though I enjoyed amateur acting, a theatrical career seemed unlikely, and I continued to check the popular Sunday newspapers, which carried sensational stories about people who had 'changed sex'. One report, I recall, featured a 'drag queen' whose ample bosom was due to cross-gender hormones. I realise now that the newspaper had probably wrongly labelled this person a 'drag queen'. Instead, she was presumably transitioning and supporting herself by performing in pubs, but it reinforced the supposed connection between gender variance and entertainment.

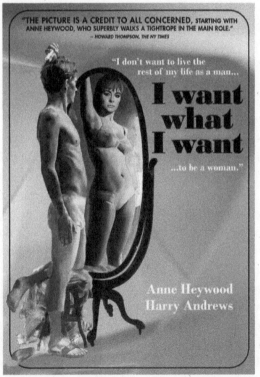

The book *I Want What I Want* became a 1972 film of the same name starring Anne Heywood.

Another article described an ordinary person living happily as a woman. I identified with her and knew I wanted to do that, but many of these features made transsexual people sound seedy. We were also considered odd. I watched presenter Sheridan Morley's BBC Two *Late Night Line-Up* interview with transgender theorist and publicist Dr Virginia Prince. The next day, one television critic wrote that it was the 'weirdest thing' he had seen on air. To me she had appeared articulate and smartly dressed, making nuanced distinctions between sex and gender, but the social stigma then was considerable and inhibited me from acting on my female gender identity.

Vocation was another factor. From the age of twelve I had wondered if I should offer myself as a priest. Priests were men, yet many seemed androgynous. They didn't go 'out to work' for example, their hands were soft compared to the working-class men in my family; some even had high-pitched fluting voices. Perhaps I could 'blend in'. The discernment process, as it is now called, took a while and I was in full-time education for eight years in total: a wonderful excuse to avoid my body by living mainly in my head.

Reading religious studies at Sussex University, I met my partner Rob. He was secretary of the recently formed Sussex branch of the Campaign for Homosexual Equality (CHE). This was 1972, just five years after the decriminalisation of homosexuality. What was I doing there? As social historian Professor Will Brooker notes, in the seventies the term 'gay' included trans people within what was then called 'drag' culture. Here was the contemporary link again between trans people and performance.

Gender and sexuality were blurred in that era. When the gay magazine *Lunch* was launched, gay icon Quentin Crisp asked rhetorically what a gay magazine might contain: advice on how to shave one's legs over the bath? It was a world in which I felt relatively comfortable, even if not fully able to be myself. Rob was happy with my femininity and the 'theatrical' aspects of gay culture enabled us to talk, but in general terms only about how I identified. As a research student in Cambridge in the mid-seventies I consulted Roger Baker's book, *Drag: A History of Female Impersonation in the Performing Arts*, and read about Robyn, neither drag queen nor cross-dresser, but on a journey to her gendered self. I was vaguely aware of another graduate in transition, but I held back, mainly because I had been accepted for ordination.

Coming out – twice

In the seventies the personal lives of those offering themselves for ordination in the Church of England were less scrutinised than they are today. Near the end of ministerial training, circumstances required me to tell the college principal about Rob. From then on anyone who needed to know – ordaining bishop, training priest, etc. – was informed that I had a male partner. What they saw was a gay male couple, my female gender identity being hidden and hard to admit to, even to myself. Working long hours, within a culture of self-denial and putting others' needs first, allowed me to sidestep the issue of my identity at this time, during which women's ordination as priests continued to be delayed.

In 1980 I had been working as an assistant priest in a parish for two years when the BBC screened their documentary *A Change of Sex*, about the male-to-female transition of Julia Grant. She was having a tough time with her paternalistic clinician, Dr John Randell, at Charing Cross Gender Identity Clinic and, even more alarmingly, lost her job as an NHS catering manager simply for transitioning. After watching it I knew that I ought to see my GP, but I was concerned about my future if I did. The Church had invested in training me for my role. Did I really want to throw it away? I carried on, but employability would become an issue.

Compared to today, the Church of England was still a relatively safe place for gay clergy who then, as now, formed a significant percentage of the workforce. There was nevertheless much secrecy. In the mid-eighties conservative Christians wished to purge the Church of England of gay clergy. A positive-leaning Church of England report begun in 1979 was shelved in 1981. Events climaxed in the 1987 General Synod debate, proposed by the Rev. Tony Higton, founder of Action for Biblical Witness to Our Nation (ABWON). The Synod concluded that heterosexual marriage was 'the only proper context for sex'; homosexual genital acts 'fell short of this ideal', and should be met by 'repentance and the exercise of compassion'.

The debate left many people feeling bruised. My own reaction went something like this: 'If the Church is unable to accept the kind of relationship I am assumed to be in (presumed gay) and which people in authority had assured me was acceptable, how will it deal with the real me: the female self who I have so far suppressed?' It was an unhappy time, but I was now in charge of two parishes, drawn there by two women colleagues who were training for a priestly ministry that did not yet exist for women. I became a member of the campaigning group Priests for the Ordination of Women.

Two years after the General Synod debate, in November 1989, a personal breakthrough occurred when I came out during a sermon. On waking one morning this sentence was fully formed in my mind: 'God loves me, including the fact that I'm gay.' The effect was dramatic and I could easily have lost my job. Perhaps I'd intended that, so that I could transition, but I had a vocation and it seemed important to carry on. People knew about Rob, of course, but it was rare then for those in public office to out themselves. Hitherto I had rarely discussed my self-understanding with others. Coming out publicly enabled me to look at myself, and inevitably that included my feminine gender identity.

Soon after coming out someone congratulated me on what I'd said, adding that it was a good role model to see a gay man in a caring profession. I immediately said to myself, 'But I never said that I was a man.' I had used the word 'gay' in that broad seventies sense that included trans. 'Queer' might have been better, but it had not yet been rehabilitated as a term. I now felt able to talk to trusted friends and colleagues about my female gender identity, though I did not transition for another decade, during which time women began to be ordained as priests. The legislation to enable women's ordination was passed in 1993 and the first women were ordained in March 1994. I also attended many dance and movement classes, which connected me with my body and with other women.

Even in the nineties, prior to widespread adoption of the Internet, it was hard for trans people to find basic information about transition. One book that helped me was the 1985 photo anthology *Men in Frocks* edited by Kris Kirk and Ed Heath. Mainly about drag – so once again linking gender variance and performance – the book included a few people who, as the authors acknowledged, could no longer be considered men, since they had transitioned to female. Among those examples was the magician Fay Presto. I was moved to read how her GP explained that she needn't continue living a half-life and that he could help her. Those words stayed with me. I also networked with the London TV/TS society (see chapter 3) but never found the courage to attend any meetings.

In 1997 I was due a sabbatical. It began at Chisenhale Dance Space with the five-day intensive workshop 'Gender in Performance' led by New York-based drag king Diane Torr (1948–2017). Here, at last, I could explore the theatrical aspect of gender variance. It was amazing, but when it ended I knew that I did not want to shuttle between male and female like Diane – 'the best of both worlds' in her words – and that I needed to transition permanently.

Working like the rest of us

Transitioning in a public role seemed daunting, but the year 2000 was approaching and I had no wish to enter the new millennium other than as myself: Christina. I discussed this endlessly with Rob.

In 1989 my parishes and bishop had supported my coming out as gay. I also had 'freehold', which means one can only be removed by doing something criminal or immoral. Being gay is insufficient cause. What about being trans? Once I was ready to explore this, it seemed unfair to test it out on parishes which had generously supported me once already. I had been in post for over a decade and was ready to move, ideally to chaplaincy, which has better boundaries between work and home. Living in a vicarage offers little privacy. But it proved difficult to find a new post. Was this because I'd said that I was gay, or because interviewers intuited I was now addressing my gender identity?

Since I was already difficult to redeploy, I concluded that I should just be myself and face the consequences. Besides, I was in my late forties and felt that time was running out. How long would I delay transition? My dreams were littered with alarm clocks. I networked with the Sibyls, the Christian spirituality group for transgender people, founded by Jay Walmsley in 1996. Sibyls weekends allowed me to meet a range of trans people who also shared my religious faith. In November 1999 I made an appointment with a clinician who I knew would prescribe hormones without a lengthy wait. It was a decision of sorts. Shortly afterwards, in June 2000, I was appointed as a part-time hospital chaplain in Shoreham-by-Sea in Sussex.

I then heard that another priest was transitioning. Announced in 2000, this turned out to be my theological college contemporary from the mid-seventies, the late Rev. Carol Stone – so far the only Church of England parish priest to have transitioned in post. Carol's transition was supported by senior clergy, whereas mine went on to be contested by my bishops and queried by my NHS chief executive when I transitioned at work in 2001. The bishops did not withdraw my licence (my authorisation for that particular post) as had been threatened, but they limited my ministry to the hospital where I was based. This restriction continued for a time on moving to another post in London. I had survived, though, thanks to the non-discrimination protection conferred by the Sex Discrimination (Gender Reassignment) Regulations (1999), and assisted by the human rights NGO Liberty, the trans rights campaign Press for Change and the Sibyls. I then went on to have a successful career as a health-care chaplain. Prior to leaving Sussex I co-founded the Clare Project, based in Brighton and Hove, for people exploring issues of gender.

My experience underlines just how important it was that the law changed to protect trans people's employment. Gender transition isn't an overnight affair. Clinical protocols for mandating treatments entail (even today) a Real Life Experience (RLE), which stipulated at that time that one must be employed, in voluntary work, or a student. However, prior to the amendment to the Sex Discrimination Act (1975) in 1999, which introduced employment rights for those who propose to undergo, are undergoing, or have undergone gender reassignment, people could lose their jobs for transitioning, as Julia Grant did in that 1980 documentary. It was a Catch-22: if you embarked on the RLE you could lose your job. If you lost your job your clinical progress was stalled.

One case I noticed involved a former airline pilot, Kristina Sheffield, who was obliged to work in the sex industry, as many people were then forced to do. NHS protocols insisted that people live and work in role for a year before hormones were prescribed, making them vulnerable at work. Those who could afford it sought private medical care so as to access medication sooner than the NHS permitted. Self-employed people were also often in a better position, as you can't dismiss yourself and the relationship with those you work for is often quite different.

Scenes of clerical life

Before the new millennium there were no role models for UK clergy contemplating transition. Anecdotally, at least one person transitioned in this earlier era but their ministry is said to have ended abruptly. In the late nineties a rumour circulated that two male Church of England clergy had transitioned from female to male. Never confirmed, it seems unlikely. This was long before the days of the Gender Recognition Act (which wasn't enacted until 2004), so they would have been legally women in the eyes of both Church and State. This was precisely the bind faced by an earlier transitioner, Mark Rees, during his unsuccessful attempts to have his priestly vocation recognised in the seventies (see chapter 7). Two US clergy transitioned as male in the Episcopal Church at the millennium, but in the Church of England clergy transitions have been man to woman. Prior to transition all except me were heterosexually married; some are still.

In 1995 a priest transitioned on retirement. Carol Stone's transition followed in 2000 and mine in 2001. The next year another priest approached their bishop about transition, but was given the ultimatum: 'Drop this or go!' She returned to secular employment. In 2004 a priest was persuaded by their bishop to step down from parish ministry 'temporarily' in order to transition, but the bishop never offered her another position. She supported herself and her family for more than a decade and has only recently returned to parish ministry. A Church of Ireland priest, who lost her parish on transition, found a home in the Church of England, but has not resumed priestly ministry.

Apart from Carol Stone, the deployment of clergy who transition has been problematic. Those who transitioned first and then offered themselves for ministry have fared better. Less visible, a policy was put in place for transgender candidates, among them the Rev. Sarah Jones and the Rev. Rachel Mann, who would have been in discernment for ordination when Carol and I transitioned. This was also the period leading up to the Gender Recognition Act (2004), so the Church of England was under pressure from several directions to reach a view on what it referred to as 'transsexualism'.

Some issues in human sexuality

Early in the twenty-first century a working party of four bishops was formed to review the Church of England's position on homosexuality and, almost for the first time, gender variance. Their findings were published in 2003 as *Some Issues in Human Sexuality: A Guide to the Debate*. Chapter seven is entitled 'Transsexualism' and its principal author, Dr Martin Davie, presumably liaised with the former Bishop of Winchester, the late Michael Scott-Joynt. Scott-Joynt had emerged as the lead bishop on this topic, possibly because the priest who transitioned on retirement had been working in his diocese. Judging by this chapter, Scott-Joynt was no advocate for trans people.

The chapter relied heavily on the earlier report *Transsexuality* (2000) published as a book by the Evangelical Alliance (EA), which was fiercely opposed to the UK's proposals for gender recognition legislation. The EA is theologically conservative and, to some extent, biblically literalist. *Transsexuality* argued, on the basis of Genesis 1:26–27, that biological sex is God-given, and hence the mind of someone experiencing gender dysphoria should be adjusted to the body. *Some Issues* referred to this as the 'traditional' theological view, contrasting it with what it called the 'revisionary' position, which considers gender variance, whatever its biological basis, to be authentic, and is supportive of transition. The two were presented as debatable alternatives. Like *Transsexuality*, the chapter showed scant engagement with clinical literature or practice and I critiqued it in the academic journal *Theology*. I also wrote pastoral guidelines for churches, published by the Gender Trust, to counteract the dogmatic approach of these two documents.

The impression given by *Some Issues* – that the two positions on trans people remained undecided – was disingenuous, as the House of Bishops had already agreed, prior to its publication, that both were acceptable in the Church of England. This paved the way for a trans person recognised as their 'acquired gender' by the Gender Recognition Act (2004) to marry someone of the opposite sex in a Church of England church, and for a minister with conscientious objections not to officiate at such a marriage. It is a model that the Church of England could have adopted for equal marriage a decade later, had any bishops been willing to break ranks and speak in its favour.

However, in 2003 there were advocates for trans people among the bishops, including Carol Stone's bishop, Barry Rogerson, and even more outspokenly, the former Bishop of Worcester, Peter Selby. Most Church documents about trans people read as if the authors had never knowingly met a trans person. Bishop Peter had first-hand experience, having facilitated the continuing ministry of the priest who transitioned on retirement when she moved to his diocese. He was also a powerful opponent of an amendment to the Gender Recognition Bill, proposed by Baroness O'Cathain, designed to permit religious groups to exclude trans people. Defeated in the House of Lords, it was reinstated via statutory instrument in 2005.

What sympathetic bishops have not managed to alter is the Church of England's implacable opposition to same-sex marriage, and its reservations about civil partnerships (which it began to appreciate only in the wake of equal marriage). This had unfortunate consequences for trans people who were heterosexually married, as the Gender Recognition Act (2004) stipulated that they could only obtain full gender recognition by first divorcing their spouse and then, if they wished, contracting a civil partnership. It was odd to find the Church's position apparently encouraging divorce. This anomaly was only overturned with the legalisation of same-sex marriage in 2013, but because heterosexual civil partnerships remain illegal, civilly partnered trans people can only obtain full gender recognition by converting to marriage. These examples illustrate the complex interface of sexuality and gender for trans people.

The personal is political

The *Some Issues* chapter noted that one person's transition – presumably mine – was treated differently to Carol Stone's. Perhaps our relationship status was a factor. Carol, who was twice married, was by then single, but presumably this was less significant than the Church's inconsistent attitude to women. Based in Bristol Diocese, Carol's bishop had presided over the first ordinations of women to the priesthood in March 1994, whereas I was then in Chichester Diocese, whose bishops did not believe that women could be ordained, so news of my impending transition must have been a shock. Women's full inclusion in ministry has involved campaigning and compromise. The struggle is not yet over and this affects trans women clergy as well.

I was also on the brink of being outed in the press when I approached my bishop about transition. He was unhappy I had not informed him earlier, but my therapist had advised caution, and maybe I had come to distrust 'need to know' paternalism by then. Being outed, I almost lost control of my narrative, but the press officer at the hospital where I worked as Chaplain helped me wrest it back again.

My experience of discrimination and press intrusion turned me into an advocate for trans inclusion in the Church. I was the first Changing Attitude England Trustee for trans people from 2006 to 2013, and co-edited the Sibyls' book *This Is My Body: Hearing the Theology of Transgender Christians*, published in 2016. Carol chose not to campaign. Her transition attracted more publicity than mine, so her wish to concentrate on her parish and avoid further attention is understandable. As I discovered, twice over, coming out in an organisation that is deeply conservative about gender and sexual orientation is as much a political act as a personal statement, and can be sufficient in itself.

Part Two

Activism

I declared that although it was an apparent defeat the government had not heard the last of the matter. My case was the first but others would follow, of that I was certain. It was not possible for the matter to 'be kept under review' indefinitely. The court would grow weary of a succession of similar cases. We would not give up and would eventually win. The only uncertain factor was when that would happen.

Mark Rees, chapter 7

A Question of Human Rights

The thing that is most surprising, looking back, is that the evolutionary arc of trans people in Britain took so long to birth an activist movement. From the formation of the Beaumont Society in 1966 and the opening of regional support groups in Manchester, London, Leeds, Nottingham and elsewhere during the seventies, the focus was very much on self-help and providing little oases of safety and community in a hostile world.

Progress was steady rather than dramatic. As writers have shown in part one, the overwhelming majority of people taking advantage of these groups and networks were at first cross-dressing men. Transsexual people (women or men) – even if they might be helping to run the groups – were a tiny minority by comparison. And that minority status was compounded by being spread thin around the country without many opportunities to meet just as people sharing the experience of transitioning.

What compounded this further was the pressure on clients of doctors like John Randell to buckle down to show that they could survive as their target gender – a process referred to in those days as the Real Life Test, later renamed Real Life Experience to defuse the idea of it being a 'test' you had to pass. Patients, especially with the NHS, needed to show they could make it in life as the woman or man they sought to be – holding down an approved kind of job (something stereotypically feminine, like office work, for the trans women). Evidence of being involved with your own kind could undermine that. The worst accusation to be levelled by a clinician was that you weren't completely committed. For those trans people trying to 'pass' and live without being seen as trans by employers or neighbours, socialising with others of your kind could also lead to being unmasked. Being discovered to be trans could lead to the sack – there was no employment protection until the late nineties. Being outed could indeed lead to violence from the neighbouring community. And any of these outcomes could lead to 'failing' that all-important Real Life Test.

For cross-dressers and trans people who hadn't yet fully burned their boats with permanent transition, the equation was different. Certainly there were ever-present fears about being 'outed'. The threat of losing a job or family or getting something nasty through your letterbox was a major concern. But, for those who were able to revert their style of dress after a night out, the ability to carry on the rest of life more or less normally meant there wasn't a big activism imperative among the majority. Yes, it was bad that people caught cross-dressing would have a dreadful ride from the police and local press but, so long as trans-friendly venues had somewhere to dress, this risk could be circumvented by arriving for a social event incognito, and changing outfits at the start and end of the evening. Regulars at transvestite-dominated venues would be more likely to get engrossed with talking about steam engines and computers and where to buy clothes than questioning whether their legal status and harassment by police and tabloid journalists could be addressed.

The division between transvestite and transsexual interests took shape in the early eighties with the emergence of the first organisation specifically focused on the needs and interests of transsexual people. The Self Help Association for Transsexuals (SHAFT) – possibly the most inappropriate acronym ever devised – was started by a trans woman called Judy Cousins in 1980. Cousins (1917–1993) was a keen golfer and professional sculptor who, on transition, faked her own disappearance (and implied death) in order to spare her family the shock and shame of learning she was transsexual – a course judged pretty indefensible even by contemporaries. Still, that alone tells you a great deal about the climate in those days.

Surprisingly little is ever said about SHAFT, other than the fact that Judy Cousins appeared to be completely blind to the glaring inappropriateness of the name for her organisation. The group was eventually rechristened the Gender Dysphoria Trust, but its days were numbered. The group fell apart amidst recriminations, yet it did underline the vital need for something

SHAFT was the first group in Britain specifically for transsexual people. The magazine was edited by Alice Purnell, who joined the group in 1984.

in the same vein that would be more focused on the interests of transsexual people.

In 1988 Alice Purnell and others jointly founded a new organisation to fill the void created by the collapse of SHAFT. The Gender Trust was the second British charity now focused on supporting trans people and it expanded rapidly, soon gaining well over a thousand members. Its greatest contribution – apart from being there for a growing number of emerging gender diverse people – was to provide a widely read membership magazine, *GEMS News* (again edited by Alice Purnell), a formidable mailing list (which would later be essential for letter-writing activism), and the basis for staging a vital series of conferences which brought clinicians, lawyers and trans people together to exchange ideas and present papers. The basis for serious intellectual discussion about trans people's lives was taking shape.

The credit for the Gendys conferences must again be attributed to Alice Purnell, using the experience she had built up as a Beaumont Society and Beaumont Trust principal. A 1990 conference held at Hulme Hall in Rusholme, Manchester, under the aegis of the Beaumont Society, demonstrated the need and proved the formula. Subsequently, Gendys-branded

conferences were organised every two years from 1992 until 2004 by Alice and her associate Jed Bland. The formula – a quasi-academic interdisciplinary event with papers and presentations from all sides – was what made the occasions so valuable.

Gendys encouraged

Boy's Own No.19

Robert Allen: born and registered as a girl in 1914; married to a man at the age of 19, served in the forces during the war and for 30 years lived ostensibly as a woman. A change of identity was officially recognsied in 1944 and then he married a woman.

The FTM Newsletter, April 1996
BM Network, London, WC1N 3XX

Supplied by Lee Gale

The Gender Trust, which welcomed all types of trans people – men as well as women – was complemented by the FtM Network, which focused on the particular support needs of trans men. Just as the Gender Trust had *GEMS News*, the FtM Network had *Boy's Own* magazine. This cover from 1996 highlights another of the many trans men from the 1940s.

people to write papers and follow-up articles. It provided an outlet for trans-friendly clinicians as well as thinking trans people. And it made it possible for everyone in newly emerging organisations to get together face-to-face at a time when email was still rare and social media was some years away from being invented and becoming what it is today. For the first time, clinical professionals in Britain found that they needed to present and justify their ideas to a critical client audience that would challenge flawed thinking. Some patriarchal doctors found that uncomfortable at first. Crucially, trans intellectuals also got to present new ideas to each other. It's hard to convey how transformative that was, and how much synergy resulted. Trans people were beginning to form a coherent political narrative about the factors that had kept them marginalised, powerless and afraid.

Those negative factors in trans people's lives had been building throughout the previous thirty years, from the first aggressive newspaper exposés of people like Michael Dillon and April Ashley. Fear of being outed by the press was a powerful enough force to keep people down, but another event was to become the killer blow.

In 1960 (the year before her newspaper exposure) April Ashley had met Arthur Corbett, the son and heir of Lord Rowallan. The couple became close and married in 1963, as transsexual people had proven they could do with a corrected birth certificate. The marriage was not to last, however. They

Alice Purnell pictured at the final Gendys conference in Manchester, 2004.

became estranged and in 1966 April pursued Arthur for maintenance payments. He responded by challenging the whole validity and existence of their marriage, on the grounds that April was legally a man. The dispute went to court, where Justice Ormrod (a judge with a bit of a medical background) devised a formula for deciding the sex of someone in April's position. The medical professionals giving expert evidence were divided over how to classify her – woman or man – leaving the field open for Ormrod to take the part of tie-breaker, proposing a 'test' and definition of his own. The judge suggested four criteria for determining sex, based on chromosomes, gonads (the presence or absence of testes or ovaries), genitals and psychological factors. Transsexualism was deemed to fall under the latter. The ruling, in February 1970, was that April was a man for the purposes of marriage law. The marriage was void. There was no basis for April to claim anything from Arthur.

As former Member of Parliament Dr Lynne Jones notes in chapter 8, the Divorce Reform Act (1969), which introduced the idea of 'irretrievable breakdown' as a ground for divorce, might have provided a less combative way for April and Arthur to sort things out, had it been enacted a few years sooner. History might have been very different as a result.

The *Corbett v Corbett* ruling was not just a personal disaster for April Ashley. The logic meant that the marriages of all the other quietly and happily betrothed transsexual people in Britain were also invalid. It also made transsexualism the province of mental health professionals. What's more, although the decision had concerned April's status for the purposes of marriage law, officials rapidly expanded the scope to every other circumstance where sex was relevant. It meant that trans women couldn't retire at sixty, in an age when women were expected to stop work five years earlier than men. It also meant that the law couldn't recognise rape as rape in the case of a trans woman and that such a woman could expect to be sent to a men's prison if convicted of a criminal offence. Over the years that followed, the negative consequences flowed thick and fast. At a time when gay and lesbian people were beginning to make social progress, life for transsexual people was going downhill fast.

Having a legal status that negates your lived reality is not a problem that most people would ever consider. People take their legal sex for granted – so much so that, prior to Justice Ormrod, the law had never needed to spell it out. Everyone assumed they were the gender indicated on their birth certificate and that wasn't a problem for anyone – even trans people, who had discovered how to get their birth certificates corrected. Take away that facility, however, and an unamended birth certificate was a liability. It's amazing how much official processes relied on requesting to see a person's birth certificate to prove who and what they were. Being a trans person with an uncorrected birth certificate meant that applying for a job could result in your immediate 'outing', no matter how successful and complete your transition had been. The lack of protection from employment discrimination just compounded the situation, making it difficult for trans people to even get interviewed for some jobs.

The Ormrod decision also meant that a trans man couldn't marry a woman and a trans woman couldn't marry a man – that was the whole point in April Ashley's case. Ironically, however, there was nothing in principle to prevent a lesbian trans woman from marrying another woman, or vice versa in the case of a gay trans man. Gender identity – the driving force behind needing to live as a woman or man – has no bearing on sexual orientation (who you want to have sex with). Trans people are as diverse in terms of sexual attraction as everyone else. In fact, although there are no accurate figures, most trans activists agree anecdotally that the proportion of trans women being attracted to other women is somewhat higher than the incidence of lesbianism in cisgender (non-trans) women.

With all these factors bearing down upon trans people it was inevitable that, sooner or later, someone would seek to challenge the inequity of the law. That person was Mark Rees, who tells an abridged version of his story in chapter 7.

The crux of Mark's case, which eventually found its way to the European Court of Human Rights, was that the circumstances in which trans people found themselves as a result of *Corbett v Corbett* violated two key human rights in the convention that Britain had helped draft in 1950.

Article 8 of the European Convention on Human Rights concerns the right that each of us has to 'private and family life, home and correspondence'. Clearly if the documents issued to you and demanded by the state instantly reveal your transsexual status to any official Tom, Dick or Harry, then it is hard to see how those rights can be upheld. There are arguments for weighing one person's rights against the interests of the many, but it was questionable whether the immense consequences of exposure for a man like Mark were proportionate. These were arrangements which stopped him being able to pursue his desired career and exposed him to public ridicule and worse.

Article 12 of the Convention deals with the right to marry and found a family. Again, the effects of the Corbett decision precluded any possibility of Mark settling down and marrying a woman – he wasn't the kind of person who could benefit from being able to marry another man. Besides, the mere fact of being able to marry a man thirty years before equal marriage in Britain would have been just another way of marking yourself out.

These aren't minor issues. The articles of the Human Rights Convention are not about trivial things. They are about the bedrock of security necessary for everyone to live a whole and fruitful life. There was nothing trivial or vexatious about the things Mark and those who followed him were concerned about. And this wasn't about trans people seeking 'special' rights of any kind. This was always about seeking the same rights enjoyed and taken for granted by everyone else.

As explained in chapter 7, Mark's pursuit of his rights took many years and ultimately ended in failure as far as the legal case was concerned. A majority of the international judges hearing his complaint in Strasbourg decided that, whilst the effects described in his team's evidence were real and serious, there wasn't a sufficiently settled convention between the other contracting states to rule that the UK government was out of line. But the judges weren't unanimous: the dissenting views of the minority contained arguments that were to grow in significance in future years. The most important gift of the court was to leave the way clear for other litigants like Mark to follow in future. The matter wasn't to be regarded as completely settled. And indeed it wasn't long before another British litigant came along: Caroline Cossey (aka 'Tula'), the model and television hostess who had been outed by the *News of the World* in 1982, reached the same court with a very similar case in 1990. Again she lost, but with a much smaller margin of difference among the judges. Things were already moving.

Mark Rees describes in his chapter how his court case became the catalyst necessary to create an activist movement. And it was the involvement of the lawyers, including people like trans man Stephen Whittle, that set the tone for the activism.

Some people seek change with big demonstrations and attention-grabbing stunts. That was out of the question for trans people – there were too few and the consequences of protesting in public were too dire. The trans formula for activism was to educate people, make friends in high places, win arguments on the facts and use strategic litigation to break down an unwilling government. Mark's case had been strategic. Many others were to follow.

Looking back, the synergy is remarkable. Mark Rees's and Caroline Cossey's cases (and the resulting publicity) energised trans people around the country. It led to a surge of interest in support groups like the new Gender Trust and the FtM Network (set up for trans men) – there were by then thousands of people who had transitioned in Britain. In turn the Gender Trust and the associated Gendys conferences provided the forum for the new activist group Press for Change to recruit support, build a mailing list, raise money and develop its talking points.

That period – especially in 1992 – constitutes the second big milestone in modern trans history. It was in February of that year that Press for Change was formed, and it was in September that the new group could launch itself to a substantial audience at the first full Gendys conference. There was a sense of possibility in the air. Things were no longer totally, overwhelmingly hopeless. People could see that maybe – not right away, but soon – there might be a way to change the status quo.

It was to be a long haul, as it happens – it took twelve years from the formation of Press for Change in 1992 to the passage of the Gender Recognition Act in 2004. In chapter 8 a former Member of Parliament and key ally, Dr Lynne Jones, describes that haul from her perspective – a fascinating angle which complements the more common accounts of the campaign by trans activists.

There were many intermediate steps along the way:

1993 to 1999: The lengthy legal process that led to trans people being protected from unfair dismissal, as a result of a judgment in the European Court of Justice. The case of *P v S and Cornwall County Council* was the first instance in which a carefully planned legal case by a single individual led to a court decision requiring the government to change national laws. This is what is meant by 'strategic litigation'.

1994: The establishment of a cross-party Parliamentary Forum on Transsexualism, further helping to bring together trans people, clinicians, lawyers and politicians. This was another embodiment of the Press for Change philosophy: making friends and alliances and winning people over with good arguments. It has become fashionable of late to characterise trans activists as strident and unreasonable, yet this couldn't be further from the truth. Trans activists weren't for shutting down debate – they were all for trying to cultivate it in the highest circles.

1996: An attempt to legislate for legal recognition of transsexual people via a private members' bill drafted by Sir Alex Carlile

In this iconic photograph from October 1997 a group of trans people are seen marching from 10 Downing Street (where a petition had been delivered) to a press conference in Westminster. This was one of only two times that Press for Change ever asked trans people to gather in public like this (the other was at the Royal Society of Medicine in 2002).

MP and Terrence Walton (April Ashley's solicitor in *Corbett v Corbett*). Eight years before the actual Gender Recognition Act (2004) this attempt by a senior parliamentary ally was doomed to fail – private members' bills don't succeed unless the government of the day wishes them to do so – but the cause got unprecedented numbers of trans people writing to their MPs to ask for support and helped put Press for Change on the map.

1997: The founding of the Gender Identity Research and Education Society (GIRES), initially intended as a charitable research offshoot of Press for Change. Also the delivery of a 10,000-signature paper petition to 10 Downing Street and an unsuccessful case by Stephen Whittle in the European Court of Human Rights, concerning his status as father to his partner's children. This was also the year when Labour swept into power in a landslide election victory. As Lynne Jones reflects in chapter 8, that didn't help as much as people might have imagined.

In October 1997 Press for Change organised a booth at the Labour Party Conference in Brighton. Visitors included several new government ministers and the Prime Minister's lawyer wife, Cherie Blair. Pictured L-R Alex Whinnom, Christine Burns, Mo Mowlam MP and Michelle Wilson.

1998: The arrival of a trans character, Hayley Patterson (soon to become Hayley Cropper), in *Coronation Street* (albeit played by a non-trans actress, Julie Hesmondhalgh) and Dana International's win in the Eurovision Song Contest – all signs of greater visibility and a social awareness. Also a key High Court ruling confirming that trans people had the right to treatment by the NHS, and another failed attempt in the European Court of Human Rights by two further litigants, Rachael Horsham and Kristina Sheffield. Strategic litigation failed some of the time, yet even the failures tended to move the campaign forwards. In this case the court's judges were so divided in their opinion that the case would have been won if just one had voted the other way. It was a signal that time was running out for the British government.

1999: The Sex Discrimination (Gender Reassignment) Regulations represented the first legislative success for Press for Change, after a year-long battle with civil servants at the Department for Education and Employment. The new provisions meant people were formally protected by the law if they were intending to undergo, were undergoing or had undergone gender reassignment treatment.

2000: A landmark report from a committee of twelve government departments reviewing the government's options for what to do about transsexual people's rights.

2002: The landmark unanimous European Court of Human Rights decision in yet another case brought by transsexual people (*Christine Goodwin (and T) v United Kingdom*), signalling the need for the government to legislate. This time the European Court had had enough and signalled its displeasure that the British government, with over fifteen years to address the issue of legal recognition, had done nothing.

And finally…

2004: The passage of the Gender Recognition Act, largely due to the work put in behind the scenes by Press for Change activists to shape the legislation. It wasn't perfect – Lynne Jones makes clear the Labour government's culpability on that front – but it was the best legislation in the world for its time.

None of this happened in a vacuum of course. The other constant factor throughout this period was decidedly hostile press and media. In chapter 9 the trans journalist and writer Jane Fae examines the history and trends in the way the press dealt with trans people. And in chapter 10 actress Annie Wallace gives the same treatment to film and television. There is also more on this topic from Helen Belcher of Trans Media Watch in part three.

Likewise, these affairs in the activism of trans people cannot be divorced from a consideration of what else was going on at the same time. In 1987, when the government was arguing that Mark Rees wasn't denied the ability to marry – 'he could marry a man,' they said – the Thatcher government back in Westminster was getting ready to introduce the notorious Section 28 of the Local Government Act (1988), targeting education about the lives of gay and lesbian people. It was the time of AIDS, which can affect trans people as well – especially those forced into prostitution to support themselves. It was a period of growth in LGB organising, which eventually saw the inclusion of the letter 'T' for trans. In chapter 11, Sue Sanders of Schools OUT and a founder of LGBT History Month provides a reminder of some of that background and, especially, how the LGBT history movement came to curate and celebrate trans history like this as well.

That period, from the late eighties to the early noughties – and especially the first twelve years of the Press for Change campaign – constituted the second big milestone in modern trans history in Britain, marked by the transition from support to activism and from underdog status to winning international legal cases and pioneering primary legislation.

To have lived through the whirlwind, as this writer did, was to experience the realisation that even the impossible can happen and the most insurmountable-seeming obstacles can be climbed. It was exhausting but exhilarating and life-affirming. And it wasn't the end of the story by far. Changing the law – opening up marriage, protecting privacy and employment and the access to health care – were all essential goals in themselves, but they don't immediately change attitudes within the public at large. Having the law on your side is cold comfort if people still treat you badly – if doctors still obstruct care and if the press, television and film still portray your life as a freak show.

These are not things that you can alter with Acts of Parliament or by taking people to court. They require a social rather than legal revolution, led by many more people with the stamina to fight. By the mid-noughties the activists of the nineties were burned out. In part three we will look at the new activist wave that arose to take their place.

7

Taking to the Law

**MARK REES WITH THE
ASSISTANCE OF KATHERINE
O'DONNELL**

Mark Rees was a vital contributor to the birth of trans activism in the UK. His autobiography, *Dear Sir or Madam*, first published in 1996, told the story of Mark's own life: from birth in December 1942, through childhood, joining the Navy, transitioning to live as a man in 1971, taking his case to Europe in the 1980s and making the vital connections that sparked the campaign that won the rights trans people enjoy in Britain and eventually brought about the Gender Recognition Act (2004). Sir Alex (now Lord) Carlile QC described Mark's autobiography as 'a brave and honest plea for justice… a story of suffering and success'. The *New Law Journal* described it as 'not only moving but required reading for anyone legally and medically concerned'. With Mark's cooperation this is an abridged version of that inspiring story.

A few months after my sixty-fifth birthday, in 2007, I made a formal application for my gender recognition certificate (GRC). This slip of paper, among other things, allows the issue of a new birth certificate with the preferred gender – in my case male – and pronounces the state's certainty that henceforth and for all legal purposes, the holder is of the gender he, or she, says they are.

In short, the certificate and the act that brought it into being is the fruit of more than thirty years of campaigning for the right to live as the man I am and not be stamped by society and the state as the female I could never be. Had it only been available sooner, or perhaps better still never required at all, much of the preceding sixty-four years would likely have been very different indeed and, on balance, my life and circumstances more comfortable.

So it was to my surprise, and considerable annoyance, that my application was sent back. Had I not, after all, had more than a hand in bringing about the legislation that made the GRC possible?

The panel considering my application wrote that to satisfy them I must submit not just a letter from my GP, as I had done, but a report from one of an approved list of specialists in gender dysphoria, confirming a diagnosis and giving details of how the diagnosis was made.

This presented something of a problem. I had made the transition to living as Mark in 1971. While I recognised some of the names on the approved list – having met the doctors concerned at conferences and sometimes in television studios – few had been in practice and some not even born at the time of my transition. I had not been a patient of any of them. As for my original specialist, Dr Randell, it would have been very difficult to make contact with him without either an exhumation certificate or an excellent medium, because he had died years earlier.

It was Dr Randell who had been the first specialist to tell me that my overwhelming need to transition to life as a man was not an impossibility. He had prescribed the testosterone that changed my body and deepened my voice from alto to bass and had firmly offered his professional backing for the moment when I had to explain the situation to the dean of the university where I was studying dentistry. At the time I saw him as my saviour. Yet he continued referring to me in the female pronoun, even years after I had become Mark. Although willing to give me the treatment, Dr Randell made it clear at an early stage that, in his eyes, I was a female and a lesbian and deluded. He never wavered from his assertion that it was solely a psychiatric condition. I never wavered from mine that it was not.

I was born one of premature twins in Kent in December 1942 looking, my father said, like skinned rabbits. My sister, Carol, lived for just five days. Three years later a younger sister, Jane, arrived.

As a child, dressing up was one of my favourite activities because it gave me the opportunity to wear male clothes. I wanted to be a boy even then but, as many of my peers were also tomboys, it was not considered unusual, just something we would grow out of.

At the age of ten I was happily ignorant of any problem of gender identity and still assumed that all girls wanted to be boys, but if I was unaware of my own situation, other people already had inklings. Years after my gender reassignment my mother admitted that she had taken me as a small child to the family doctor because she was concerned about the size of my clitoris and thought I was changing sex. The doctor assured her that there was no cause for anxiety.

In 1980, in the absence of any close family in addition to my mother, 'Aunt' Rose, our long-term neighbour and family friend, made a supporting statutory declaration for my appeal to the European Commission for Human Rights. My mother had stated in her declaration that she had had a job to get me to wear girls' clothes, even when very young. Rose said that from very early days I had exhibited masculine behaviour and even when wearing frocks had not looked like a girl and had always walked with a masculine gait. My subsequent change of role had been no surprise to Rose or any other close neighbours.

Their awareness was, however, of little help in those days. Had I been born thirty years later it is possible that diagnosis and treatment could have been obtained at an early age because St George's Hospital at Tooting in London later opened a clinic for children and adolescents suffering from gender identity problems (gender dysphoria). If my role change had taken place earlier in my life than it did, then much suffering could have been avoided, both for my family and me – for puberty, when it came, was shattering.

Desperately I had prayed to be spared, but at fourteen, later than all my classmates, menstruation began. I was horrified and disgusted and tried to ignore the whole messy business, pretending that it wasn't happening, but it was useless. My mother had to be told. 'You're a woman now,' she said, almost proudly. To her it must have been an immense relief, confirming that I was normal, but few words have brought me so much pain.

In common with my school friends, I went through the 'crush' stage, but unlike them did not go on to find boys attractive. Instead, the objects of attraction were young women – but I never envisaged having a relationship with a woman as a woman; such an idea was abhorrent. My body was, to me, so repulsive that I didn't want to see it myself, let alone allow anyone else to do so. Sometimes mocked outside of school for my mannish dress and manner, I realised that what others took for granted – sexual relationships – would be barred from me.

That is not to say that it was to be a life without friends – and it was to friends that in time I confided what I felt to be my terrible secret and even eventually to an exceptional and sympathetic GP. Their love and kindness was deeply moving but nobody imagined, at the dawn of the sixties, that anything could be done about it. After school, I experienced depression, followed by a few weeks in a mental hospital. I had a succession of dead-end jobs and a disastrous two-year spell in the Women's Royal Naval Service. All of it failed to dispel the certainty I felt that I could not live my life as a woman. By 1971 I was at university, being treated by Dr Randell and about to start again as Mark at the beginning of the autumn term.

I was doubtful that it would be possible for me to pass as a man by then but had to trust Dr Randell's assurance that all would be well. I was changing roles but once, whereas he'd seen it many times. The results of the hormone therapy were more immediate than I'd expected. Menstruation ceased almost immediately, to my profound relief, and within a few weeks my voice was changing enough for people to ask what was wrong with my throat. Any enquiries I answered by explaining that it was a bad bout of catarrh, which was partially true. The friendly lady in the students' union cloakroom continued to enquire about my 'bad throat' for some weeks.

'You should see someone about it.'

'Don't worry, Elsie. I'm seeing a doctor!'

I told my sister before approaching our mother. She was supportive and positive – and for a while the only member of my immediate family who was. I had supposed that my mother had always had some inkling. It seemed not and it took her some time to come around. But when she did, it was with unstinting love and fierce protectiveness.

Around this time a solicitor told me that I'd be able to alter every document except my birth certificate, which meant of course that marriage to a woman would be impossible. It didn't worry me unduly at that point, but lack of legal recognition and the impact it would have – not just on marriage, but on my privacy, on employment and parental rights, access to appropriate health care and so on – would eventually prompt me to take up a campaign which would change my life.

My personal fight started in 1972, when I wrote to Renée Short MP. Over the next ten years or so I was to write many letters to many MPs but the result was always the same: the MP usually wrote to the Home Office or the Registrar General and would then pass on a copy of the reply with a note of sympathy. The reply would say that the sex description on the birth certificate was an historical fact and therefore an alteration would allow us to 'deceive others' as to our 'true sex'.

What the replies never stated was that until the *Corbett v Corbett* divorce case in 1970, transsexual people did get their birth certificates amended. I know of one who legally married in her new role.

The Corbett case was cited ad nauseam in defence of the government's stance. It involved male-to-female April Corbett, née Ashley, whose husband Arthur wanted a divorce. Mr Justice Ormrod ruled that a change of sex was impossible. For the purposes of marriage April was a man and therefore the marriage was void. Although the judge stated that his definition of sex applied specifically to marriage it had since been used by the government whenever sex was legally relevant, so that transsexual people had no legal standing in their adopted roles. In law they remained of their natal sex description.

Angry but undaunted, I plodded on and even got friends to write to their MPs. It seemed a very lone campaign; surely other transsexual people ought to have been doing something too? Then a friend said that she'd heard of a Belgian female-to-male who had taken a case to the European Court of Human Rights, and why didn't I?

So I did. In 1979 I wrote to Liberty (then the National Council for Civil Liberties) and was recommended a lawyer, David Burgess, who was willing to do this. In turn he briefed Nick Blake as counsel. I could not have had a better or more caring team.

David (later Sonia) Burgess (1947-2010) was a lawyer who went on to specialise for most of their career in immigration cases, achieving several landmark successes in both the domestic courts and the European Court of Human Rights. Mark may not have been aware at the time, but Burgess was transgender and eventually transitioned as Sonia in 2005, retaining the name David just for legal work. Then in 2010, in a strange twist, Sonia was pushed in front of an Underground train by a mentally disturbed transgender client, sparking an angry online controversy about the way they were both described by the press reporting the event. The event coincided with the rise of a new generation of activists concerned about the way trans people were treated by the press (see Helen Belcher in chapter 17) but only one or two ever made the connection between Burgess's advocacy for a trans pioneer in the eighties and being posthumously defended by another trans generation thirty years later. What is certain is that Mark Rees was in the best of hands.

Five years and mountains of paper later we flew to Strasbourg for the hearing before the European Commission for Human Rights. 'You are brave to do this!' people said. 'Fancy facing all those judges.' In truth I was more anxious about flying than coping with the hearing, although my heart thumped furiously against my ribs as I sat before the commission listening to Nick present my case and the government lawyer oppose it. I felt a great sense of unreality. It was difficult to realise that 'the applicant' to whom they were referring was me.

My application, which was heard on 14 March 1984, was declared admissible by the commission. The procedure was that the commission would then invite the parties to reach a friendly settlement, which usually took a few months. The government, predictably, was not prepared to do this, so on 18 March 1986, two years later, my application was taken by the commission to the European Court of Human Rights (ECHR).

Unlike the earlier hearing, which had been held in private, this was in open court with seventeen judges. It was somewhat daunting, although Nick of course did all the speaking. 'Whatever happens,' David whispered, 'you'll now go down in the law books and journals. You're making history.'

It had not been my intention to do that, but he was right. I was the first UK transsexual individual to take action against the government and subsequently saw my name many times in various journals, '*Rees v United Kingdom*'. 'David and Goliath,' I thought.

Unfortunately, on this occasion, Goliath won. On 17 October of that year, judgment was finally handed down. We had lost. It was a shock and a great disappointment. I was greatly saddened that all the efforts of Nick and David were apparently wasted. Nonetheless I was determined to persist. We would just have to carry on our battles on a different front.

David described the judgment as a Pyrrhic victory, and it was clear that the court did not consider its dismissal of my appeal as the final word on the matter, because the judges recommended that 'the need for appropriate legal measures should therefore be kept under review having regard particularly to scientific and societal developments'.

In the subsequent inevitable media interviews I declared that although it was an apparent defeat the government had not heard the last of the matter. My case was the first but others would follow, of that I was certain. It was not possible for the matter to 'be kept under review' indefinitely. The court would grow weary of a succession of similar cases. We would not give up and would eventually win. The only uncertain factor was when that would happen.

Ah, but the media… that was Strasbourg's unwitting gift to me. Having promised not to identify me, the press were handed my full name and address on court documents shortly before the hearing.

My details were there for all to see. Like it or not, I was exposed. My private life was now public property. It was especially ironic in view of the fact that one of the articles cited in my appeal was 'respect for private life' (Article 8). David Burgess was equally angry. He said we could withdraw the case and start the whole process again, but I didn't want to waste another six years.

'I'll risk it. We'll carry on. At least I know what to expect.'

It was inevitable that there would be media interest; after all I was a pioneer, and, even more interesting for some people, a 'sex-change'. A journalist friend, Wendy Cooper, advised me to speak to the serious press if approached. This would stop the gutter press, who were only interested in 'exclusives'.

I 'came out' on 7 March 1986 with a report on the BBC One *Nine O'Clock News*. This was eleven days before the court hearing in Strasbourg. John Harrison came to interview me and my mother. He was the first television journalist I'd ever met and undoubtedly one of the best. When John was killed in a car accident during his time as the BBC's Southern Africa correspondent, I felt that I'd lost a friend.

On the same day as my first interview with John, Jenny Cuffe interviewed me for *Woman's Hour*. This was broadcast as I was about to leave for the airport and Strasbourg. Jenny was also an interviewer of great integrity and sensitivity. Subsequent experience taught me that not all journalists possessed these qualities.

I have, over the succeeding years, had many encounters with journalists and TV interviewers. There were times when it felt almost like a one-night stand. Great interest and sympathy would be affected, they'd get their story – then vanish. I was an object, a story to be exploited at minimum cost. In a way, the media were guilty of abusing us. There were certain TV programmes that clearly regarded us as entertainment. One researcher actually used that term when telephoning me to invite me onto a programme. She did not gain my co-operation. At first I did agree to such invitations, idealistically believing that perhaps it would help people to understand the situation. It might have done to a certain extent but it was often obvious that the minimum amount of research, if any, had been done.

The other 'trick' of the programme makers was to find someone willing to oppose us. Sometimes they had difficulties in finding people to do this so they ended up with one or two 'professional' antagonists whom we'd meet again and again! I wondered if the programme makers felt it necessary to find opponents to treatment when discussing other medical conditions?

It seemed that many in the media were obsessed by sex and incapable of interviewing any transsexual person or partner without asking them, 'What do you do for sex?' A friend's partner gave a superb response, which I shamelessly repeated when in a similar situation: 'Well, what do you do?'

To be fair, however, I have also encountered people from all parts of the media who took the topic seriously and researched carefully. They were caring and courteous and I was pleased to take part in their thoughtful and responsible programmes which undoubtedly did a great deal to ease the lot of the transsexual community.

My initial reaction to my unexpected media exposure had been one of total dismay but I soon realised that it was very positive. No longer was I looking over my shoulder and wondering 'who knows?' Nor was I afraid of someone passing on my 'dreadful secret', nor could I ever be blackmailed. I lost no friends but made more. The 'monster' of revelation had turned out to be a friendly kitten.

It was a liberation. I was freed from a fear that had long haunted me, and also freed to educate others, either directly or by just being seen to live a normal life. I was also made aware of the support of many people, some of whom were unknown to me. Total strangers stopped me in the street, both in my home area and elsewhere, to express their support. By hiding I'd been saying to the world 'this is shameful' and 'I cannot believe that you have the capacity to show love'. Of course there were a few who were unpleasant, but only a very few.

The transsexual community adopted me and I began to receive newsletters from the various self-help groups. Most had not existed when I was changing roles, and by this time I did not need their support, but I contributed to their newsletters, and I hope that some of my articles may have helped people.

After years of isolation, and as I began to meet other transsexual people, I became convinced that we were as diverse as any other section of society; in fact we were a microcosm of society as a whole. No one can describe a typical transsexual individual. When invited to address an FtM (female-to-male) group I was interested to see that the audience was made up of everyone from yuppies to bovver boys! It was also interesting to observe that the average height was about five foot four, so I felt less conscious of my small stature. I was delighted to see a number of family members, partners and friends at that meeting. One thing which has struck me about the FtM network is that as a group it is very caring. There is a great deal of mutual support.

When the news of the ECHR judgment broke I received many messages of sympathy and encouragement. One of the most notable people to contact me at the time was the Liberal Democrat MP and lawyer, Alex (later Lord) Carlile, QC, who later wrote the preface to the first edition of my memoir *Dear Sir or Madam*, published in 1996. His words of support were put into action and he was to campaign doggedly on our behalf until the battle was won.

As I had been a lone campaigner for transsexual rights, so too for some time was Alex within the parliamentary sphere. Legal recognition for transsexual people was not likely to be a vote-winner or an opening to high office. As he stated in his preface, he attempted to interest other politicians 'with mixed success'. I suspect that he had some scornful comments; it was after all a subject that still aroused such reactions. We were very fortunate that he continued to battle on our behalf. Eventually many MPs of all parties would support the cause.

It had undoubtedly been difficult to fight a cause almost single-handedly, but the publicity surrounding my ECHR case resulted in other transsexual people coming forward. I saw my long-held desire to see a campaign group formed becoming a real possibility.

With Alex's backing I organised a fringe meeting at the Liberal Democrat Federal Conference in 1991. It was a total act of faith. I was not certain that it would be possible to get other speakers as well as Alex, whether there would be any interest on the part of the delegates or how I could afford the costs. I asked myself: whatever was I doing booking a room in a smart Bournemouth hotel?

Thanks to the generosity of some of the transsexual people with whom I had made contact and of a lawyer and a medical specialist who kindly gave their time, the meeting took place. Alex expertly chaired, for which I was very grateful. To my relief I was not the only transsexual person present. One of those who accepted my invitation to attend and speak was Stephen Whittle, a law lecturer. He was to become very active and involved in the subsequent campaign, and was later to receive official recognition of his expertise and very hard work on behalf of people like us.

Alex had ensured that we had some reasonable press coverage. We did not want to address just a few conference delegates, however understanding they might be. Generally the coverage was sympathetic, though a subsequent article by Claudia FitzHerbert in the *Telegraph* left Alex incandescent. It was an appalling piece but we agreed that perhaps it was better to ignore the matter rather than keep it boiling, which can sometimes be counterproductive. Certainly it was a reminder that we had more than the challenge to get the law changed; we had also to overcome people's attitudes. As this piece had shown, a 'good education' was not necessarily a guarantee of an accepting attitude. Claudia FitzHerbert's very unpleasant stance was negated by a sympathetic and informed article in *The Times* by Liz Hodgkinson, who had previously written well-researched books about the subject. We had reason to be grateful to responsible journalists like Liz who fully supported us.

By 1991 my privacy was no longer an issue and the chances of my ever being in a position to marry were very remote, so why did I feel driven to carry on the battle for legal recognition? In spite of being open about my situation, it gave me concern to see my screen on the Jobcentre computer: 'Mark Rees. Single Female'. It was also very unsettling to know that we had no legal protection. Had I been in employment at that time it would have been quite lawful for my employer to dismiss me solely for being transsexual. Or I could have been in trouble for using the gents toilet. Given that I had a red beard and was clearly socially accepted as male I would probably also have found myself in trouble if I used the ladies.

In having contact with an increasing number of transsexual people, I began to learn of the problems some experienced because of the lack of legal status congruent with our social roles. A male-to-female transsexual person who was living unobtrusively with a man she had married (unlawfully because she was legally still male) was betrayed and subsequently arrested. The friend of a deceased transsexual person went to collect the latter's death certificate. Thanks to a vindictive person who had telephoned the registrar, the certificate read, 'Mary Smith. Male.' Transsexual people could very easily become victims of such individuals.

My friend Stephen Whittle was also in an untenable legal situation. He had been living with his girlfriend, Sarah, for about twenty years. After undergoing much investigation, the couple was allowed to start a family by artificial insemination. Sarah eventually had four children. Anyone who knew this family would have been very impressed by the loving and stable home which Stephen and Sarah gave to the children, something that many offspring of so-called 'normal' parents are denied. Yet at that time Stephen, being legally female, could neither marry Sarah nor become the children's adoptive father. Had Sarah died, the children could have been quite lawfully removed from Stephen's care because he had no parental rights.

These few examples show how the then-current legal situation was causing distress, not only to transsexual individuals but also to other people who were close to them. It could also be disconcerting for the officials (such as registrars, police and Jobcentre staff) whose roles demanded that they follow the law. Legal recognition, then, would ease life for a wide range of people.

The fringe meeting at the Liberal Democrat Conference had been successful in a very important way; it had brought some of us together, which gave me the incentive to move matters on. Again with Alex Carlile's support, I contacted several interested people – both transsexual and sympathetic professionals – and organised a meeting that was held in Alex's office at the House of Commons on 27 February 1992. Alex's wisdom and parliamentary expertise was of great help. It was clear from the outset that, although relatively few in number, there were enough enthusiastic and competent people for a campaigning group to start. I felt very happy to see my dream becoming a reality.

A general election was looming and Alex advised us to write to every MP in the new Parliament and ensure that our letter would be one of the first to land on each of their desks. He didn't think that we'd get much of a response – and he was right – but at least we had some replies. It was a beginning.

Alex's final recommendation to us that afternoon was to repair to Grandma Lee's café opposite the House of Commons. Having firmly decided to set up a group we wondered about a suitable name. Suddenly someone said, 'Press for Change!' It was a spark of inspiration. We all agreed and thus the movement was born and named.

Press for Change, or PFC as it became commonly known, was to grow and become influential in a way far beyond anything I could have envisaged. Its full story is too grand for a simple chapter and, besides, has been told elsewhere. But of my role I

The very first campaign literature produced by Press for Change was a two-sided A4 leaflet, sent to members of Parliament and distributed for supporters to use. Mark Rees was pictured on one side and another early activist, Myka Scott, on the other. From the beginning PFC was a campaign about both trans women and trans men.

will say this: my prediction, made after my unsuccessful appeal to the ECHR in 1986, that others would follow me to Strasbourg, was beginning to be realised. The trickle of appellants to that court and others, both European and domestic, developed into a steady flow, with PFC encouraging transsexual people to take action whenever possible.

The case of *P v S and Cornwall County Council* was heard before the European Court of Justice in 1996. In its judgment the court declared unlawful the dismissal of people from employment on the grounds of their transsexual condition. This declaration was formally incorporated into law in April 1999 as the Sex Discrimination (Gender Reassignment) Regulations. At last employers were no longer able to sack employees purely on the grounds of their transsexual status. Although it was to be a few more years before we were given full legal recognition, this was a very welcome move forward. The refusal of a health authority to sanction gender reassignment treatment of transsexual people was successfully challenged in the courts and upheld on appeal (also in 1999). Others took action over pension rights of partners.

We wanted to be seen as apolitical but most PFC campaigners admitted that the election of a Tory government in 1992 was a disappointment. Certainly there were some Tory MPs who were sympathetic to our cause, but whatever our individual party allegiances, it was generally felt that there would be a greater chance of getting a change in the law under a Labour administration.

Nonetheless we had a lot of work to do if we wanted to gain support from both Parliament and the British people. Few MPs would want to vote for legislation that had no support from the voters. I had always perceived the campaign as one of water on stone, a slow and gentle attrition of the resistance. We would get there. Some members of our community, understandably perhaps, were quite belligerent, wanting immediate results, but my view was that it was more productive to be patient and always polite. The seemingly awkward civil servants and politicians were, in the main, not 'enemies'. It was just that many of them were bound by rules and woefully ignorant of our situation, as was the general public. With the exception of a very few people who were determined to remain bigots, our only 'enemy' was ignorance, which we would gradually overcome. We were to find that we had many potential friends, both in Parliament and outside. It was a source of great pride to see PFC become an organisation that was respected by those with whom it dealt because of its professionalism and courtesy.

Whilst some people wanted change immediately, the wiser members of our community realised that good legislation was not made in a rush. Frustrating as it might have seemed, there was now opportunity to prepare the ground carefully. PFC spent the period between 1992 and the election of a Labour government in 1997 very fruitfully. With the advent of the Internet, small organisations like PFC were able to communicate with many people in a way hitherto impossible. It was soon gaining much support from members of the transsexual community and also giving them a chance to contribute to the campaign in many ways. No longer did they feel isolated in their efforts, as I had done twenty years earlier.

Other PFC campaigners took up my idea of fringe meetings at party conferences, so we thus made ourselves known to all three major parties and elicited support from other MPs. One of these was Labour Member Dr Lynne Jones (chapter 8) who, together with Alex Carlile, set up an all-party Parliamentary Forum on Transsexualism in 1994. They were joined later by Conservative MP Roger Sims, who was recruited to the cause by leading PFC campaigners Stephen Whittle and Christine Burns at the 1995 Conservative Conference fringe meeting.

Alex was elevated to the House of Lords and Roger Sims retired from the Commons at the next general election in May 1997, leaving Lynne as the sole chair of the Forum. The Forum consisted not only of MPs but also medical specialists, lawyers and activists.

In 1997 Tony Blair moved into Downing Street and Britain had a Labour government. We were confident that things would improve for us, although not immediately. Thanks largely to the effort of the Parliamentary Forum and PFC, an interdepartmental working group (IWG) was established in 1999 by then Home Secretary, Jack Straw, to examine the legal status of transsexual people and recommend possible provisions which should be made to alleviate the situation. There were other cumulative factors that possibly contributed to this action: recent cases at the European Court of Human Rights indicated that the court was losing sympathy with the government, and the contemporary story in the soap opera *Coronation Street* regarding the transsexual character Hayley had evoked considerable public interest and sympathy.

The IWG consisted of representatives of twelve government departments and deliberated for a year. To its credit it also met members of the transsexual community before completion of its task. Its report was published in the spring of 2000 and this was to contribute greatly to the development of subsequent legislation. I reflected on the letters received from the Home Office twenty or more years earlier which told me that a change of registration would not be acceptable because it would enable us to deceive others as to our 'true sex'. By contrast my PFC colleagues, some of whom were specialists in lobbying, problem-solving and the law, formed good relationships with the government officials, to the benefit of all.

It is sometimes the case that those who initiate projects are not the people who then run them. This was certainly so with PFC. Although the initiator of the group, I soon realised that others had administrative and legal skills which I certainly lacked. At the beginning I was also disadvantaged by not having a computer. Technology and expertise overtook my amateur efforts, added to which I was geographically distant from what had become the hub of PFC in Manchester. After twenty-five years of almost lone campaigning I had lost much of my drive and also felt very strongly that I wanted to do much more with my life than just spend the rest of it in the campaign. Eventually I resigned from PFC.

The court battles and lobbying continued into the new millennium, and eventually the legal victory we had so long sought came about. In July 2002, sixteen years after my appeal to the European Court of Human Rights (*Rees v United Kingdom*), the Strasbourg judges ruled *unanimously* in the case brought by two other transsexual people, Christine Goodwin and one known anonymously as 'I', that the UK had breached Articles 8 and 12 of the European Convention. These were the same articles under which my case was heard. After a succession of similar cases brought against the UK government, the Court of Human Rights had clearly lost patience. Something now had to be done. After having been 'on hold' for a couple of years the interdepartmental working group was reconvened and, after much discussion and hard work with Press for Change and other concerned groups, the draft Gender Recognition Bill was introduced in July 2003.

We were nearly there.

After the successful and aptly named Goodwin case I was once more contacted by the BBC. Clearly they expected me to be euphoric, but I was not. After thirty years of campaigning it seemed unreal. Besides, for me, it was too late in one very big respect. Although I've not mentioned it before in this account, the Church had played a great part in my life and the many people of faith I had known had so often offered friendship and understanding when others had not. My ambition had been to enter the priesthood when I was younger, but that was at a time when my legal status as female completely disqualified me.

Indeed, it was the refusal of the Church of England to consider me for ordination, because of its stance on women priests, which had driven me first to agnosticism and ultimately to Strasbourg. The chances of my following that calling at the age of nearly sixty seemed very remote and marriage was equally unlikely. As an ageing transsexual person of very limited means and with a poor cardiac prognosis, it was unrealistic to hope that anyone would want to share my life.

My personal disappointments apart, I still felt it necessary to liaise with the Church of England at least, on behalf of transsexual people.

In November 2000, after much correspondence with the Church of England's Board for Social Responsibility, I was invited to meet the secretary, David Skidmore, and Michael Scott-Joynt, Bishop of Winchester. I was pleased to have PFC's Susan Marshall, a practising Anglican, former naval officer and qualified barrister, with me for this meeting. The bishop seemed interested to hear what we had to say and we were pleased to know that at long last the Church was willing to have a dialogue with us. The case of the Rev. Carol (née Peter) Stone was in the news at the time, and we thought that perhaps we would be able to give the bishop some relevant information. We were assured that there was to be a working party of bishops, chaired by Bishop Michael, which would be examining the issue and ultimately publishing its conclusions.

At least the C of E had invited us to meet them, which is more than can be said for the Evangelical Alliance (EA), which, early in the spring of 2001, published its report *Transsexuality*, which declared that transsexual people were deluded and their lifestyles incompatible with the will of God. They called for the government not to grant us legal recognition.

We wondered why the EA had made transsexualism such a major campaign. It was almost an obsession. Weren't there more important issues for them as Christians to consider? As well as opposing the Gender Recognition Bill they were also against gender reassignment treatment and asserted that the condition could be cured. Since it was unlikely that many transsexual people would want to have anything to do with them and therefore would not 'taint' their gatherings, why their concern? On a wider scale, as one of our activists remarked, even if we received legal recognition, the trains would still run.

Regrettably, some clergy and others took the EA report as authoritative with the result that some transsexual people were treated with less than Christian understanding and left their churches in distress. At the other end of the ecclesiastical spectrum, in early 2003, the Vatican declared that it would not recognise change of gender roles, which it regarded as sinful. Those Catholics who had undergone such would not be permitted to marry in their new roles, or become priests, monks or nuns.

Ironically (or deliberately?) this announcement was made whilst the Lord Chancellor's Department was working hard with representatives of the transsexual community to frame legislation which would be acceptable to all. It seemed that the secular world often had greater love for transsexual people than the body that so often preached the importance of love – the Church. Yet we did have much support from many church people, both ordained and lay. History tells us that it has usually been the bishops (Lords Spiritual) who have opposed compassionate and socially beneficial legislation in Parliament. One has only to look at their efforts to block the reforming acts of the 1830s to see this trait. It is hard to reconcile such attitudes with those of Jesus of Nazareth.

Whilst the bill received overwhelming support in the Commons (by 355 to 46) its prior passage through the Lords was less smooth. An unholy alliance of Norman Tebbit, Detta O'Cathain of the Christian Institute and a few bishops of the Church of England, amongst others, did their best to destroy the legislation. O'Cathain described those of us who had taken our cases to the European courts as 'nasty and devious', which prompted a very angry reaction from Alex Carlile, who pointed out that he knew me personally. One of the leading episcopal opponents to the bill was Michael Scott-Joynt, Bishop of Winchester. This was somewhat ironic and disappointing, given that Susan and I had earlier spent some time with him at Church House, carefully explaining our situation. At least, unlike some, he was courteous.

In spite of their efforts, the Evangelical Alliance and other Christian fundamentalists lost their fight to destroy the bill. The Gender Recognition Act received royal assent in July 2004. Yet they refused to give up gracefully and persisted with their campaign. In April 2005 a statutory instrument (SI) was added to the act. This concerned disclosure of a person's transsexual status for, inter alia, legal, medical and religious purposes.

Probably few of us would have been too upset by this provision, given safeguards, for legal and medical purposes. Yet, as a result of the fundamentalists' persistence, the SI also gave this right to religious bodies to check whether or not a person was transsexual. They pressed for this so that they could refuse to officiate or permit a marriage of such a person, bar them from ministry or any other employment, office or post within a church, including religious orders, and even deny church membership to the individual. Additionally, this exclusion enabled churches to decide 'whether the person was eligible to receive or take part in any religious sacrament, ordinance or rite, or take part in any act of worship or prayer, according to the practices of an organised religion'. A licence for intolerance and bigotry had sullied a compassionate piece of legislation.

In June 2008 I was invited to address a meeting of Changing Attitude, England, a predominantly Anglican group concerned with the treatment of lesbian, gay, bisexual and transgender people in the church. I read to them an extract from the statutory instrument. They had not been aware of it and were shocked and angry to learn of its contents. One lady, a member of General Synod, was considering raising the matter at Synod. They asked how it could have come about. I had assumed that the extremists had been responsible for this appalling measure but promised to make further enquiries. Christine Burns was able to confirm what had happened. She wrote:

> To answer your question, the government was subjected to very determined lobbying by the Christian Institute and Evangelical Alliance – the latter claiming, of course, to represent one million Christians. The civil servants showed me a huge trolley containing 10,000 letters that had been sent to the Prime Minister – each saying how they feared their faith was under threat if they couldn't know if their Church might be marrying a transsexual or (worse still) promoting one to a lay position within their congregations. (These are the same people, of course, who also painted stereotypes of the 'you can always tell' variety). The civil servants and ministers were hearing no alternative viewpoint. Church House was silent on the matter; so was Lambeth. So what do you expect? They were already so scared of wrecking the precarious deal they'd got to get the Civil Partnership bill through (and remember this was to follow the GRA) so they didn't want to rock the boat and appeasement was the order of the day.

People assumed that as one of the old campaigners I would be among the first to take advantage of the Gender Recognition Act (2004), change my registration and acquire a new birth certificate showing my present male status. I did not. As a woman in law I had been entitled to the State Retirement Pension when I reached the age of sixty in December 2002. At first I was unwilling to accept this – after all, I was living in a male role – but then a friend bluntly said, 'The government has buggered you up for years, grab the money!' After reflecting upon the difficulties that had come my way I realised she was right, so accepted the pension. Since I was working only part-time the extra money from the pension was very welcome, although half of it went back in tax.

Which was why, at sixty-five, I found myself on the wrong end of the very process of recognition I had played a part in creating. I should not have worried. The friendships forged at PFC came to my rescue in the form of Christine Burns, who contacted a sympathetic psychiatrist she knew, Stuart Lorimer, who was one of the GIC team in Fulham, formerly at Charing Cross Hospital. He was very willing to write a report but, quite understandably, wanted to meet me. It was a very agreeable encounter. Stuart asked and I answered all the right questions, although he already knew how I would reply, having read my book. I thought it likely that most of the present specialists were probably still unborn when I changed roles and Stuart confirmed that he was then one year old. Nonetheless his report was accepted and I was grateful to him.

On 30 May 2008 I heard the post arrive. A large 'DO NOT BEND' envelope dropped onto my doormat – bent by the postman because he did not bother to knock at the door. It was my gender recognition certificate. After a wait of thirty-six years I was now legally male. It was a strange feeling but also a little anti-climactic. The accompanying information informed me that I now had the rights appropriate to a person of my acquired gender, including the right to marry someone of the opposite gender. 'It's a bit late now,' I thought.

My new birth certificate arrived later. This had a more profound and unexpected effect on me than the gender recognition certificate. Suddenly I thought, 'This is wrong!' I was not born a boy or male. Yet I knew that I was never a normal girl. The discussions I had had with David Burgess at the time of my Human Rights appeal came back to me. Our concern was not so much the birth certificate as legal recognition of one's current gender status. The major problem had been caused by the use of a birth certificate in order to prove identity. That would have been less of a problem if transsexual people had been totally accepted in society. Would the answer have been identity cards for all which showed current status? Or birth certificates that left gender blank until the child's status was certain? Given that sex is a spectrum, with more people than generally realised falling between the two poles, that would surely have been a more realistic and humane approach. Or is it necessary to put any gender at all?

After a short period of wrestling with my conscience I decided that it was a reflection of my social status. What had been possible had been done medically and surgically but it was a compromise. Compromises might not always be comfortable but they can be more so than the alternatives. I put the new certificate away in the deed box to join its predecessor, one marking the start of my life and my campaign for legal recognition, the other marking its success.

Over the years I had come to realise that whether committed to a particular faith or not, in seeking reassignment, transgender people are ultimately seeking wholeness. This is surely a religious, indeed a spiritual quest. Probably no human being will ever find total wholeness but, for the gender dysphoric person, gender reassignment will certainly be movement towards it.

It is ironic that whilst in the twenty-first century some religious people seek to deny those who are transsexual basic rights, there were ancient mythologies and civilisations that recognised the male and female in each person, and accepted into their societies those who were probably transsexual. A clergyman wrote to me of the Maori attitude to an individual who was different: 'To treat that person as special, not suspect. To ask what contribution such a person can make to the common good, not whether they belong or not.'

Whilst these and similar cultures may not have the medical and surgical means to help the transsexual person, they give what is more important – acceptance (which is not synonymous with 'tolerance') into the community. Even with our advanced techniques, a transsexual person's treatment is less than fully effective if this integration into society is not available. Some may see legal recognition as the ultimate acceptance, but I believe that the love of those around is more important than an amended document.

I have received much love, not only from my beloved late mother, family and friends, but also from caring professionals and people I've hardly known. Neither their love nor medical science has made me 'fully male' but it has made me more fully myself, and thus able to contribute to the common good.

My role-change was almost a religious experience. It freed me to live a life that was infinitely more fulfilling than I had ever dreamed possible. It gave me the opportunity to experience love, both given and received, in a much richer and deeper way than before. For that I am truly thankful.

8

The Parliamentarian

DR LYNNE JONES

For eighteen years – between the 1992 general election and her decision to step down in 2010 – Dr Lynne Jones was the Member of Parliament for the Birmingham Selly Oak constituency. A biochemist by training (she earned her Ph.D. in 1979) Lynne joined the Labour Party in 1974 and became a councillor on Birmingham City Council before standing for Parliament for her home constituency. Her politics  came from personal experience of poverty and of mental illness in the family. She always stood up for disadvantaged people and against policies she saw as irrational, even if it meant defying the party line. Her involvement in the political campaign for trans rights came about by chance early in her parliamentary career and became one of her proudest achievements.

It was my Friday 'surgery', about a year after I had been elected MP for Birmingham (Selly Oak) in 1992. An anxious-looking man entered the room and proceeded to quiz me about confidentiality. He had not come on his own behalf but to test me out to see whether I could be trusted with some personal information about his partner. I managed to reassure him that I would never disclose anything told in confidence and we agreed to meet again the following week to talk through his partner's concerns. Nevertheless, when the time came, she – I will call her J – still didn't feel sufficiently secure to appear herself but was represented by a friend, Zoë Playdon. J was what was then called a male to female transsexual. Nowadays, the consensus amongst transgender people themselves is to use the terms trans woman and trans man. Henceforth in this memoir I will use those terms (apart from in quotations) even though they were not in use in the earlier years covered. Looking back, I am embarrassed to find reminders of the occasions I too referred to trans people as transsexuals. In mitigation, even trans people themselves used it. For example, in the second edition of his book *Dear Sir or Madam*, Mark Rees, co-founder with Stephen Whittle of the pressure group Press for Change, wrote, 'Although "transsexual" is a term which I have used throughout this book it is one I abhor.'

Zoë explained that J wanted to marry her partner, but was unable to do so, because she couldn't correct her birth certificate. Not being a great fan of the patriarchal institution of marriage, I was not particularly vexed by this. Besides, if I am honest, what little thought I had given to trans people would have been to unthinkingly dismiss them as rather weird in wanting to 'change sex'. The idea that people would actually choose to go through such a mutilating process meant that they must be disordered or seeking some deviant form of sexual gratification. I had never even considered how cruel such a view was or understood that, like being gay, it was not a matter of choice. However, at that precise time, what really fired my indignation over J's case was to learn that she had no legal protection from dismissal from her job and could be sacked simply for having been assigned as male at birth. Should this become known to her employer, they would be completely within their legal rights to stop employing her and so ruin the career she had worked hard for.

If I was not that bothered about marriage, I was clear that everyone had a right to be able to work and to use their talents to the full. Although I was vaguely aware of the April Ashley case, I did not know that this judgment had denied trans people the opportunity, previously available, of getting a corrected version of their birth certificate. I had no idea that this judgment meant that being asked for a copy of your birth certificate, something everyone else takes with a pinch of salt, could potentially have catastrophic effects for a trans person. Not only would the privacy of their medical history be invaded but they could lose their ability to earn a living. It also compounded the fears of exposure and ridicule, which were already very real for trans men and women. I felt ashamed of my own ignorant complicity in the culture that created such injustice.

I soon realised that my lack of knowledge meant that I was not well-equipped to deal with J's case. Fortunately, Zoë was there to help. She was head of education at South Thames Postgraduate Medical Deanery. Through her work, she had access to all the clinicians with expertise in the field of transsexualism. She was also working with the legal team that was bringing the case of *P v S and Cornwall County Council*. This case was brought by a former senior manager working for Cornwall County Council, who was 'made redundant' when the council learned that 'he' was to have gender reassignment treatment. In 1993, the Truro employment tribunal found that the true reason for P being sacked was her intention to undergo gender reassignment. However, because a female to male trans person would have been treated in the same way, the Sex Discrimination Act (1975) provided no protection. The tribunal referred the case to the European Court of Justice (ECJ) for a decision on whether the employment rights of trans people were protected by the European Directive on Equal Treatment. I was outraged that we had to depend on the ECJ to decide this. Our own government had the power to amend the act if necessary. Surely they would want to put things right?

My first task was to take up my constituent's concerns with the government. I remember the heartfelt letter to the relevant minister in the Department for Employment urging that J and other trans people should be protected from arbitrary dismissal. The minister replying was Ann Widdecombe. As far as she was concerned, it was perfectly justifiable for an employer to sack a trans person as other employees or customers might be offended by their presence in the workplace. I found this quite shocking. I have not liked her since. She also opposed the Gender Recognition Bill in 2004.

Clearly I had a campaign on my hands, including on equal rights concerning marriage. Whatever my attitude to that institution, I had myself married in order to ensure that the father of my children had a spouse's rights to my parliamentary pension. Why shouldn't a trans individual (or indeed a gay person) have the same rights as me?

At that time, two relevant cases, *Rees v United Kingdom* and *Cossey v United Kingdom* had been heard in the European Court of Human Rights (a body of the Council of Europe that oversees the European Convention on Human Rights and distinct from the ECJ, which is a European Union institution). These cases were quoted by another minister, Charles Wardle, Minister of State in the Home Office, in response to my further representations. Both cases, he said, showed that the ECHR upheld the view that Article 12 of the European Convention on Human Rights on the right to marry and found a family referred to the traditional marriage between persons of the opposite sex (because of the 'found a family' bit). So Article 12 could not be invoked to change the then status quo that fixed sex as that at birth.

In his letter, Charles Wardle also stated that someone who identified with the opposite of the gender assigned at birth but who, for medical reasons, could not undergo surgery, was not a transsexual but a transvestite. This was because she retained the ability to bear children. In medical textbooks, transsexualism or gender dysphoria was classified as a mental illness. Treatment was to pacify the delusion that a person had been born in the wrong body by means of hormonal and surgical intervention that changed their primary and secondary sex characteristics. This implied the existence of a sort of third sex called a transsexual. This attitude was, and still is, endemic in those opposing equal treatment for trans men and trans women with their cis counterparts. Some feminists have even argued that trans women cannot be 'real' women and even that their very existence is some kind of male supremacist plot.

In passing on this reply, I noted that it contained elements that seemed rather contradictory. It had obviously been drafted by civil servants from several departments. Interestingly, in one section of the letter, it was acknowledged that, if the sex assigned at birth is a fact, so is the sex of a person that has undergone sex change surgery. So this could be considered to be the more relevant fact in existence at the time of any complaint of discrimination. Whoever had drafted this section helpfully highlighted two employment appeal judgments that had conceded that a person could properly be found 'by suitable tests' to be female at the material date, even though the same tests might have indicated that the person was male at some earlier time.

Later on, I learned that four dissenting judges in the Cossey case strongly criticised the view that procreation is the basis of marriage. Their argument was that marriage is far more than a union that legitimises sexual acts having the potential for procreation. Legal opinion on Article 12 was on the move!

The minister's letter also covered other issues I had raised such as the gender specificity of the crime of rape and the treatment of trans people by the police and prison services. He concluded that 'this is clearly a complex area in which knowledge and experience continue to develop'. I could not disagree with that.

By early 1994, Zoë, if not me, realised that we needed to have some mechanism that brought together expertise on these 'complex' issues with the parliamentary process that could achieve change in the outdated attitudes and laws that pervaded at the time. I say 'complex' in quotes because that word features so often in letters written by ministers and officials who don't want to do something.

Zoë and I hoped that other people affected would also contact their MPs. This would help in the task of creating a more sympathetic political environment for the legal changes that were needed to give trans people full civil rights.

The truth is that most MPs are willing to listen to the concerns of their constituents and usually react sympathetically, but it is impossible to become an expert in all the issues thrown at them. They usually resort to being a postbox, passing on concerns to the relevant minister and leaving it to them. This paper chase had been going on ever since the decision in *Corbett v Corbett* (the April Ashley case) had ruled that the law regarded a person's sex to be fixed at birth. This meant the Corbett marriage had been contracted between two persons to be regarded as being of the same sex. The marriage could therefore be annulled without the need for a divorce. At that time, divorce was only possible on the grounds of adultery, insanity or cruelty, none of which applied to the Corbetts. Only a year later, the law was changed to allow divorce by mutual consent. Had the Corbetts been able to end their marriage mutually, their case would not have had such devastating consequences for trans people.

Mark Rees sent me copies of letters he had received in 1973 from Labour MP Renée Short. In one she asked for permission to submit his case to the Home Secretary. She realised his position was difficult and delicate and added that she was glad to know he had found suitable psychiatric help. In the other she passed on a reply from a junior minister with the results of his consultations with the Registrar General. As was to be expected, this merely reiterated the position that a person's sex was fixed at birth.

Trans people must have continued to receive such letters in the decades that followed, demonstrating that, like me initially, most MPs, however sympathetic to an individual's plight, were still of the view that transsexual people suffered from some kind of psychiatric disorder.

Meanwhile, this was still the time of the stifling influence of Section 28, which was based on the idea that homosexuality could be promoted (and that aversion therapy was a suitable treatment). The then Tory government, being party to the institutional homophobia in our culture, were unlikely to challenge it. Trans people were a numerically much smaller group, yet, based on similar misunderstandings that theirs was a lifestyle choice or a mental illness, even more greatly despised. Thus it was unrealistic to hope that the government could be persuaded to take action to reverse the unintended consequences of the breakdown of the Corbett marriage. Litigation seemed the only route to take to achieve change for the better. Cases were having to be appealed to the ECHR or ECJ, which had the power to override domestic law.

One of my fellow members of Parliament – a Liberal, Alex Carlile – had had a similar conversion to the cause of trans rights just after his own election some years previously. As he put it in 1996, in his preface to the first edition of Mark Rees's book *Dear Sir or Madam*, a letter from Mark had made him aware of 'a group of people who, despite all the developments in rights legislation since 1945, had been left disregarded and without sympathy'. In October 1993, with Tory MP Jerry Hayes as a co-signatory, we had a cross-party letter published in *The Times* headed 'Unhappy plight of trans-sexuals' (sic).

This letter referred to the deficit in legal rights suffered by 'this misunderstood and maligned minority' requiring them to 'be labelled as freaks ... despite the fact that there is clear and respected medical evidence that transsexualism arises from biological and physiological causes'. We pointed out that, over four years previously, the European Parliament had passed a resolution calling on member states to grant legal recognition to 'trans-sexuals' and it was about time the matter was addressed. It was to take more than ten years for this to happen.

My constituent, J, had contacts with Stephen Whittle, who sent me a list of MPs whom members of Press for Change (PFC) had canvassed for support for the principle of trans equality. I got some rather surprised looks when I approached them about forming an All Party Parliamentary Group (APPG) on the issue. They had either forgotten, or were embarrassed about these interactions and I could not raise enough support to set up an officially recognised APPG.

Instead, I agreed to convene a meeting in the House of Commons with speakers in the medical and legal fields. The intention was to try to set up a body that could coordinate efforts to combat the endemic discrimination against trans people. We drew up a list of invitees: parliamentarians who seemed sympathetic, PFC members, medical and legal

Stephen Whittle of Press for Change pictured in 2004.

practitioners, academics and others with an interest in tackling legalised discrimination against trans people and in challenging the way they were perceived by the medical profession and society in general.

The meeting was held on 30 June 1994 in the Jubilee Room at the House of Commons. Papers were presented on the medical aspects (Dr Russell Reid) and socio-cultural aspects (Zoë Playdon) of 'transsexualism'. Madeleine Rees, the solicitor representing 'P' in *P vs S and Cornwall County Council*, explained the basis of the test case against Cornwall County Council, and Vereena Jones from the Equal Opportunities Commission, which was funding the case, also spoke. Looking back on the notes of the meeting, there was a significant intervention by another medical practitioner, Dr Domenico Di Ceglie from the Tavistock Clinic, which provided gender identity services for children. He made the point that medicine treated many conditions for which it had no idea of the causes and that the modern medical approach should be focused on getting a good outcome for the patient rather than aetiology. This was an argument that would come up in the Forum time and again over the coming years – it could be considered an enlightened view or one that meant doctor knows best!

Alex Carlile, Lord Beaumont (a Green) and I were the only parliamentarians present, but several sent their apologies. It was agreed to set up two groups to analyse existing legal and medical positions and to identify the next steps to be taken. The press release I issued the following day was headed 'Britain in the Dock on Transsexual Rights' and compared the UK's poor record with that of other European countries. It announced that MPs were working with legal and medical experts to challenge legal discrimination against transsexuals.

Thus began the Parliamentary Forum on Transsexualism (later Gender Identity). The significant other MPs involved were Alex Carlile and the Conservative MP Roger Sims. As with the letter to *The Times*, we always sought cross-party support, and Roger came on board a little later. Very few parliamentarians ever attended our meetings but, in practice, that was no different to formally constituted APPGs.

Over the years that followed, more MPs became aware of the issues we were raising, especially when contacted by their own constituents. Slowly we built up a reputation that government came to respect. The catalyst for this was the government's realisation that they lacked the necessary expertise to implement the changes forced upon them as a result of the ECJ and ECHR judgments, which overturned UK law on employment and gender recognition.

Through my work with the Forum, I was able to meet many more trans people and I found them to be just as diverse (and sometimes as bloody-minded) as other sections of society. They held different views about how to bring about acceptance of trans people and achieve their human rights, and they wanted different levels of involvement in the fight. Some, like my own constituents, offered their stories and experience to aid understanding whilst generally wishing to be anonymous or at least to keep a low profile. Some were involved in landmark legal cases. These were pivotal in forcing reluctant politicians to make the necessary changes in our laws. It was vital to respect the anonymity of people pursuing such cases, if that was what they wanted. They must not be deterred from pursuing their rights for fear of attracting the prurient interest of the gutter press. However, others eschewed anonymity to challenge public opinion and to help get their stories into the consciousness of lawmakers. Some had their privacy invaded and were pilloried in the press. Some were unable to take the pressure and took their own lives. All played their part in the battle for fairness and justice. It has been a privilege to have met so many impressive people.

Chairing the Forum was not an easy task, however, and required levels of diplomacy that were not expected from someone stereotypically labelled as one of the 'awkward squad'. Actually what that meant was that I was willing to listen to evidence (my scientific background helped) and not just toe the line. Throughout my political career, starting on Birmingham City Council, I hated the patronage that required elected politicians to support a leader whose policies went against the fundamental values of the party in order to further their career.

The Forum's first ever round of fringe meetings, organised with PFC, was held at the party conferences in September 1995. The meeting room at the Labour Conference was upstairs in a Brighton hotel. I arrived to chair the meeting at the same time as a couple of female hacks from tabloid papers. We got in the lift together. They felt no embarrassment in the presence of a complete stranger (me) in denigrating trans people and suggesting that the meeting would be 'good fun'. Our main speaker was Christine Burns, a vice-president of PFC, who was to talk about her experiences as a trans woman and why current UK law violated her human rights. I had never met Christine before. She turned out to be an ordinary-looking, middle-aged person in the sort of suit befitting a member of the Conservative Party, which she then was. I took some pleasure from the reaction of the two 'journalists' as they realised that their expectations of being treated to a 'freak show' would not be met. Clearly they never intended to cover the serious issues being discussed and I noticed that they crept out as soon as they could.

Christine was inspiring, but the attendance was poor and the meeting failed to recruit any more MPs or activists to the cause. However, this incident also made me question my own attitudes and realise that there was always a deep-seated hope in me that, whenever I was seen to be challenging the social stigma from which trans people suffered, the individuals in the public eye should be as congruent as possible with their correct gender identity. It seemed easier that way. It seemed a path that was more likely to ensure success in changing society's prejudiced attitudes.

Through my work with the Forum, I became more aware of research into differences in the physiology of the male and female brain, and the evidence that people expressing gender identities at variance with their genetic/gonadal sex had the brain physiology to match that identity. This brought into question my own perception that so-called masculine and feminine characteristics were exaggerated by cultural and religious conventions that were responsible for the persistence of discrimination against women and girls. I remember playing 'taking the school register' with my son. We wrote down the names of his classmates as he called them out. At the end of the exercise, I realised that all the boys' and girls' names were grouped together, which must mean that separate registers were kept for boys and girls (and probably boys first). Hadn't such separation been abandoned years ago? I took this up with his school and the chief education officer. I wanted to see differences in the sexes minimised, especially pre-puberty. Yet here I was, championing the idea of distinct masculine and feminine brains. I had always thought that real, as opposed to cultural, differences between the sexes, were simply due to the physiological variation necessary for evolutionarily advantageous sexual reproduction. Now I had evidence that people could identify as being male or female without the gonadal differentiation of their sexual identity.

Chairing the Forum, I came into regular contact with trans people who did not conform to accepted notions of the binary divide between male and female that, to my mind, had persisted for far too long. I became familiar with the concept of gender fluidity and non-gendered identity. Many trans people sought to be as congruent as possible with the prevailing image of their correct gender. Others felt they should not have to kowtow to society's unthinking norms and did not wish or were physically unable to undergo all the medical and cosmetic procedures that were previously seen as necessary in order to be able to be accepted in their own self-identity.

Maybe my earlier beliefs were not so stupid after all. Tolerating a situation that pressurises people to conform to some idealised notions of the masculine and feminine was the cause of much unhappiness. It was as important to fight against the discrimination that resulted as it was to combat any other form of discrimination. To hell with physical appearance, whatever people looked like they were deserving of respect and acceptance. Requiring someone to make changes in their body that they did not want was unacceptable but, equally, someone unhappy with their physical appearance should be helped to make changes that would allow them to feel more at ease in themselves.

By the time of the Labour landslide of 1997, when Tony Blair became Prime Minister, not much progress had been made. Several legal cases were chugging along. I was not enamoured of 'New' Labour, as Blair had branded us, and felt its appeal shallow and lacking substance. Blair's predecessor, John Smith, had died of a heart attack, a tragedy from which the Labour Party has only just started to recover. I didn't know John well but I was privileged, only a couple of weeks before he died, to eat dinner with him in the Members' Dining Room. He just came down and sat beside this new backbencher. As we talked, I formed the impression that he blamed himself, as Shadow Chancellor, for Labour losing the 1992 election. This seemed to be weighing heavily on him. I never saw either of his two successors, Blair and Brown, even eat in MPs' communal facilities, let alone sit with the likes of me. Labour

MPs, from right to left, mourned his death. As for the cause of the loss of the election in 1992, I always put the blame on the public's distrust of the then leader, Neil Kinnock, who gave the impression of being a politician who would ditch cherished beliefs in order to get elected: 'U'-turns on nuclear weapons and electoral reform come to mind. As Theresa May discovered in 2017, the public do not trust politicians who are seen to chop and change to gain or keep office.

So it was that, in 1997, I had no great expectations that the new government would achieve the radical changes I felt necessary in the financing and delivery of public services after years of cutbacks under the Tories. What I did hope was that Labour would be strong on upholding and improving civil liberties. After all, this generally did not require deviation from the nonsensical pledge to stick to Tory spending levels.

At Labour's Party Conference in 1997, I attended Stonewall's fringe meeting. There were great expectations that the incoming government would sweep away the legal obstacles to gay and lesbian rights. We heard from an employee of a train company who was taking legal action against her employer on the basis that they discriminated against gay couples by not providing them with the same free travel that was available to married couples. One of the issues I had been working on (again arising from constituency casework) was the different treatment of gay couples compared with heterosexual couples by the immigration system, and this was also raised. But Alun Michael, newly appointed minister in the Home Office, dampened the expectations of everyone present and I think most people were left in no doubt that they were not going to get much help from the government in achieving their rights. I could not help but be dismayed by the realisation that if this was the attitude to gay rights, what chance had gender variant people? The sad fact was that, in this and other areas, senior Labour politicians were unwilling to be associated with what they saw as unpopular issues. Despite having a majority big enough to give the freedom to pursue progressive, libertarian policies in tune with Labour principles of equality and fairness, the Labour government would, like its Tory predecessor, have to be dragged kicking and screaming into the light by legal judgments in the ECJ and ECHR.

The first significant judgment bequeathed to Blair's government was that in the case of *P v S and Cornwall County Council*. In 1996, the ECJ had found that P's dismissal constituted discrimination under the terms of the Equal Treatment Directive, as she would not have been sacked had she remained a man. This meant that the government had to ensure that UK law was consistent with the ECJ interpretation of the EU's Equal Treatment Directive.

In February 1998, a consultation on draft regulations to amend the Sex Discrimination Act 1975 (SDA) was finally issued by the Department for Education and Employment (DfEE) but allowed only six weeks for response. The whole thrust of the document was that a person would cast aside their sex at birth at some moment in time when they become 'transexual'. Then, at the point of believing that 'they would, when observed by a reasonable person, *appear* [my italics] to be of the new sexual identity' they would have the right to request a change of identity. Four years after Charles Wardle's reply, civil servants were still of the mindset that trans people were some deviant kind of third sex. Such was the inherent prejudice in the proposed regulations that one of the questions in the consultation was whether discrimination should still be permitted for jobs that involved working with children.

Despite the short consultation period, such was the outcry within the trans community that the DfEE received over 300 written submissions of objection. I managed to organise a meeting between members of the Forum and Alan Howarth, the responsible minister. He promised there would be further consultation following the preparation of draft guidelines for employers. Four Forum members were given confidential access to the revised drafts and had to respond within a week. In the event, the regulations were published before the week was up. Although the four responded before the publication of the regulations, no changes were made. They were approved by a process that required no parliamentary debate.

Dissatisfied with the initial lack of official guidance on employment rights, the Parliamentary Forum and Press for Change published an independent guide, *Transsexual People in the Workplace: A Code of Practice*. This was a time before widespread adoption of the World Wide Web, when printing a booklet was still the preferred way to disseminate information.

Bizarrely, the regulations had the effect of reinstating protection for discrimination that was already being ruled unlawful by employment tribunals acting upon the judgment in the P case. These regulations would surely be subjected to further case law. After Alan Howarth was replaced by Margaret Hodge, the Forum's representations were received more sympathetically and civil servants' assumptions questioned. Forum members drafted guidelines for employers and these were largely adopted, though with fewer 'best practice' examples. I was startled to find that the DfEE publication included the acknowledgement that 'This Guide was produced in consultation with the Parliamentary Forum on Transsexualism, chaired by Dr Lynne Jones MP'. This was the only time my name ever appeared in any government publication and, looking back, this formal recognition must have been one of the highlights of my political career – or maybe not!

It should also be noted that the government failed to use the opportunity of the P judgment to make other amendments to the SDA to ensure that provisions outlawing sex discrimination in the supply of goods and services were also extended to trans people. Ministers would go not one step further than they were required to do by the ECJ judgment.

It has to be concluded that unthinking prejudice was rife within government at this time. But this was changing. Several factors contributed to the slow raising of awareness. Through the work of the Forum, civil servants were coming into contact with highly capable people who had direct and indirect experience of being trans. In addition, more and more trans people were contacting their own MPs to talk of the societal and institutional prejudice they faced on a daily basis. Then a big boost to the cause came with the arrival of a trans character, Hayley Patterson (soon to become Mrs Cropper), on *Coronation Street*.

Initially I was sceptical about the authenticity that Julie Hesmondhalgh, the actor cast as Hayley, could bring to the role. I was quoted in the press as saying 'getting a non-transexual to play the part may detract from the message that transsexuals are just ordinary people'. I still like the sentiment, but Julie's portrayal of Hayley was brilliant. It is interesting that journalists reporting my views thought it relevant to include commentary to the effect that, despite being happily married with young children, Lynne Jones was championing the rights of 'transexuals who spark fear, confusion and anger among "normal" people'!

We later learned that Julie had at first been banned from contacting trans organisations for advice lest there was a leak of the storyline (described at the time as 'explosive' – and which boosted ratings up to eighteen million). Julie described my parliamentary motion, which congratulated the writers, producers and especially herself for the sensitive portrayal of Hayley, as one of the best moments of her life. She said that she knew things were changing when old ladies came up to her in Asda to ask when she was going to get married to her character's fictional boyfriend Roy, adding that 'when they make transexual weddings legal, then I will be a happy woman'.

In actual fact, marriages in which one of the partners was trans had continued to take place despite the Corbett judgment. Registrars did not ask to see birth certificates and so presided over marriages that were actually illegal. Liz Bellinger was an example of a 'real' Hayley who, for twenty years, lived an anonymous life as the wife of Michael and mother to his daughter. They married after the death of Michael's first wife and Liz had been granted parental responsibility by a judge who knew the truth about her status. By 'outing' herself to pursue *Bellinger v Bellinger* (2003), testing the legal status of her marriage, and involving the Forum, Liz was another trans person who told their story and thus contributed to the changes in attitude that were undoubtedly taking place.

In April 1999, around the time that Hayley's fictional and problem-strewn 'wedding' to Roy was broadcast, I was asked to table a planted written question asking what plans the government had to review the status of transexual people. This is a device governments frequently adopt to make announcements 'by the back door'. I had added the word 'people' to the draft question I was given but this was ignored in the Home Secretary, Jack Straw's, reply. This announced the 'setting up of an inter-departmental working group on transsexuals to consider, with particular reference to birth certificates, the need for appropriate legal measures to address the problems experienced by transsexuals'. Regard would be had for scientific and societal developments and measures undertaken in other countries.

Thus began the process leading to the passing of the Gender Recognition Act (2004) – but this was to take another five years and require another legal ruling in Europe.

In setting up the working group, Jack Straw seemed to genuinely want to improve the lives of trans people. In the press release accompanying its July 2000 report, he referred to his constituency casework. Nevertheless, someone must have decided to put this initiative on the back burner. The report was shelved until 2002 and was only dusted down after Christine Goodwin won her case at the ECHR, overturning previous judgments such as *Rees v United Kingdom* and *Cossey v United Kingdom*, thus forcing the government to legislate for gender recognition.

Meanwhile, the Forum had continued our work in exposing and seeking to bring about an end to the institutional abuse and humiliation of trans people. Trans men and women seemed to regard me as a focal point for telling their stories and seeking redress for the injustices they experienced. I came to be seen as the 'MP for trans people', something of which I was, and remain, very proud. I received several letters from trans women treated unsympathetically in male prisons, including one who had committed a bungled armed robbery in order to fund her medical treatment, which had been denied by the NHS. The low standards that were common in newspaper reports about trans people plunged to new depths in such cases but the Press

Home Office
BUILDING A SAFE, JUST
AND TOLERANT SOCIETY

REPORT OF THE INTERDEPARTMENTAL WORKING GROUP ON TRANSSEXUAL PEOPLE

April 2000

HMSO

The report of the government's Interdepartmental Working Group on Transsexual People, published in the spring of 2000, drew heavily on talking points supplied in submissions by trans groups like PFC and the Parliamentary Forum. Out of three options explored, the committee concluded that there was no workable solution to transsexual people's discrimination short of full legal recognition. However, the report was initially shelved until the cases of *Christine Goodwin (and T) v United Kingdom* in 2002 left no option but to act.

Complaints Commission refused to exert any influence on the newspapers responsible. The then chair of the Press Complaints Commission, Lord Wakeham, was good at making speeches claiming that discrimination 'in any of its ugly forms' has no place in the media, but could apparently do nothing to act against the prurient reporting that was drawn to his attention.

The everyday experiences of trans people informed the rigorous work being undertaken by the Forum's legal and medical experts. Under the auspices of the Forum, documents and guidelines were produced and fed into relevant departments and organisations. If PFC was particularly hot on the legal issues, GIRES (Gender Identity Research and Education Society) organised the drafting of the Forum's medical papers and published them on their website. In this we had input from some of the leading academics and practitioners both in the UK and internationally. This included medical practitioners who were themselves trans. We had members from all walks of life, including the police and armed forces, who were able to transform attitudes in their organisations. We lobbied on medical education and outdated textbooks, the treatment of prisoners, reform of the press complaints system and on changing the upsetting practice whereby death certificates recorded the sex of a deceased trans person as that on their birth certificate. When West Yorkshire Police insisted on taking an employment discrimination case to the House of Lords, which unsurprisingly reiterated the judgments of lower courts, we deplored this huge waste of public funds. When progress was made, as in the development of guidelines for the employment of trans police officers by Essex Police, we helped publicise improved practice.

By the time of the publication of the draft Gender Recognition Bill in 2003, all this work had paid off. The government had finally grasped that being trans is not a mental health condition. The proposals were groundbreaking in that they did not require individuals to undergo surgical sterilisation prior to recognition in the gender that most closely reflected their gender identity. However, there were other aspects of the gender recognition process that were not so welcome. For example, the bill included a measure that was a blow to the small number of trans people who remained married after one partner's transition: they must divorce. Such couples, by definition, must have demonstrated exceptionally strong devotion to one another, surely something to be applauded? Nevertheless, they were to be forced to choose between their marriage and the right of one partner to be recognised in their correct gender.

To fit in with other business, the bill was introduced in the House of Lords, and the process in the Commons began in January 2004 with second reading (a general debate about the principles of a bill). There is a tradition that MPs who speak at second reading are asked by the whips to serve on the committee scrutinising a bill at the next stage (standing committee). However, this rarely applied to me as I was considered unreliable: I didn't always do as I was told. During my eighteen years as an MP, I was appointed to only three standing committees – on Sunday trading, high hedges and gender recognition. These were quite tightly defined issues in which I did not generally disagree with the party line. However, because the government made sure it had a majority even without me, the bill scrutiny consisted solely of probing amendments, designed to raise issues in the hope of voluntary concessions, but never put to the vote. These were primarily focused on the forced divorce issue and pension rights. The only concession we were able to achieve was the offer to produce guidance for the National Association of Pension Funds. The bill went through unamended to report stage, involving all MPs.

At report, Andrew Mitchell, a Tory, unexpectedly forced a vote on his amendment that would allow a gender identity certificate to be granted to someone in a subsisting marriage. I did not have time to brief Labour MPs on this, so almost all went into the 'No' lobby as guided by the whips. Most Liberal Democrats and SNP MPs, together with a substantial number of Tories, voted for the amendment, but only Jeremy Corbyn, Diane Abbott and John McDonnell joined me in the 'Aye' lobby. The amendment was defeated. Some consolation was provided to married couples forced to divorce by the simultaneous introduction of civil partnerships, which gave them the option of converting their marriage into a civil partnership.

One of the speeches in support of Mitchell's amendment was from Shaun Woodward. Woodward had been a Conservative MP. In 1999, he was sacked from the Tory front bench after voting to repeal Section 28. Soon after, he defected to Labour. He was pilloried by the press who felt it appropriate not only to speculate whether he was gay, but also to publicise that his sister had been born his brother, making jokes about them both having 'crossed over' – MPs who changed sides were said to have 'crossed the floor of the House'. Referring to the reluctance to even permit the continuance of a marriage that had been entered into legally because it might imply condoning same-sex marriage, Woodward commented: 'In fifty years we will look back at this in perverse wonder.' He was right, of course, but it didn't take fifty years.

The first same-sex marriage in the UK took place on 29 March 2014, only ten years later. Interviewed on 23 March 2014 by Richard Coles on Radio 4, Tony Blair suggested that, with hindsight, he could have gone for equal marriage and not just civil partnerships. Previously he had proclaimed 'we are best when we are bold', but Blair will be remembered as a Prime

Minister who failed to live up to the hope he inspired when first elected and who, with the exception of the peace process in Northern Ireland (a great achievement currently at risk) was only bold when he was wrong.

In the years between the Gender Recognition Act (2004) coming into force and my decision to step down as an MP in 2010, the big issue for the Forum was the appalling institutional transphobia within the health service. We were also concerned about the policy of refusing to prescribe reversible puberty blockers for teenagers (see chapter 4). The government had accepted that people who sought help with gender reassignment were not suffering from a mental illness. However, the NHS continued to demand that they be forced to undergo two or more years of psychiatric assessment if they were to access the full range of medical interventions available – a shocking state of affairs and a waste of precious resources. Despite a legal ruling in 1999 that it was illegal to impose a blanket ban on medical treatment for the purposes of gender reassignment, service commissioners continued to fund unnecessary and unwanted psychiatric assessment and then go on to deny surgery for financial reasons.

Charing Cross Hospital was the main NHS provider of surgery (particularly male to female), operating a virtual monopoly. The surgeons there were able to insist that a person referred to them by gender identity clinics outside London should undergo further assessment by psychiatrists at Charing Cross GIC next door. This meant that the NHS was funding the same process twice, but 'clinical freedom' to insist on such duplication meant that, apparently, nothing could be done about this.

Many trans people felt they were subjected to humiliating treatment, even amounting to abuse. The government had, rightly, been emphasising the need for a patient-centred approach – no decision about me, without me – but this did not seem to apply to services for trans men and women. We took up standards of care at Charing Cross GIC with their medical director, James Barrett, suggesting that they consider abandoning the term 'transsexual' as patients found this offensive and that they undertake an audit of patient satisfaction with the services they provided. We were given short shrift. Terms that were considered unacceptable by the people referred to were not unacceptable to Barrett. He seemed to take exception to the statement that patient satisfaction audits should be undertaken, since satisfaction did not, in his opinion, bear any relationship to patient outcomes.

And so I retired from Parliament knowing I had helped bring about changes that improved the lives of trans people but also knowing there remained a lot more to be done. I passed the baton over to Baroness Joyce Gould. In 2015 the Women and Equalities Committee of the House of Commons produced a report that, rightly, described the Gender Recognition Act (2004) as not fit for purpose and made other recommendations for improving the lives of trans people. In response, the government promised a review to streamline and de-medicalise the gender recognition process. They committed to finding a way of transferring services from mental health to another specialism or a new specialism and agreed that assessment prior to treatment should meet only clinically necessary criteria. NHS England has begun the process for agreeing 'a joint and co-ordinated action plan for improving health services for transgendered [*sic*] people'.

It is almost a quarter of a century since the establishment of the Forum. During that time, there has been a sea change in social attitudes and it is common parlance to refer to the importance of LGBT rights. We should never forget the vital role played in this by both the ECJ and the ECHR. In 2010, I received an award from GIRES referring to me as a

'Parliamentary champion for trans people at a time when few parliamentarians took an interest and attitudes were significantly more prejudiced'. The award hangs proudly in my home in Wales.

In writing this chapter I would like to acknowledge the work of my parliamentary assistant, Ingrid Davidson, who provided administrative support for the Forum and Professor Zoë Playdon who provided me with invaluable help in retrieving archives.

9

The Press

JANE FAE

Jane Fae is a feminist, journalist and campaigner on political and sexual liberty who also knows a bit about IT, the law and policing. In between times, she can be found amusing London audiences with alternative stand-up. Fae writes for national media, including the *Guardian*, *Daily Mail* and *Independent*, as well as more niche publications, such as *GayStarNews* (on LGBT issues), the *Register* and *OpenDemocracy* (on IT and privacy) and *Freedom in a Puritan Age* and *Index on Censorship* (on free speech and censorship). Her most recent book, *Taming the Beast*, provides an in-depth analysis of legislative and regulatory responses to concerns over online pornography and sexualisation.

The relationship between the trans community and the press has long been fraught. Over the last few decades, much coverage of trans people and issues has been problematic: at best disrespectful, treating individuals as curiosities whose lives the press is uniquely entitled to expose, exploit and lay waste to.

Even the better coverage has, mostly, been not very good. To dismiss all this as simple transphobia is to miss the point. As this chapter highlights, narratives have changed and evolved, and while some things have improved, others have taken a turn for the worse.

In the early days, from the 1930s through to the 1950s, coverage of trans stories was relatively neutral. Perhaps this reflected a less sensationalist press. Whatever the reason, by the sixties, that was changing, and the trans community joined the roster of minorities singled out for sensational, often sexualised reporting, because they lacked the political clout to stop such abuse.

Arguably, this phenomenon is not quite as common now, in part following the Leveson Inquiry (see chapter 17), in part as a consequence of the tragic death of Lucy Meadows, a trans woman who killed herself in late 2012 following significant hounding by the press, particularly the *Daily Mail*.

Instead, as political recognition of trans issues has increased, and the trans community has begun to have some impact on those issues, some press, some journalists, have become more partisan, more overtly dedicated to undermining trans people. The result, from 2015 onward, has been a significant and concerted rise in anti-trans sentiment, from writers with little experience of the trans community, often dressed up as 'concern' for trans welfare, with every least advance now under attack or questioned.

The focus of this chapter is on print media – the press. Other media – particularly broadcast media – are not beyond reproach: rather, it would take at least one extra chapter to cover the issues in respect to TV and radio, as well as the wider entertainment and advertising industries.

Early coverage: vicars, tarts and legal shenanigans

After 1967, and the partial decriminalisation of homosexuality, there was little awareness of trans as a category separate from gay or lesbian. That is understandable: prior to that date, if there was any consideration of LGBT issues at all, it was that homosexuals were criminals and/or mentally ill. Trans people, if they fitted this world view at all, were considered merely a sub-category of homosexual.

At the same time, the public knew so little about trans people that *any* trans-related story was likely to make the cut because the mere fact of being trans was news and their story – allegedly – in the public interest.

For the first few decades, the print media split.

'Freak show' aptly describes much of the coverage – in the tabloid press especially, but also in more mainstream reporting. The general tone was, 'Oh, look, it's a man in a dress!' accompanied by allegations of kink, explicit or presumed.

There was something considered not quite right about cross-dressing, which for the most part was how transition was perceived, while many equated it explicitly or otherwise with gayness. In the seventies, glam rock and David Bowie also helped put 'gender bending' on the agenda (see chapter 5), prompting conservative outrage. But, broadly speaking, this was an era of vicars and tarts (and vicars dressed as tarts): of trans as panto dame, treated as titillation for Sunday readers.

Press behaviour over several decades is summarised by the press bingo card below:

Language	Content	Conduct
Misgendering	Sexual(ised) focus	Public interest
'Sex change'/'sex swap'	Fake/fraud	Outing
Deadnaming	Deviant/pervert	Intrusion/privacy breach
	Shock	Chasing (stalking)
	The transition narrative	Law-breaking
	Before/after images	Invention
	Trivialisation	

Misgendering, deadnaming – quoting an individual's pre-transition name – and use of specific terms such as 'sex swap' are the clearest trans-specific abuses; so too is the fairly common habit of framing trans people as fake or fraudulent – essentially contesting the authenticity of trans narratives.

Otherwise little here is unique to trans reporting. Tabloids sex up stories. Period. The in-depth 'transition narrative' – more prominent in later years – is also stock in trade for 'personal interest' stories, from 'slimmer of the year' to celebrity divorces.

Newspaper readers – and not just tabloid readers – obsess over the different, the way out, the 'odd': and, since trans people are vulnerable, not 'the norm', and are relatively powerless, why wouldn't they be co-opted by Fleet Street editors as a useful punchbag?

And if that means people get hurt – literally – then so be it.

Likewise the tabloid penchant for outing people or, as they put it, 'exposing' them. Leveson revealed how intrusive tactics, breaches of privacy and stalking, up to and including law-breaking, were all commonplace. For tabloids claimed that a

The outing of Caroline Cossey by the *News of the World* in 1981.

'public interest' in a story, however tenuous, entitled them to expose every slight detail.

A flavour of how this worked is illustrated by the outing of Caroline Cossey in 1981.

Caroline, also known as 'Tula', was famous as an international model and Bond girl. In May 1989, she had the UK government on the ropes when she persuaded the European Court of Human Rights to recognise her as legally a woman. Success was short-lived: the government appealed and by September 1990, the law was back where it had been previously.

In 1981, however, the *News of the World* had outed Caroline as trans – in the process ticking multiple boxes on the trans bingo card.

Their language demonstrated the usual nod to 'sex change'. This was par for the course: a search of the NewsBank newspaper database for this period reveals that tabloids, in particular, were significantly more likely to reference 'sex swap'/'sex change' than 'trans'/'transgender'.

There was, however, little misgendering, possibly because Caroline/Tula was so strongly established in her female persona that it would have confused readers to describe her as anything other than a woman.

There were, though, other issues:

- Subheadings such as 'fake' and 'shocked' simultaneously questioned Caroline's authenticity, while promoting a sense of outrage to justify her exposure.
- Prurience: the focus on Caroline's breast op; the pin-up illustration.
- Dubious practices: allegedly bribing individuals at a gender identity clinic to provide records.

Then, there was the most fundamental question of all: why was this piece justified? In what way was the gender identity of a popular model a matter of public interest, especially when, according to Caroline, 'the *News of the World* exposé ruined my career'?

But then at least they had the excuse that Caroline was famous − she was later described as 'the world's most famous transgender woman'. Yet others who weren't famous were also targeted, with no more justification than that they were trans.

The headlines below took just a few minutes to cull from a selection of press coverage of trans issues over the period from 1970 to 2000. Bad puns and sensationalising abound, from the obsession with a 'sex swap cop' wearing 'frilly knickers' − a detail that was likely either invented, or obtained through underhand methods − to hints of sexual deviance. Past names and circumstances were sprinkled around these pieces, with an utter disregard for the individuals whose lives were being turned over to public scrutiny.

As for justification? Merely being trans and having any public presence seems to have justified every least detail of your

A sample of typical headlines from decades of newspaper coverage.

life being made public, while any attempt to hold on to one's privacy was recast as inappropriately secretive and thus justified the intrusion the press intended in the first place. Suspicions raised, aspersions cast: it is hard to read these pieces without concluding that there is something not right about trans people.

Worse, this banal procession of stories – hundreds thoughtlessly published in this period – all spread and encouraged the same dangerous (for trans people) narrative.

Despite this, some papers, some individual journalists, did better.

The case of trans woman April Ashley hit the headlines in 1970 after a court voided Ashley's marriage on the grounds that she was still biologically male, and therefore not properly married to the man she was divorcing.

Coverage of Ashley was divided, with some papers, including the *Guardian*, staying relatively respectful. They even – as not all papers did – reported her gender correctly: 'April Ashley, the model, was told by a divorce court yesterday that she was a man and ... her marriage ... was void'.

'Miss Ashley ...'

Rather more problematic was the language in a piece, also from the *Guardian*, that appeared just a couple of years later: 'Martha is doing alright. He [*sic*] is holding down a job, accepted by women as one of themselves, causing no trouble.' The tone was respectful, but the language was not, suggesting an author trying hard to be fair, but lacking the tools or training to do better.

Here is the same paper, a little over a decade later. Clearly, some journalists are trying: 'Mark Rees walks like a man, talks like a man and looks like a man. Yet his birth certificate says he is female and unless there is a reform of British law, legally he will remain a woman.'

Mark Rees, a trans man who took on the legal system to fight for his rights, received a more generally respectful press, perhaps because FtM (female to male) transition was viewed as less threatening/more serious than MtF.

Daily Mail coverage nowadays causes much concern. Then, though, it was often more balanced than it has since become. Some boxes on the bingo card are ticked – but not every time. On the other hand, when it came to one of their pet battles – against the European Court of Human Rights – they were not above bundling up trans people with a range of other 'deviants', from drug dealers to terrorists and murderers, as a means to make their point.

So, to sum up: the press treatment of trans affairs during much of the sixties and seventies – the 'vicars and tarts' era – was a mixed bag. Some papers can be seen trying to pursue stories in a sensitive way – not always successfully – but their failures were often attributable to lack of knowledge rather than an agenda. Other titles – those for whom reader titillation was the stock in trade – just added trans people to the roster of subjects to be treated in a particularly exploitative way. There was no specific editorial plan: coverage was opportunity-led, and it was generally about individuals unlucky enough to stray onto their radar, rather than issues.

Trans stories become 'a thing'

An early hint that trans people's stories might be something else – something more than just titillation – came with reporting of April Ashley's divorce (*Corbett v Corbett, 1970*) and Jan Morris's transition: two very different stories that are worth comparing. The latter, a historian, author and travel writer, generated interest with her decision to transition medically in the mid-sixties and the publication of her own story – a somewhat upmarket first person transition account – in 1974. This was an articulate professional journalist prepared to take readers beyond the veneer of 'sex change' as shock headline and invite them to examine what her journey contributed to our understanding of the human condition – something of *worth* perhaps.

Ashley's story, by contrast – the tabloid-friendly tale of a social-climbing working-class transgender outsider who dared aspire to marriage and social advancement and was slapped down – was more of a harbinger of things to come.

As trans people became more visible, it turned out that, like their LGB cousins, they had requests: for rights, in respect of basic issues such as marriage, employment and pensions – all of which demanded that the system recognise their gender identity – and for specialist health care. Of course, those core issues – the questions raised in *Corbett v Corbett* about the nature of sex and its legal recognition for matters such as marriage and inheritance – were easily lost when there was a simpler, more scandalous story to write.

What we see emerging here are two very different ways of writing about trans people and their travails. Coverage on the one hand came from legal correspondents, who were generally objective. Clare Dyer and Sally Weale at the *Guardian*, Liz Hodgkinson in *The Times* and Joshua Rozenberg at the *Telegraph* all understood the basic legal points raised by the emergence of trans people. Likewise, Vincent Hanna of the BBC and LBC was, before his abrupt death in 1997, increasingly supportive. For the *Guardian*, Wendy Cooper wrote over many years about the issues faced by trans people, and in 1996 she provided a straightforward explanation of why Alex Carlile MP was introducing a private members' bill to allow for change of gender on birth certificates.

This type of coverage contrasted sharply with the sensationalist narratives then dominating the rest of the press.

Not yet on the agenda, however, was the claim that trans matters in general – and specifically trans women – could be a (political) thing. The seeds for this were sown with the publication of Janice Raymond's *The Transsexual Empire* in 1979, which made a series of assertions, including:

- Sex is determined by chromosomes: XY is always male; XX always female.
- The experience of being raised as a girl and menstruating determines a woman.
- Transsexualism is caused exclusively by the sex stereotyping of patriarchal society; the support of professionals – surgeons, psychiatrists, counsellors, electrologists, etc. – who persuade foolish persons to change is a secondary reason.

Her primary focus was on trans women: trans men she barely considered and otherwise dismissed as 'the tokens that save face for the transsexual empire'. The patriarchy, Raymond argued, has introduced sex changes as a means of controlling gender stereotypes, which act in the interests of men. Once extra-natal conception is introduced, biological women will become redundant. 'All transsexuals rape women's bodies,' Raymond wrote, 'by reducing the real female form to an artefact, and appropriating this body for themselves.' As for those trans women who would be allies – described by Raymond as 'lesbian-feminists' – they 'show yet another face of patriarchy', in that they attempt 'to possess women at a deeper level, this time under the guise of challenging rather than conforming to the role and behaviour of stereotyped femininity'. Her solution: 'I contend that the problem with transsexualism would best be served by morally mandating it out of existence.'

The impact of Raymond's work in the US was deadly. The National Center for Health Care Technology (NCHCT) co-opted her to write a report on the ethics of trans medical care. Despite subsequent protestations of innocence, Raymond's claim that trans health care was ethically controversial is argued by some to have played a major part in having such therapy routinely excluded from both public and private health insurance plans during the period 1989 to 2013, a policy which, activists have since claimed, led to the death of hundreds of trans individuals.

Raymond was also accused of seeking to limit the influence of trans activist Sandy Stone, who had some standing in feminist circles, by a persistent and aggressive campaign.

At the time, Raymond's writing attracted little attention in the UK. Without the Internet to propel it more widely in those days, *The Transsexual Empire* and Raymond's hostile attitude to trans people was little more than a footnote in speeches given in the UK by some feminist leaders. Nonetheless, Raymond may be viewed as the grandmother of the anti-trans strand of feminism: the naysayers and haters were starting to gather.

Sometimes, it was simply a case of 'news begets comment' – even if much of the commentary was written by cis persons with little or no understanding of trans issues. As trans moved up the news agenda, so the comment pieces proliferated. Following a documentary about trans kids by Oliver Morse in 1996, for instance, regular columnist Nigella Lawson felt impelled to respond in *The Times*. As journalist Paris Lees later wrote, Lawson 'clearly wrote a whole feature about transsexual people – including whether or not we should receive NHS treatment, the suggestion that we're delusional, and sweeping generalisations – without doing much more research than watching a Channel 4 documentary. It beggars belief.'

There were also other triggers for press comment and response. A fringe meeting at the Liberal Democrat annual conference, organised by Mark Rees, testing the water on legal gender recognition (and paving the way for Alex Carlile's private members' bill on that topic) drew out many positive responses, as well as one decidedly hostile one from *Telegraph* journalist Claudia FitzHerbert. Similarly chequered coverage followed the case of a training manager from Cornwall, dismissed from her job for being trans. The subsequent case – *P v S and Cornwall County Council* – was decided in the European Court of Justice in April 1996.

It is unlikely that editors commissioned such articles at random: rather, a group of interested, like-minded columnists saw a trans rights advance as the cue to pitch a piece. Some were allies, some not; either way, a common thread emerged in this period of trans issues as fair game for non-trans commentators to talk and write about. Trans matters were a story – but not one that belonged to trans people.

From head-scratching to hostility
By the late eighties, press coverage of trans issues was often clumsy, clichéd, offensive and much else besides. But apart from the occasional diatribe from a writer with a bee in their bonnet, this was still random stuff. The real, concerted nastiness was about to arrive. In 1989, perhaps responding to Caroline Cossey's case at the European Court of Human Rights, perhaps in homage to the re-release of *The Transsexual Empire*, Germaine Greer took to the *Independent* to unleash a tirade of viciousness in the direction of the trans community. Greer's description of an encounter with a trans woman gives the flavour:

> I should have said, 'You're a man. *The Female Eunuch* has done less than nothing for you. Piss off.' The transvestite [*sic*] held me in a rapist's grip... Knee-jerk etiquette demanded that I humour this gross parody of my sex by accepting him as female, even to the point of allowing him to come to the lavatory with me.

This was significant on several levels: first the absolute intolerant language, unthinkable in respect of any other minority; second, Greer's status as feminist royalty; and third, and most significantly, the ideological nature of this attack.

Ironically, many press commentators now talk about the 'trans agenda'; some even represent it as a political position, rather than – as it is – a desperate attempt to survive. The real politicisation of trans issues, however, is by certain high-profile ideologues, whose primary rejection of trans people springs from the fact that they do not fit their (political) world view, and are inconvenient for their analysis. Greer's attacks were ahead of their time, but they presaged the more concerted ideological backlash that was to come. Until the Millennium, attacks on trans people remained sporadic, ad hoc, tailored to the particular analysis of individual writers; soon, though, this would change.

In the first half of the noughties came an event whose coverage, though it was not realised at the time, would prove pivotal in empowering and recruiting to the transphobe cause. This was the complaint to the General Medical Council (GMC) that psychiatrist Russell Reid had improperly authorised a number of gender re-assignment cases – and his subsequent censure.

The problem? Most trans people would agree that medical malpractice, of whatever nature, should be pursued and reported upon. But there was significant concern at the selective nature of the concern being voiced. As the later impromptu Twitter-led #TransDocFail campaign revealed, trans people are routinely discriminated against by the NHS, with hundreds of medical practitioners implicated in their mistreatment. Yet the one case the press highlighted was that against a practitioner who, for all his failings, was broadly seen as positively inclined towards trans people.

A small number of journalists took interest, including the freelance writer Julie Bindel. Many activists read this reporting on Russell Reid as concern trolling: the pursuit, by non-trans writers, of narratives that could disadvantage trans people, while simultaneously claiming to be acting for trans people – 'we only have your best interests at heart'. Here, for instance, is the conclusion of an interview by Bindel, published in the *Guardian*, following the GMC's verdict:

> As gender-reassignment surgery becomes more commonplace in the UK, with more than 400 operations carried out each year, and since the recent implementation of the gender recognition bill, which allows those who have had reassignment surgery to change their passports and birth certificates to reflect their new sex, society seems to be becoming more accepting of a person's right to decide to change their gender. For Claudia and others who regret having surgery, this is not good news.
>
> 'If we allowed people to be as they wish, whether that is a man being camp and feminine or a woman butch and unadorned,' says Claudia, 'then the need to chop up healthy bodies to achieve that acceptance would diminish.'

These two themes feature large in subsequent years:

1 The regret narrative: the claim, despite evidence to the contrary, that there exists a large and unrepresented pool of transitioners with regrets.
2 The cis focus: an insistence on pursuing key trans issues – such as regret or medical malpractice – while excluding mainstream trans perspectives or reporting selectively.

Equally important is that this particular episode, combined with Bindel's coverage of related topics (for instance, a rape crisis centre in Canada that objected to employing a trans woman), set in train a lasting feud between her and the trans community that has proven damaging to both: to the former, because it has created a rift with many progressive groups and, as a result, led bodies such as Manchester University's students' union to 'no-platform' her for her anti-trans views; and for the latter because, as the anti-trans backlash gains pace, to other slurs against the trans community has been added the claim that it is opposed to free speech.

Backlash

For a while, despite the odd foray from radical/old school feminists such as Greer and Bindel, the trans community made gains. In 2004, the UK government passed the Gender Recognition Act which, despite flaws, cleared away several of the issues that had been dogging the community since 1970. In 2010, transgender status was included in the Equality Act as a protected characteristic giving, in theory, an unprecedented level of protection to (parts of) the trans community.

This was an era of peak sympathy for trans people, in which many trans writers and community leaders began to be heard. The press may not have been favourable – there was a continued focus on prurient investigation – but boundaries were being set. Public trust in the press was at an all-time low, following the Leveson Inquiry, at which trans activist Helen Belcher (chapter 17) gave powerful evidence of the way in which trans issues are treated.

This was also an era of 'teacup storms': for instance, a social media spat between columnist Suzanne Moore and the trans community led to her one-time colleague Julie Burchill writing a piece for the *Observer* in 2013 – subsequently withdrawn –

that described trans women as 'bed-wetters in bad wigs' and 'd**** in chicks' clothing'.

Meanwhile, widespread outrage following the death of trans teacher Lucy Meadows, and a demonstration outside the offices of the *Daily Mail*, led to a public outpouring of sympathy for the trans community, and at least a temporary rowing back by the *Mail*. Two organisations contributed to that success story. Trans Media Watch, founded in 2010, is a charity that works with the press to improve media coverage of trans and intersex issues. It also complains about poor treatment when necessary. All About Trans began life in October 2011, and aims to encourage better understanding of trans people and to promote trans voices in the media by engaging media professionals with trans topics in creative ways.

A further positive step, in 2016, was a parliamentary inquiry into transgender rights by the Women and Equalities Select Committee. This was the first time that an official body had sought to systematically examine the state of trans experiences by interviewing activists and by interrogating officials on what they were and were not doing. It took evidence in public – people could watch on television and online – and the significant thing was that the published report, based on all the oral and written evidence, reinforced all the things trans activists had been saying for years about the discrimination people experienced across the board.

Yet in 2017, the press are still publishing extreme and hostile stories about the trans community with alarming regularity. Reasons for this include:

- The emergence of difficult issues: e.g., trans rights in prisons and the treatment of children.
- The emergence of distinct non-binary concepts and activism (virtually invisible in the press before 2007),

which has created new demands, from rights to facilities, that are in some cases at odds with the now familiar binary trans model. Some commentators genuinely have difficulty with this, while others have exploited differences for polemic purposes.

- The Trump victory and anti-LGBT backlash in the US, which has led to some issues (for instance, women's safety in public toilets) being imported into the UK.
- The failure of attempts to reform the press.
- The branding of a wide range of issues around gender as 'trans issues': for instance, Royal Air Force policy on skirts is not a trans issue, but was widely reported as such.

These issues have been readily exploited by centres of hostility, including radical feminists, evangelical Christians and anti-LGBT gender traditionalists. Those centres have some very clear foci in the press: publications as diverse as the *New Statesman*, *Christianity Today*, *Spiked* magazine and the Institute of Ideas, and the *Daily Mail*. *Spiked* magazine and the Institute of Ideas are both successors to the Revolutionary Communist Party: the former boasts as editor strongly anti-trans editor Brendan O'Neill, while the latter has links to the *Observer* which, far more than its sister paper the *Guardian*, has been a channel for some significantly anti-trans commentary. In the case of the *Daily Mail*, the issues are both with specific columnists, such as Richard Littlejohn, and more generally the paper's selection of news and comment.

Add in occasional columnists, such as the BBC's Jenni Murray, asserting that trans women can never be 'real women', or Fay Weldon claiming that trans women transition for 'frivolous' purposes, and you get a picture of the climate today. Public safety, free speech, trans children: everything is up for debate, which is now seen as an end in itself – even if 'debate' simply boils down to questioning the authenticity and rights of trans people.

The only constant is that this is 'about us without us'. Some trans writers have broken through on the margins, yet most major publications prefer to publish pieces about trans issues by writers who are uninformed or hostile – or both.

Meanwhile, trans people are accused of silencing debate. The reality is quite the opposite: by denying them a platform, mainstream press silences trans voices – and by seeking a spurious balance, in which experts are rebutted by non-experts, they undermine real debate. As far as the current backlash goes, we have seen the beginning, but the end remains unclear. What we can say is that there is a purposiveness to it that was not there in the early days of reporting trans affairs in the UK. Depending on how events in the wider world play out, things may yet get worse before they get better.

10

Film and Television

ANNIE WALLACE

Annie Wallace is a British actress best known for her portrayal of Sally St Claire, the headmistress of the local high school in the regular Channel 4 series *Hollyoaks*. Her acting career began when she won a place at the National Youth Theatre in 1980. She later played a crucial role as an advisor to the writers of ITV's *Coronation Street* from 1998, when the fictional transgender character Hayley Cropper (née Patterson)  was first introduced to viewers. She won the 'Celebrity of the Year' award at the 2016 National Diversity Awards, was runner-up at the Icon Awards as 'Cultural Icon of the Year', and was the first transgender actress to be nominated for a Scottish BAFTA award in 2016.

There is a bit of a misconception amongst certain sections of the public that transgender people are some kind of new phenomenon, only emerging over the last twenty years or so. You might hear people venting that it's largely a result of the 'permissive society', and maybe a product of the partial decriminalisation of homosexuality in 1967, despite the fact that gender and sexuality are two very different things.

Trans people have certainly had an increasing profile since 1970, but this is largely thanks to a few celebrated and courageous people who were prepared to talk about it openly; sometimes voluntarily, but often due to being 'outed' by a lascivious press, keen to expose so-called 'perversions' for their own gutter gains.

Film and television material usually preferred to portray those who cross-dress as sick or twisted, and almost exclusively focused on male-to-female trans people. An early film from 1953, however – *Glen or Glenda*, directed by Ed Wood, himself a cross-dresser – tried to shine a sympathetic light on the subject at a time when such things frightened and horrified most of the general public. Notable negative examples followed, including Norman Bates in *Psycho*, Bobbi in *Dressed to Kill* and Sister Hyde in *Dr Jekyll and Sister Hyde*. Men who dressed as women, whether because they were transgender, cross-dressed, or for other reasons, were to be feared and hated.

There are notable British names, of course, who came to prominence in the twentieth century: Roberta Cowell in 1954, Jan Morris, who published her memoir *Conundrum* in 1974, and of course April Ashley, whose 1970 legally contested divorce from her estranged husband at the time, Arthur Corbett, made the headlines, and had the side-effect of depriving trans people of legal rights in their correct gender for over thirty years.

The first mainstream television exposure to trans issues that the public saw was the groundbreaking series *A Change of Sex* in 1979–80, featuring Julia Grant's transition and medical journey. This was the first time that the process had been recorded for television and, whilst it shocked many, it is seen as a landmark fly-on-the-wall documentary, exposing the painful and often judgemental and harsh process of gender confirmation treatment, surgery and transition to a new life.

The combative psychiatrist Dr Randell, seen in the series, later achieved notoriety as the basis for the character of the rude and dismissive Dr Ira Carlton in *The League of Gentlemen*. Randell controlled Julia's transitional progress, punishing her for taking personal initiatives by delaying her sought-after final surgery. It's worth noting that although this was the late seventies, this kind of 'gatekeeping' was still in place until relatively recently.

Around this time, a flurry of British and international stories were making the media, including about the model and actress Caroline Cossey (also known professionally as Tula), who was outed by the press after her appearance as a Bond girl in *For Your Eyes Only* in 1981. It's important to note that, during this period, trans people were overwhelmingly seen as figures of fun and derision, and trans men were rarely mentioned at all. British newspapers such as the now defunct *News of the World*, the *Sunday People* and other tabloids regularly took it upon themselves to out trans people, usually by getting tip-offs from work colleagues or neighbours, which would then lead to a reporter turning up on someone's doorstep with an ultimatum of 'tell us your story with pics or we'll publish anyway without your co-operation'. Trans people were seen as fair game. Unprotected by privacy laws and having no legal rights in their confirmed gender, they had little recourse to justice once outed. Many lost families, jobs and livelihoods as a result.

As the eighties progressed, trans people were being mentioned or featured more in movies and television, largely from the United States, including Chris Sarandon's character in *Dog Day Afternoon*, Eric Idle's Loretta in *Life of Brian*, Roberta in *The World According to Garp*, Denise in *Twin Peaks*, and Dil in *The Crying Game*. In a few of these cases, the trans character was portrayed positively, but mostly not. In 1992, *The Crying Game*, for instance, used a sex scene to reveal that the protagonist Dil was a pre-operative trans woman, which led to her boyfriend Fergus (Stephen Rea) running to the toilet to throw up in disgust. This rather gross and unpleasant reaction was subsequently rehashed by comedies such as *Family Guy* and *Ace Ventura: Pet Detective*, amongst others. It was clearly and offensively stating that dating or sleeping with a trans person was utterly disgusting. *Ace Ventura* in particular spent a lot of time mocking or being disgusted by trans people in general – all the worse for trying to make it funny.

Eventually, though, as the nineties progressed, we started to see stories more regularly where the trans character was sympathetic, rather than derisory. One landmark movie was *Different for Girls* in 1996, which told the story of two childhood friends who meet up later in life after one has transitioned from male to female. After some friction, the two eventually end up together, giving a trans person a happy ending for once. The positive aspects of this film were certainly influenced by the producers getting a real trans person to advise them. Actress and singer Adele Anderson (from the acclaimed group Fascinating Aïda, and herself a pioneer trans actress) was consulted extensively and proved what a valuable asset such a liaison could be, instead of writers working in limbo and relying largely upon anecdotal or out-of-date information.

A year later, something would happen in British television which would rewrite the rulebook for the representation of trans characters forever, in the UK at least: the then thirty-seven-year-old, cosy, early evening soap opera *Coronation Street* introduced a trans woman into the regular cast.

The character of Hayley Patterson was created by the writers as one of a series of dates for the awkward and socially inexperienced Roy Cropper, the popular café owner in the series. It was by no means intended as a permanent arrangement – the writers planned that Roy would go on to meet other dates too – but things didn't quite turn out like that.

The casting directors had had their eye on a versatile actress called Julie Hesmondhalgh for a while. She was an experienced theatre and television actress from Accrington with a broad Lancashire accent and an engaging style. They selected her for audition and, shortly afterwards, offered her the role, which she was really keen to get. It was not only an excellent opportunity for her as a performer, but also, as a keen advocate for social justice and LGBT rights, an opportunity to play a unique character who could help the public understand the issues better.

Hayley appeared on screen for the first time on 26 January 1998, having filmed her first scenes just before Christmas 1997. She was quite plain, a bit shy and nervous and working alongside established characters Alma Baldwin and Curly Watts in the Firman's Freezers shop. She was introduced to Roy at a dinner party hosted by Alma, and a clear chemistry between the characters and actors was evident. The general public, previously rather hostile to the idea of a transgender character on their favourite soap opera – on their tellies at 7.30 in the evening – warmed to the gentle love story that was unfolding. Even when Hayley revealed her secret, much to Roy's distress, the public *wanted* this couple to work – so much so that Hayley was written into the show as a regular character. This gave the writers much more time and scope to not only allow their relationship to grow naturally and slowly, but to also explore what life is like for a trans person, socially and legally.

In order to do this tale justice, and after some initial criticism from some quarters about stereotyping, *Coronation Street* turned to the trans advocacy group Press for Change for assistance. Press for Change had been campaigning for the legal rights of trans people for several years by this point and, in the months prior to this, I had been helping the group on the periphery, campaigning at a local level and talking to MPs about the total lack of legal rights afforded to trans people in their present gender at that time. I had already expressed an interest in *Coronation Street*, as I felt that Hayley resembled the 'old me' quite a lot. Christine Burns, one of the vice-presidents of Press for Change, approached me to see if I would be interested in stepping up to the mark and helping on the series. I jumped at the chance and eagerly visited the studios in April 1998, where a long and detailed interview took place. This was recorded, transcribed, and copies given to the writers. My interview became a primer for them, giving them insight into a trans woman's life, events and feelings.

After this initial interaction, contact was made regularly for about eighteen months or so – whenever the writers needed some details or thoughts. A particularly crucial example of this consultation involved the planned wedding of Roy and Hayley, which the producers wanted to stage in 1999. Such a marriage was, at the time, not legally possible, so the compromise of a religious 'blessing' was planned for the story.

The 'Hayley and Roy's Wedding' storyline became a major television event, viewed by over eighteen million fans of the show. It was at that very time that the Labour government of the day finally, after much lobbying and persuasion, announced the formation of a working group to investigate how best to grant trans people full legal status in their new gender. I don't believe that this was entirely coincidental, as Hayley's story had, by this time, won round much of the initially hostile public to her plight. They just wanted Roy and Hayley to marry and be happy – which, after all, was the goal of many trans people in general.

Five years later, the Gender Recognition Act (2004) came into being, granting trans people the rights for which they had fought for so long. It wasn't a perfect bill by any means, but perhaps the best that could be achieved at the time, given the continued opposition from the right wing and some Christian groups. To this day, several parts of the bill remain contentious, such as the 'spousal veto', introduced after the Marriage (Same Sex Couples) Act (2013), allowing a trans person's husband or wife the right to refuse the granting of a gender recognition certificate. At the time of writing (2017), consultations are underway about an overhaul of the system.

After fifteen years in the role, and keen to diversify her work into theatre, radio and film, Julie Hesmondhalgh decided to hang up Hayley's famous red anorak for the last time. Given that Roy and Hayley were such a devoted couple, her exit would necessitate a plot involving Hayley's death. It was simply unthinkable that the couple would be parted for any other reason. After a diagnosis of pancreatic cancer, we saw Hayley decline over six months and, towards the end, she was plagued with nightmares about her pre-transition past, leading her to eventually take her own life, rather than let the cancer torture her to death. Hayley's death was screened on 22 January 2014, nearly sixteen years to the day of her first appearance.

Over in the United States, supportive films about trans people were starting to break into the mainstream and more films and TV were featuring trans characters, such as the Oscar-winning 1999 movie *Boys Don't Cry*, about the brutal transphobic murder of young trans man Brandon Teena, portrayed by actress Hilary Swank. In 2005, *Transamerica* told the story of Bree, a trans woman played by actress Felicity Huffman, who discovers she has a son, and the subsequent journey they undertake, real and figurative. This movie too benefited from having a trans consultant, Andrea James, to ground the story in reality.

Filmmakers were now interested in telling trans people's stories, but the one hurdle yet to be overcome was the casting. Ninety-nine per cent of trans characters were being played by non-trans (or cisgender) actors and actresses. The reason usually given for this was that trans actors were few and far between. This may have been true, but then again they weren't really being sought out. It was easier, and more bankable, to cast established performers (like Swank and Huffman), who often garnered accolades for their performances, in these roles. Trans actors were largely ignored or, as is often the case, invisible. Even if granted the opportunity, the reality for actual trans actors was that coming out as trans would certainly have limited their castability.

By the mid-noughties, a few notable performers had begun to break through into US mainstream media, most famously Laverne Cox, who went on to great acclaim as inmate Sophia in the TV series *Orange Is the New Black* in 2013. This started to turn heads in the film and TV industries, as it was not only a more truthful way to tell a story but it was also revealing new talent.

Transparent debuted on US TV in 2014, and tells the story of an older father, played by Jeffrey Tambor, transitioning to female. The show deals with the effect this event has on her children. This series also made it their business to bring trans actors into the project, both in front of the camera and in writing and production roles. A 'transfirmative action' programme, put in place by the show's creator Jill Soloway, saw almost eighty trans people involved in the first season alone. These included Zackary Drucker and Rhys Ernst (consultants and co-producers), Our Lady J (the first trans writer on the show) and Trace Lysette (who plays the part of Shea). As trans actors started to become more noticeable, criticism began to appear when trans characters continued being played by non-trans people. There were several notorious examples, such as Jared Leto's performance of the character Rayon in 2013's *Dallas Buyers Club*. Now, instead of being seen as skilled, cisgender actors playing trans roles started being seen as patronising. 2015's *The Danish Girl*, featuring Eddie Redmayne as trans woman Lili Elbe, and the 2017 film *About Ray*, featuring Elle Fanning as young trans man Ray, attracted much criticism. In both of those cases, however, the characters spend much of the time on screen in their birth gender, and the transition is part of the story. Personally, I don't have a problem with casting cisgender actors in that context. But where a character is post-transition and established, the excuses for *not* casting a trans actor are becoming fewer and fewer.

Back in the UK, in 2013, the BBC Writers Room, in conjunction with the trans media liaison group All About Trans, ran the Trans Comedy Award in order to find some new ideas for a transgender-based sitcom to be made and broadcast by the BBC. Two finalists were chosen: *Boy Meets Girl* and *Nobody's Perfect*. The first of these was a romantic comedy, and the second a comedy about a very twenty-first-century family – the parents being a cisgender woman and her trans partner. I took the plunge and auditioned for the latter in late 2013 and, although I was one of the final few recalled, it was *Boy Meets Girl*, starring Rebecca Root, which was chosen to be developed into a full series.

Early in 2014, Channel 4 ran a series called *Cucumber*, written by *Doctor Who* and *Queer as Folk* writer Russell T. Davies. In the series, and its spinoff, *Banana*, a trans character called Helen was featured. It was stated that ideally they wanted to cast a trans woman in the role. Open castings were held in 2013 and, eventually, comedian and actress Bethany Black was cast, becoming the first openly trans actress to play a leading trans character in a major TV series. To all intents and purposes, the glass ceiling had been broken.

Hollyoaks, the Channel 4 soap opera, watched largely by a sixteen to thirty age-group audience, had also featured a couple of trans characters: Jason, a young trans man played by Victoria Atkin in 2010, and Blessing, a young trans woman played by Modupe Adeyeye in 2014 – both cisgender actors. The selection of Adeyeye attracted criticism because she wasn't a trans actor and so the production team decided to develop a trans character for the future. To achieve this they set about discovering a 'pool of talent' in the trans acting community. An open casting call was announced and a workshop of script work and improvised scenarios was staged for around thirty actors. After that, half a dozen were recalled and more work was done. It took nearly a year for the trans character to be developed and written into the show but, by July 2015, they were ready to cast. Auditions and screen tests for this role were carried out in early July, leading to me being cast in the role of Sally St Claire, headmistress of Hollyoaks High School, and secret parent of the popular and established character John Paul McQueen.

Since her first appearance on 29 October 2015, Sally St Claire has been involved in several big storylines and I'm happy to say that, thanks to her popularity, there are many more adventures planned for the strict headmistress with the heart of gold.

EastEnders, the BBC soap opera, had also had their eye on the times in 2015, and planned their own trans part. In this case they chose to create the character of Kyle Slater, a young trans man and the half-brother of regular character Stacey Slater. Riley Carter Millington was cast in the role after similar open auditions. Kyle made his debut on 30 October 2015 and started being featured more extensively in December of that year.

These characters became part of the phenomenon known colloquially as the 'Year of Trans Visibility', which had featured many media-based representations of trans people, both in fiction and reality. Caitlyn Jenner's internationally reported coming out, Janet Mock's TV presentation and well-received autobiography *Redefining Realness*, young Jazz Jennings's reality series on satellite and cable TV *I am Jazz*, Laverne Cox's Tussauds waxwork, and the many supportive news articles on the increased profile of trans people in the media all contributed to a sense that our time had come.

Unfortunately, this wasn't entirely the case, and there are still issues as regards casting for film and television. By early 2016 it seemed as though a right-wing backlash had started in the usual places, such as the *Daily Mail*, *Breitbart*, the *Sun* and so forth, fuelled by an outrage that uppity trans people didn't know their place anymore and were actually demanding, and receiving, equality and respect, as well as supportive media attention and representation. Clearly this had to stop. Supported by well-funded US Christian fundamentalist-led groups such as Focus on the Family, and the rhetoric of individuals like televangelist Pat Robertson and president of Liberty University Jerry Falwell, their agenda was to stop this progress in its tracks. It manifested in many different ways, such as the creation of 'bathroom bills' (crafted by Liberty Counsel) in the southern US states, forcing trans people to only use toilets of their birth gender, and (in the UK) the demonisation of parents for daring to support and help their trans children – accusing them, and the organisation which supports them, Mermaids, of all manner of abuse.

On television, Caitlyn Jenner's reality show about her transition, *I Am Cait*, was cancelled, *EastEnders* dropped Kyle Slater from the cast, Rebecca Root's *Boy Meets Girl* wasn't renewed for a third series and, in film, Elle Fanning, a cisgender actress, was cast as trans man Ray in *About Ray*. Back to square one?

I'd like to think that it was more a case of 'three steps forward, one step back'. The media is notoriously faddy and, whilst trans people's visibility was certainly increased, the media moves on relentlessly to other stories. They'll come back. As I said, the glass ceiling *has* been broken and trans visibility has been vastly improved. As I write this, there are more trans writers, directors and performers than ever before, and we are now part of the entertainment industry, rather than remaining on its outskirts. The campaign continues.

11

Section 28 and the Journey from the Gay Teachers' Group to LGBT History Month

PROFESSOR EMERITUS SUE SANDERS OF THE HARVEY MILK INSTITUTE

With the assistance of Jeanne Nadeau

Sue Sanders is Emeritus Professor of the Harvey Milk Institute, an 'out and proud' lesbian, and an LGBT rights activist. Since 1967 she has been a teacher, tutor and lecturer on women's studies, drama and homophobia. Having been an active member of Schools OUT UK, a group working for the visibility of LGBT people in the education system, she became their chair in 2000. She was a founder member of the LGBT advisory group to the Metropolitan Police and worked closely with the criminal justice system on hate crime. In 2004 she instituted the UK's first LGBT History Month and in 2008 was responsible for the website 'the Classroom', which has over seventy lesson plans that usualise LGBT people for all ages across the curriculum.

Since records began in our Western-dominated culture, LGBT people have had many barriers to contend with, both legally and culturally. Their effects on our communities have been both devastating and strengthening. In response, we have learned to challenge oppression, make common cause and forge links with a variety of friends and allies. We have witnessed discrimination and violence visited on our minorities and women, and continue to do so, as society struggles and fails to meet us with the human rights we all deserve. Sometimes that aggression shows itself in individual acts of violence in school or on the street, or it is enshrined in law as an official act that is designed to undermine our rights and/or existence.

The legal position of gay people, before the Sexual Offences Act (1967), was that all homosexual sex involving men was illegal. The act decriminalised homosexual behaviour between consenting men over the age of twenty-one in private, a seemingly major advance for that time. But far more was needed. After the act, the legal situation for gay men remained precarious because they could still face a barrage of threats, such as accusations of importuning and cottaging. The result was that more annual arrests of gay men were made *after* 1967 than before.

Though the change in the law undeniably contributed to a more liberated atmosphere, it endorsed rather than challenged public hostility towards gay people, by underlining the extent of what remained unlawful or unclear. Lord Arran's comment at the time says it all:

I ask one thing and I ask it earnestly. I ask those who have, as it were, been in bondage and for whom the prison doors are now open to show their thanks by comporting themselves quietly and with dignity. This is no occasion for jubilation; certainly not for celebration. Any form of ostentatious behaviour, now or in the future, any form of public flaunting, would be utterly distasteful and would, I believe, make the sponsors of the Bill regret that they have done what they have done. Homosexuals must continue to remember that while there may be nothing bad in being a homosexual, there is certainly nothing good.

This too was the climate in which the divorce of transsexual socialite April Ashley and her husband Arthur Corbett was judged in 1969–70. Just as Parliament was conservative about how much to decriminalise gay relationships, the courts really were not likely to uphold a marriage which they observed to be between two men. The language of the judgment expressed this view: April Ashley was to be considered a male for the purposes of the Marriage Law. In consequence there could be no question of a divorce settlement as, in law, April's and Arthur's marriage had simply never existed.

Moving on to the seventies, we had national laws to prohibit discrimination on the grounds of sex and race, and they gave some rights to disabled people. The law ignored lesbians, bisexuals and trans people. However, they found it necessary to hide their identities to protect themselves from the hateful attitudes and acts they experienced from our homophobic society that labelled them all 'perverts'.

The personal challenge to come to terms with one's sexual and gender identity is daunting and painful when there is a pernicious atmosphere.

Until fairly recently, lesbians and gays have been perceived in our society as constituting an imperceptibly tiny minority. Virtually all lesbians and gays can and commonly do 'pass' – for at least part of the time, at work for instance – as heterosexuals. This has affected our ability to organise ourselves politically in the sense that, very often, we have literally been unable to identify each other. It also limits the public recognition of our existence and experience. There are both parallels and contrasts to be drawn here with the position of disabled and trans people. In the former case, disabled people are often concealed from one another by their restricted access to the public realm. In the case of trans people, the pressure to 'pass' as cisgender, and to assimilate as such, could keep them from both meeting each other and being 'seen to be there' by the public.

In the eighties, with the rise of the women's movement, it was painful to see how often lesbians were either ignored or vilified by both the press and the movement itself. In 1984, I gave a paper at a women's studies conference, entitled 'Where Are the Lesbians in Women's Studies?' Press coverage of the 1981 peace camp at Greenham Common usually included vicious attacks on the sort of women there, declaring them man-hating, hairy, aggressive lesbians. Lesbians were challenging the threats to a woman's right to choose and violence against women, but we were encouraged to keep a low profile lest we scare the 'straight' women. It's easy to forget how, in those early days of second-wave feminism, lesbian women were ostracised by straight women – in much the same way that most lesbian feminists later went on to ostracise trans women.

Schools OUT UK, of which I have been the chair for over twenty years, was founded in 1974 as the Gay Teachers Group. In those days 'gay' was a word that was used to mean both gay men and lesbians. We were vague as to whether it included bisexuals and it certainly did not include trans people – the latter were barely visible both in the press and in our activists' circles. The group was mainly a social framework to support gay teachers who were isolated and frequently under attack by school bureaucracy, as there were no laws to support them. The group did gradually become more active and morphed into Schools OUT UK, which progressively included LGBT people.

During the seventies, attempts by the Gay Teachers Group to move forward were thwarted. However, with the election of Ken Livingstone to the Greater London Council (GLC) in 1981, things began to change.

Work to include lesbian and gay people in schools and in youth groups was now supported by a few Labour politicians. The fact that they were called the 'loony left' by both the right and the mainstream left, says much about the culture of the time. However, in London, Manchester, Leicester and other cities teachers were beginning to be encouraged by their Local Education Authorities (LEAs) to include and reference lesbian and gay issues in the classroom.

Many councils supported inclusive work, with notable examples including Haringey LEA's *Mirror Round the Walls* booklet and the Inner London Education Authority's (ILEA) *Relationships and Sexuality* project. Paul Patrick (1950–2008) worked for the ILEA on the latter and he was later to be my co-chair at Schools OUT.

Such projects came under sustained fire by the right-wing press, who frequently used the concepts of 'family', 'loony left' and 'wasting taxpayers' money' to undermine and destroy them.

This was particularly the case with initiatives in education. In more than one authority, ill-thought-out promises of action on heterosexism in schools were left unexplained and undefended in the face of accusations that councillors were seeking to encourage children to grow up gay. Compare that with the way some commentators nowadays accuse trans activists of 'trying to turn children trans'.

The real brunt of this kind of behaviour was borne by lesbians and gays, whose position in the community was publicly undermined by growing prejudice, eagerly encouraged by Tory politicians and the right-wing press. In April 1986 the Thatcher government, enacting a policy set out in its 1983 manifesto, abolished the Greater London Council and six top-tier Metropolitan County Councils (MCCs) – the elected bodies thought of as being most 'to blame'.

The year 1986 also saw the first signs of what was to become the notorious Section 28 of the Local Government Act (1988), preambled by the government's previous vicious attack on local democracy.

In 1986, the Earl of Halsbury tabled a private members' bill dubbed 'An Act to Restrain Local Authorities from Promoting Homosexuality'. Moving for a second reading of the bill, he said:

I did not think... that lesbians were a problem. They do not molest little girls. They do not indulge in disgusting and unnatural practices like buggery. They are not wildly promiscuous and do not spread venereal disease. It is part of the softening up propaganda that lesbians and gays are nearly always referred to in that order. The relatively harmless lesbian leads on the vicious gay. That was what I thought... and what I still in part continue to think, but I have been warned that the loony Left is hardening up the lesbian camp and that they are becoming increasingly aggressive.

Writing about this at the time we were clear:

Presumably it was basic male chauvinism which prevented the noble Earl from suspecting that the opposite was true: the policies of the so-called 'loony Left', far from politicising lesbians, had instead begun to develop following many years' hard work and agitation by lesbian activists. Yet his observation does reveal a crucial point about the attitudes towards lesbians current among today's authoritarian Right: what they find unforgivable is that we are becoming visibly involved in the political process, and are demanding a larger share of social resources. This, of course, is classic patriarchal misogyny in operation. Halsbury's use of the words 'hardening' and 'aggressive' betray a horror and fear of women who refuse to fit into traditionally accepted patterns, who are outspoken and visibly different, and who make demands.

At the same time, he clearly cannot believe that women might initiate their own actions: without the 'loony Left' to stir us up; he appears to think we would not be, in his terms, a 'problem'.

These attitudes were prominent in the press and the women's movement were slow to challenge them. Halsbury continued:

One of the characteristics of our time is that we have for several decades past been emancipating minorities who claimed that they were disadvantaged. Are they grateful? Not a bit. We emancipated races and got inverted racism. We emancipate homosexuals and they condemn heterosexism as chauvinist sexism, male oppression and so on. They will push us off the pavement if we give them a chance.

Our contemporary analysis from the same chapter again:

Underlying this speech is an awareness that demands are being made which, if met, will change society as we know it and lead to the erosion of the existing bases of power. The projection here is unmistakable; it is after all, the members of the ruling class who hitherto have successfully colluded to keep Blacks, lesbians and gays (among so many others) 'off the pavement'. Hence the fear that, given half a chance, we would do the same to them.[1]

1   Quoted from 'Section 28 and Education' by Sue Sanders and Gill Spraggs in the book *Learning our Lines: Sexuality and Social Control in Education*, edited by Carol Jones and Pat Mahoney, London: The Women's Press, 1989.

Though Halsbury's bill was passed by the Lords, it failed in the Commons virtually by accident: the following week there was an election and the mood changed.

Throughout the process to advance the bill, trans people were invisible by name and the attitudes depicted make it clear that it was probably wise to remain that way. The attack on men and women not seen as 'normal' was vehement – although, of course, a legal challenge by trans man Mark Rees was at the time nearing the end of a long process of reaching the European Court of Human Rights.

Mr. Tony Banks: I will be brief, but I want to say something about the speech made by the hon. Member for Birmingham, Edgbaston (Dame J. Knight). I felt that her speech owed more to imagination than to truth. I listened to an interview that the hon. Lady gave on Radio 4's "Today" programme. Mr. Brian Redhead asked her to support her statement that she had a great deal of evidence about schools promoting homosexuality. Mr. Redhead asked her what evidence she had and she replied that she had not brought her files with her, but she claimed that she had the evidence. When she was pressed even further, she said "I didn't offer to name any schools." I am not surprised that the hon. Lady has received letters from parents who have been alarmed about the position. They have been alarmed by what the hon. Lady said.

Dame Jill Knight: Will the hon. Gentleman give way?

Mr. Banks: No. If the hon. Lady will wait a moment, I will give way to her, and that is more than she did to me or to anyone else.

It is not surprising that parents have become alarmed by the kind of scare stories and fantasies that the hon. Lady has propagated in her various interviews and speeches. She has no evidence and she has never been able to produce evidence, other than that which comes from her over-fertile imagination.

Hansard. Crown Copyright

A vignette of the Lords debate on Section 28 in 1988, as recorded by Hansard.

There was a clear desire on the part of the government to lessen the power of local authorities (most of which were Labour) and erode the powers and scope of local government. This was partially done under the guise of saving money. 'The plain and simple intention of the Bill', according to Lord Campbell, was 'to curb an abuse of rates'.

The tiny sums of money allocated to lesbian and gay groups were exaggerated in the press and of course no mention was made that they too were rate-payers and tax-payers.

According to Jill Knight MP, 'Millions outside Parliament object to little children being perverted, diverted, or converted from normal family life to a lifestyle which is desperately dangerous for society and extremely dangerous for them.'

Thatcher made a special point of attacking 'hard-left education authorities and extremist teachers' on the grounds that 'children who need to be taught to respect traditional moral values are being taught that they have an inalienable right to be gay'. Section 28 stated that a Local Authority 'shall not intentionally promote homosexuality or publish material with the intention of promoting homosexuality' or 'promote the teaching in any maintained school of the acceptability of homosexuality as a pretended family relationship'. It was passed in 1988, and remained in law until 2003. Section 28 and the fight against it politicised many people.

The shift in politics which the 1997 election of the Labour government heralded involved a move to inclusion, very slowly. The rumours of a single equality act and the idea of public-sector equality duties (which would require public institutions to be proactive on diversity) seeded a change.

Schools OUT was at that time producing material to make LGB people visible. The debate about whether to be out or not was high on the list. We heard nothing at that time from trans teachers, which we thought was strange given that there was some discussion in the media about employment rights for transsexual people in 1999.

I was, however, meeting with trans people in other arenas. As I was delivering anti-racist and diversity training to the criminal justice system after the Stephen Lawrence Inquiry report in 1999, I was involved in the burgeoning diversity scene and was a member of a variety of groups and committees, both local and national. Most groups had trans members or were beginning to discuss trans issues.

The 'Inquiry into the Matters Arising from the Death of Stephen Lawrence', headed by Sir William Macpherson, was ordered by the new Labour Home Secretary Jack Straw in 1997 and reported in 1999. Although ostensibly confined to the circumstances of the young black man's death and the (mis)conduct of the police investigating it in 1993, Macpherson examined the way in which institutionalised discrimination works and made seminal recommendations for how to proactively address it and break the pernicious cycle that kept it in place. The focus was on racial discrimination, but the findings could easily be seen to apply to other minorities and women too. A key recommendation concerned the idea of placing duties upon public bodies to proactively examine ways in which their operations could (unintentionally or not) create or reinforce disadvantage. Statutory public sector equality duties (relating to race, disability and gender) would go on to become a key feature of equalities work in the noughties, obliging official bodies of all kinds to actively engage with and seek advice from women's and minority groups to carry out so-called equality impact assessments and publish plans to close gaps. This obligatory activity had far-reaching and permanent effects on the relationship between officialdom and LGBT activists.

April 1999 saw the horror of three hate-driven bombings

in London: the first being in Brixton on 17 April; the second in Brick Lane on 24 April; and a third in Soho at the Admiral Duncan Pub in Old Compton Street on 30 April.

After those outrageous and tragic events, John Grieve, then head of the Metropolitan Police Racial and Violent Crime Task Force, recognised the need for a lesbian and gay advisory group. I was in the fortunate position to hear of this and decided to help produce a truly representative and independent group. I was friends with some of the members of the Race Advisory Group who had been chosen by Grieve after his work with the black community during the Lawrence Inquiry. His lack of knowledge of the lesbian and gay community meant his ability to gather a grass-roots and accountable group was limited.

I offered to design the process and use my networks to recruit such a group and he agreed. I worked with lesbian feminists, gay men who were working with the police on homosexual issues and friends from the Race Independent Advisory Group. We drew up a job description and person specification that delivered a group of LGBT people from a variety of ethnic backgrounds, religions and abilities.

Though there were no trans people in the group that designed the structure, we ensured that their interests and later their voices would be included. The group was formed in January 2000 and made up of twenty-five volunteers; by 2001 there were two trans people included.

The run-up to the single equality act was a very long one. The Labour Party was discussing it in 2003, when they enacted the Employment Equality (Sexual Orientation) Regulations (prohibiting unreasonable discrimination for the first time); that was also the year that Section 28 was finally repealed. Trans people had already won similar employment protection in 1999 and in 2004, with the Gender Recognition Act; at last we had legislation that began to protect all LGBT people.

Given the new laws, the idea for a history festival similar to Black History Month seemed timely. Paul Patrick and I consulted with our networks and decided on February as the best time to hold it. By then the name was obvious to us. It had to be *LGBT History Month*.

Funding was granted to us by the Department for Education in November 2004, and the following month we held a launch at the Tate Modern supported by Southwark Council to announce the birth of LGBT History Month and introduce the website.

We had a panel of thirteen people on stage to ensure that the idea of inclusion was clear. Those thirteen included three trans people: Grayson Perry (by then famous as an 'out' transvestite), plus Christine Burns and Claire McNab of Press for Change (both 'out' trans women).

The Schools OUT UK committee and crew has been as inclusive as we can make it. We have had input from black and white trans members, and vital links with organisations such as GIRES, Gendered Intelligence and Mermaids, as well as the organisations and trans individuals that we worked with to support the Crown Prosecution Service to produce their guidance on homophobic and transphobic prosecution. Christine Burns and Stephen Whittle also went on to become patrons of LGBT History Month.

In 2011, LGBT History Month started the concept of 'themes', commencing with two years focused on sport to coincide with the London Olympics in 2012. Working with trans sports groups in the launches helped to expose the many issues which that particular group had to deal with in the world of sport. In 2014, LGBT History Month added the idea of having four historical figures associated with each year's theme, one from each of the LGBT communities. We have also produced twenty-five downloadable posters: one 'Voices and Visibility' poster and twenty-four curriculum-linked posters.

Christine Burns

Each year LGBT History Month has an educational theme which is reflected throughout the branding in items such as lapel pins. In 2013 the event celebrated the centenary of the birth of mathematician, code breaker and computer pioneer Alan Turing, who was persecuted for being gay.

Thus we are building resources year on year for schools, colleges, universities, libraries and museums that enable LGBT people, in all their diversity, to be visible.

Our latest development has been the LGBT National History Festival that comprises popular and academic presentations, and originally commissioned plays. The festival started with one 'hub' in Manchester during February 2015. By 2017 the festival was being run in fifteen hubs situated around the country.

The call for both the popular presentations and academic papers is wide. Over the three years we have had at least 130 popular presentations and a similar number of academic papers. We advertise widely using our activist, community and academic networks. The number of trans contributions has increased each year. The festivals provide refreshingly new spaces where people are coming to learn about LGBT history and discover untold stories. The mixture of academic and activist participation has really excited people and attracted attendance from round the world. In 2017 we had representatives from Israel, Ireland, Norway, USA and Australia. The original theatre has added a vital emotional dimension to our work and represents the telling of history through the heart. One of the plays we've produced explored a trans theme and we have had Professor Susan Stryker, a highly respected historian, come over from the USA as the keynote speaker for 2016. A trans woman herself, she educated and entertained us with her unique and dynamic take on trans politics. In 2017, among several trans presentations, Caroline Paige launched her book *True Colours*, describing her life as the first openly transgender officer in the British armed forces.

These days, even the entertainment industry is getting better at showing the issues that trans people face daily. While there's still room for improvement (as indicated by some of the critiques in this book), programmes like *My Transsexual Summer* and films such as *The Danish Girl* exemplify this move towards more mainstream representations. There is still much work to be done in our schools for trans people to feel safe and included, however, and this will be Schools OUT UK's focus in the future.

12

A Scottish History of Trans Equality Activism

JAMES MORTON

James Morton is a Scottish transgender campaigner who's been active since 2002. He is the manager of the Scottish Transgender Alliance, the leading advocacy organisation for trans people in Scotland. He gave evidence to the Women and Equalities parliamentary select committee's inquiry into trans equality in 2015, focusing on the reforms needed to the Gender Recognition Act (2004) and the Equality Act (2010).

Scotland has only a tenth of England's population and its people are widely dispersed. Not allowing themselves to be daunted by this, trans people across Scotland have together achieved a strong and distinctive trans movement. Similarly to England, early trans peer support groups generated the initial momentum for trans equality activism. However, strategy and progress in Scotland thereafter diverged from England due to different LGBT equality sector cohesion levels, availability of funding and devolved government structures.

Developing trans-inclusive Scottish LGBT activism

The Scottish trans equality movement can be traced back to 1983, when the Scottish TV/TS Group started organising social support meetings in Edinburgh. It was the first Scottish trans support group publicly known to have existed and it engaged with trans organisations based in England, such as the Beaumont Society. By 1992, the Scottish TV/TS Group's newsletter, *Tartan Skirt*, had grown into a fifty-two-page quarterly magazine distributed to over fifty subscribers, thanks to initial editor Anne Forrester, later succeeded by Julia Gordon. In addition to the Edinburgh monthly meetings and annual weekend event, there were also the Grampian Gender Group (3G) monthly meetings in Aberdeen, and Crosslynx in Glasgow ran a trans support telephone helpline as well as monthly get-togethers.

Archived copies of *Tartan Skirt* show that, by the mid-1990s, Scottish trans groups were sharing a variety of legal rights information, social spaces and helpline infrastructure with Scotland's lesbian, gay and bisexual (LGB) groups. Up in the Scottish Highlands the integration of LGBT activism was furthest ahead, with Julia Gordon running Inverness transgender support group meetings as part of her volunteer role within LGBT charity Reach Out Highland from 1995 onwards. With LGBT ceilidhs and boat cruises, media outreach, sexual health service provision, a multimedia trans information library and attendance at national equality events all being carried out via Reach Out Highland, Julia was ideally placed to recognise the benefits of collaborative LGBT activism and was able to convey this to other trans people across Scotland.

Meanwhile, the first Scottish Pride event took place in 1995, with over 3,000 people marching through Edinburgh. Inspired to make Pride Scotland an annual event, its organisers began consulting trans people about their involvement in 1997, and publicly affirmed Pride Scotland as fully LGBT in 1998. The impact that Pride Scotland's trans inclusion would have on Scottish trans equality activism was not obvious at the time and years later would be almost forgotten.

To appreciate the importance of Pride Scotland becoming trans-inclusive, it is necessary to briefly discuss the Sex Offenders Bill, which was introduced at the Westminster Parliament in 1996 with the intention of creating the UK sex offenders registry. Campaigners in London had successfully lobbied to remove from the English parts of the bill a number of discriminatory proposals that would have unfairly placed gay and bisexual men on the sex offenders registry for consensual sex – for example due to the ages of consent still being unequal. However, these discriminatory proposals had been left unchanged within the Scottish parts of the bill. Luckily, several sexual orientation activists in Scotland noticed in time and, at extremely stressful short notice, lobbied successfully for the necessary amendments to the bill. This near-miss, together with the expectation that a Scottish Parliament would soon be created, suggested to these activists that there might be a need for a new Scottish campaigning network. Barely pausing for breath, they started exploring how to consult more widely on this idea, initially under the name LGB Equality Network. This activist group overlapped with the group that ran Pride, and so a community conference to discuss the campaigning network idea was organised jointly with Pride Scotland in June 1997.

Since Pride Scotland was already at that time reaching out to trans people, the June 1997 conference included a workshop focused on trans inclusion. Julia Gordon attended the conference as part of Reach Out Highland and facilitated that workshop using the discussion topic 'Is the Equality Network willing to offer affiliation to the transgender community? What potential benefits might affiliation have?' After a bit of initial apprehension from trans people and some anti-trans opposition from a few gay and lesbian individuals, a firm agreement was reached that the Equality Network should be created in 1997 as a national LGBT equality campaigning network for Scotland.

The trans activists who helped develop the Equality Network's first manifesto in April 1999 for the new Scottish Parliament included calls for legal gender recognition, to remove gender identity discrimination from Scots sex offences law, for Scottish public bodies to adopt gender identity non-discrimination policies, and for the newly established Scottish Parliament to press Westminster to introduce gender identity equality law. Thanks to Julia, they used the words 'transgender people' and 'trans people' as equivalent fully-inclusive umbrella terms. Although preferred language has been debated, refined and expanded over the years, these terms have remained central in Scottish equality activism and peer support.

The Edinburgh youth group, which was later to grow into LGBT Youth Scotland, also swiftly became trans-inclusive in 1997, after a young person attending the group came out as a trans man and began to transition. Within that group I was a seventeen-year-old watching cautiously how it played out before deciding whether to also come out as trans.

Across Scotland the lesbian and gay switchboard helplines and nearly all local and national community support groups became trans-inclusive by the end of the 1990s. Scottish LGBT activists were then galvanised into even stronger cohesion by the intensity of the battle in early 2000 to repeal Section 28 against the multi-million-pound Keep the Clause campaign that placed homophobic billboards across the length and breadth of Scotland.

When Stonewall decided to open a Scottish office in 2000 it was clear that being only LGB would simply not be considered acceptable by activists in Scotland, and therefore Stonewall Scotland was set up from the start as LGBT. It took a further fifteen years for Stonewall to become trans inclusive in England and Wales.

Using LGBT funding to develop Scottish trans activism capacity
By 2001, the number of trans support groups in Scotland had more than quadrupled, largely thanks to the Internet enabling trans people to find each other more easily. Most meetings still took place in people's living rooms or in hotel bars and pubs. The majority were open to anyone who self-identified as trans in any way, while a minority used interviews to decide who was permitted to join.

Simon Ruth de Voil, a youth counsellor, recognised that young trans people needed specific support and therefore he set up Scotland's first trans youth group within LGBT Youth Scotland in Edinburgh in 2001. I was one of the young people who found the support of this group invaluable for developing self-esteem and finding our voices as trans activists. Meanwhile, the Sandyford Gender Identity Clinic in Glasgow started a trans support group to provide a structured support service. What was notable in comparison with all the other trans groups in existence across Scotland was that these two new groups were facilitated by paid workers who were trans people. While it was only a few hours of paid work a month, it was still a significant step forward for trans people to be paid at all for providing trans community support.

The first opportunity for trans people to carry out any paid trans equality policy work in Scotland came through the Scottish government and NHS Scotland-funded LGBT Health Equality Project, initially known simply as the INCLUSION Project and later on as Fair for All – LGBT. It ran from 2002 to 2008 and was managed by Stonewall Scotland. Trans activists Laura Aston and Nick Laird were recruited in 2003 to use a participatory appraisal research methodology to empower trans people to work together to identify their health needs and develop training for the NHS. Three initial participatory appraisal workshops were held, one for trans women, one for trans men and one for transvestite people. Several of the workshop participants, including myself, then went on to work together with Nick and Laura to develop a trans awareness training resource pack, including a thirty-minute film of trans people talking about their experiences and needs. Despite a low budget – meaning a desk light was used as a spotlight and colourful but slightly crumpled bedsheets hung behind us as backdrops – the film was extremely well received and ended up being used to train not only NHS staff but also youth workers, teachers, local council staff and the police. The film was also popular with trans people as a way to educate their families and friends. It was converted from VHS format to DVD in 2007 and remained Scotland's only trans awareness training film until 2009.

Also in 2003, Laura Aston worked for the Equality Network, facilitating a forum to enable trans people to inform and influence the Scottish parts of the Gender Recognition Bill. Birth registration is a devolved matter, so the Scottish government could have chosen to create its own gender recognition legislation. However, the Labour-Lib Dem Scottish government coalition (1999–2007) mostly preferred to give permission to the UK government to legislate for Scotland on LGBT issues. So the Gender Recognition Act (2004) was drafted at Westminster with input on Scots law issues from Scottish government civil servants. The Equality Network trans forum collectively called for a non-medicalised self-declaration gender recognition process, but it quickly became clear that the UK government was determined to draft a far more restricted and medicalised bill. The forum achieved some Scotland-specific improvements to the legislation, including preventing Scottish marriages from being voidable where a trans person has not told their spouse about their gender recognition history.

As the ink dried on both the Gender Recognition Act (2004) and the Scottish trans awareness training resource pack, Nick Laird facilitated the trans activists who had been involved in these processes to start discussing the possibility of forming a strategic alliance to progress future work. The aim of the Scottish Transgender Alliance would be to increase trans people's influence on Scottish government and public sector equality policy and practices. The idea was welcomed and Amy Redford, Brenda Colvin, Jo Long, Laura Aston, Lewis Reay, Maxwell Reay and Nick Laird spent many hours together exploring development options together with key allies from the NHS, LGBT Health and the Equality Network. It was unanimously agreed that the Scottish Transgender Alliance would be fully inclusive of all types of trans people, including non-binary people (although the terms being used in Scotland back in 2005 were androgyne and polygender) and cross-dressing people.

Establishing Scottish government funding of trans-specific equality work

At the end of 2005, the Equality Network organised a dinner bringing together Scottish Transgender Alliance activists, including myself, and representatives of the Equal Opportunities Commission and the Scottish Government Equality Unit. We used a combination of friendly charm together with emotive descriptions of discrimination peppered through the dinner conversations to illustrate to the civil servants the need for trans-specific Scottish government equality funding. The effort paid off and, in 2006, the Scottish government invited the submission of a funding application for a Scottish Transgender Alliance project worker based within the Equality Network (which had been receiving Scottish government funding to do LGBT equality work since 2001). The project never tried to create a formal federation of local groups; instead it aimed to provide flexible and open opportunities for any interested trans people to shape the project's work, share activism skills and knowledge and engage with public bodies.

By January 2007, the Scottish government funding for a one-year full-time project worker had been secured and recruitment began. It was a very different situation compared to recruitment to trans equality posts nowadays. While people were interested in the post, many were put off by the likelihood of tabloid attention and the risk of becoming unemployed twelve months later with a job title permanently outing them as a trans activist on their CV. I successfully applied for the post and began work at the start of April 2007.

In May 2007, just one month after the project started, the Scottish political landscape was turned on its head as the Labour-Lib Dem coalition which had ruled since 1999 was replaced by a Scottish National Party (SNP) minority government. There was no way of knowing what the SNP would think of its unexpectedly inherited Scottish Transgender Alliance pilot project, so future funding was very uncertain. However, the SNP were keen for the rest of Europe to recognise Scotland as a progressive, innovative country. Therefore, I encouraged the Council of Europe Commissioner for Human Rights to commend the Scottish government for being the first government in Europe to provide core funding for a trans-specific equality project. I also collected endorsements of the work of the project from a wide range of Scottish public bodies in order to demonstrate the funding was worthwhile.

Although the project funding increased the capacity of Scottish trans activism, it also brought challenges. Having one full-time paid post and everyone else working voluntarily placed a strain on activism dynamics. It also created unrealistic expectations about how quickly the trans equality work could match the capacity of longer-funded equality strands. The lack of any similar government-funded trans equality project anywhere in Europe meant there was no clear point of comparison by which to judge the work.

Thankfully, lots of trans people across Scotland were happy to help with everything from designing a logo, to media work, to running local trans community consultations, to engaging with and training public bodies. Together we tried to work through all the over-ambitious promises listed in the funding application, while worrying that if we failed to achieve sufficient results then the pilot might not receive any further funding.

At the end of the pilot year, we were very relieved and delighted when the Scottish Transgender Alliance was awarded a further three years of funding. This provided much-needed breathing space to take stock and start to be more strategic and proactive rather than reactive. Through regular community engagement events around Scotland and online surveys, the Scottish Transgender Alliance listened to diverse trans people and all the project's policy work is based on the equality priorities identified through community engagement. European Union funding from 2008 to 2011 for a learning exchange project called '...And Others!' made it possible for several Scottish Transgender Alliance activists to meet twice a year with activists from Transgender Europe (TGEU), Transgender Network Netherlands, Transgender Equality Network Ireland and TransInterQueer Berlin. This enabled sharing of activism strategy ideas, knowledge and experience. We also liaised with trans activists in other parts of the UK, but none of us had any dedicated funding for UK-wide meetings, so contact was mostly via email and telephone. At the end of 2014, the Scottish Transgender Alliance was able to secure a one-off tranche of Visit Scotland funding to bring over a hundred trans activists from across England, Wales, Northern Ireland and Ireland together with over a hundred trans activists from Scotland for a weekend-long 'Conference of the Isles' to share skills and knowledge.

Achieving non-binary inclusive trans hate crime legislation

Community consultation by the Scottish Transgender Alliance strongly identified creating fully transgender inclusive hate crime legislation as a priority. The Equality Network had been lobbying for hate crime legislation for several years and was assisting Green Party MSP Patrick Harvie to draft a hate crime members' bill at the Scottish Parliament, so we were able to be fully involved in this process. At the same time, we wanted to improve recognition that some transgender people do not identify with the binary options of man or woman. We saw the hate crime legislation as an ideal opportunity to seek to establish the concept of non-binary gender identities in Scots law. It was a hard sell to civil servants, who initially thought 'transgender' was synonymous with 'transsexual', but we succeeded in securing the groundbreaking line 'any other gender identity that is not standard male or female gender identity' in the Offences (Aggravation by Prejudice) (Scotland) Act (2009). A key way we secured this was by providing civil servants with examples of non-binary-specific hate incidents, including verbal abuse such as, 'Oi, freak, are you Pete Burns' love-child?' Being able to point out that Scots law acknowledges the existence of non-binary people has proven very useful on many occasions since it helps to persuade policymakers to take non-binary people's needs seriously.

Ensuring gender identity self-declaration works well in single-sex services

Another key priority was pushing for public services to always respect trans people's gender identities, even if they have not changed all their official documents or attended an NHS gender identity clinic. We strategised that by working intensively with the Scottish Prison Service to support them to include trans women as women on a self-declaration basis within very challenging circumstances, we would be able to ensure that all other public services should be able to do likewise. Doing this prison work was also ethically important as it helped reduce the risk of very marginalised people with complex needs experiencing human rights violations. Due to chaotic lives and mental health problems, many trans prisoners socially transition without fully changing their details on their official documents and self-medicate with hormones purchased online rather than accessing NHS gender identity clinics. This makes it particularly vital for prison policies not to make trans people's dignity, privacy and safety dependent on the quality of their paperwork. There are still many improvements needed for trans people in Scottish prisons, but the implementation of prison policy and practice respecting self-declaration of gender identity is one of Scotland's most internationally respected trans equality achievements. The learning from our prison work has made it much easier for us to assist other Scottish public services, such as NHS wards and schools, to also respect trans people's gender identities.

Together with LGBT Youth Scotland's Domestic Abuse Project, the Scottish Transgender Alliance could see how necessary it was to have strong alliances with feminist and violence against women organisations in Scotland. Most trans people are very aware that they will never be truly safe while wider gender inequality and misogynistic abuse continues in society. In Scotland, several women have been key in progressing the synergy of trans and feminist equality work. Playwright Jo Clifford, whose late partner Susie Innes was a leading second-wave feminist journalist and author, used her artistic works and positive media profile to help bring together Scotland's trans and feminist movements. Even prior to her transition, Jo had embraced and enacted feminist principles in all aspects of life. Her obvious genuine respect and enthusiasm for the positive impact of second-wave feminist academics enabled her to point out the errors in some second-wave feminist theories about trans people without creating alienation.

Very well-respected Scottish feminists, such as Lesley Irving and Nel Whiting, warmly and cogently advocated for trans inclusion while Shakti Women's Aid and the Edinburgh Rape and Sexual Abuse Centre had the confidence to lead through example by becoming trans-inclusive. By being openly trans while doing crucial violence against women sector work, such as tackling forced marriages, honour-based violence and restrictions on recourse to public funds, Mridul Wadhwa demonstrated first-hand the inaccuracy of anti-trans stereotypes. Likewise, Katherine Burrows and Jan Irvine not only provided trans-awareness training to a wide range of service providers but also held volunteer roles within Engender and Scottish Women's Aid. All Scottish government-funded violence against women services are now trans inclusive and trans activists campaign together with feminist activists on a wide range of gender equality issues.

Improving health care for trans people

Health care, especially gender reassignment services and trans equality within general mental health services, is a vital priority which trans people in Scotland have been working on for decades. The public sector equality duty within the Equality Act (2010) provided key leverage to finally get NHS Scotland to start addressing failings in gender reassignment service provision, such as year-long waiting times and wide variations in access to hair removal and various surgeries. The crucial development of the NHS Scotland Gender Reassignment Protocol in 2011 was a very fraught process. It coincided with a year of very damaging and painful infighting between some trans people in Scotland over terminology and inclusivity. Consequently two people offensively called for people who do not want genital surgery to be prevented from accessing any gender identity clinic services, including counselling and hormones. The two people did not succeed, but it nearly derailed the creation of the protocol and prevented the wording from being as clearly non-binary inclusive as it otherwise would have been.

Scottish Transgender Alliance engagement in the World Professional Association for Transgender Health (WPATH) meant we knew when version seven of their international *Standards of Care* (SoC) was likely to be released and how it would differ from version six. Therefore, we strategised during the protocol development that if we encouraged NHS Scotland to quote extensively from WPATH SoC version six, rather than write their own wording, then we would be better placed to get them to quickly improve the protocol once the new version became available.

As it happened, WPATH *Standards of Care* version seven was released in September 2011, just a few days before the NHS Scotland Gender Reassignment Protocol was due to be signed off as complete. The Scottish Transgender Alliance created a tracked-changes version of the protocol overnight and then circulated it to the NHS Scotland protocol working group asking them to please accept the updated quotes from version seven. Some of the NHS clinicians did not see any need to make the changes so we involved the Equality and Human Rights Commission and the Scottish government, pointing out clearly that by accepting the changes NHS Scotland could receive international praise as being the first country globally to implement a protocol upholding current WPATH SoC best practice, while not bothering to do the update would mean embarrassingly publishing an already out-of-date protocol. It took several tense phone calls and emails but, at the eleventh hour, the updated version of the NHS Scotland Gender Reassignment Protocol was approved. To our surprise, in 2013 NHS England announced plans to adopt the Scottish protocol as its interim protocol, which came into force in 2014.

There have been many years of further work by several different activists and groups since 2011 to try to better implement the protocol's aspirations of equity, effectiveness, patient focus and timeliness. As numbers of referrals to GICs continue to rise rapidly, waiting times for first appointments remain one of the biggest challenges.

Trans inclusion within general mental health services is another particular focus. The 2012 UK trans mental health study research collaboration between the Scottish Transgender Alliance, TransBareAll, the Trans Resource and Empowerment Centre, Traverse Research and Sheffield Hallam University has formed the basis for several peer-reviewed journal articles and training for service providers by a wide range of UK equality organisations. The emphasis in this kind of work is to ensure that trans service users are not called upon to educate the mental health professionals in every new encounter as patients and that their trans identity (which is not itself a mental illness) is not wrongly seen as a cause of, or something that overshadows, the particular issue on which they seek help. LGBT Health and Wellbeing, meanwhile, has worked on trans health issues since 2003 and has run crucial specific trans support programmes in Edinburgh and Glasgow since 2012. It has evidenced a range of trans health needs and developed trans training and resources for many health and social care services, from learning disability services to older people's care homes.

Pursuing reform of legal gender recognition

While the passage in 2004 of the Gender Recognition Act was a great achievement, trans activists acknowledged flaws in its provisions from the start. Many trans people campaigned for marriage equality to remove the need to divorce before obtaining legal gender recognition. The passage of the Marriage and Civil Partnership (Scotland) Act (2014) involved carefully planned work to secure the option for couples to choose gender-neutral ceremonies and marriage certificates and to achieve the removal of the 'spousal veto' (where a trans person cannot obtain a gender recognition certificate without the consent of their spouse). The spousal veto amendment in particular went right down to the wire and required really intensive lobbying.

Harnessing the momentum from the Equal Marriage campaign, in 2014 Scottish activists began their Equal Recognition campaign, calling for reform of the Gender Recognition Act (2004) to a self-declaration process, open to under-eighteens and providing non-binary recognition. Scottish trans activists engaged strongly in the Westminster Women and Equalities Committee's Trans Equality Inquiry in 2015 and Scottish MPs are continuing to help push trans equality at Westminster. In 2016, the Scottish government publicly committed to reforming legal gender recognition within its 2016–2021 parliamentary term.

Future trans activism in Scotland

Since it first received funding for one full-time worker in 2007, the Scottish Transgender Alliance has managed to buck the voluntary sector funding squeeze and increase its Scottish government funding sufficiently to add a second full-time staff member in 2012 and a third in 2017. More importantly, all the national LGBT equality organisations now have trans people working within their paid staff teams and many dozens of trans people across Scotland are now self-organising in diverse ways to campaign, to provide peer support and to educate service providers. The empowerment of young trans activists by LGBT Youth Scotland and also the Time for Inclusive Education campaign is rapidly progressing transgender inclusion in schools and also encouraging more and more talented and confident young activists to shape and take forward trans activism in Scotland.

Long-standing trans activists, such as Julia Gordon and Nick Laird, still remain subtly engaged in the background. While they realised at the time that their activism in the 1990s and early 2000s was making an important difference, they are now amazed and delighted to see such strength, energy and progress being harnessed by Scotland's newest generation of trans young people.

Part Three

Growth

It really is so wonderful to see how far we have come. Writing these words in mid-2017, I feel like the landscape is finally changing. Yes, there is still a way to go, but I believe there has been a genuine societal shift in understanding the fluidity of gender and the complexity of how brains form in the womb.

Stephanie Hirst, chapter 19

The Social Challenge

In the first two parts of this book we have seen how trans people began to form a community among themselves about fifty years ago, with the founding of the Beaumont Society in 1966. Many contributors have referenced the legal case (*Corbett v Corbett*) which stripped away key rights for transsexual people shortly after that in 1970, and we've seen how it took over twenty years before a legal and political campaign emerged in 1992 to address a worsening state of marginalisation. That activist-led phase, in turn, took many years to achieve its various goals: formal protection against employment discrimination on the statute book in 1999; the right to NHS treatment through case law that same year; and legal recognition through the Gender Recognition Act in 2004.

These legislative and judicial milestones didn't mean the job was done, however. Indeed, as with equality for other minorities, it seems that the job may never be completely finished – at least not on a scale measured by individual human lifetimes. The durability of a rights cause depends critically on how well it can renew itself and adapt to changed circumstances. The activists who had led for so long were in their fifties and sixties by the time the Gender Recognition Act (2004) came into force. As this book goes to print some of the older community leaders are now well into their seventies. People were burned out. A key question was how the community was not only going to refresh its activist and social leadership but also expand to address the many issues still clearly outstanding.

Movements often start with campaigns for what can be legislated. For first-wave feminists in the nineteenth and early twentieth century the initial impetus was the crucial fight for suffrage, requiring a change to electoral law. Later came Britain's Sex Discrimination Act (1975), driven by what had become an irreversible change in the labour force. Second-wave feminism was underway by the end of the sixties, particularly in the United States, but it seems as though the new law in Britain strengthened the belief that advances from that point would more often than not require social change – things you can't simply legislate for.

In the case of racial equality, the first step was the abolition of slavery from the seventeenth and eighteenth centuries and then *much later* (in various countries) the arrival of legislation tackling racial discrimination. The broader social conversation – how black and Asian people were represented in the media for instance – only really seemed to begin with having non-discrimination law in place.

You can make similar arguments for the social progress of disabled people and LGBT communities. The details vary for each marginalised group – sometimes older laws had created problems in the first place – but the general principle works across the board to a greater or lesser degree: new laws don't fix everything but they do fire the starting gun for wider social changes. Maybe that's why governments are cautious about legislating for change.

Laws only provide a new line in the sand for society. They mark altered boundaries for what is unacceptable behaviour and, sometimes, they provide sanctions to back that up. Yet what needs to follow in every case is broader social change. Populations en masse somehow need to be persuaded that previous ideas for what was acceptable have to be revised. It is not legal sanctions that ultimately bring about lasting changes, but shifting cultural norms. Discriminatory behaviour needs to become literally unthinkable rather than simply punishable after the fact.

Even before the Gender Recognition Act (2004) had been implemented (in April 2005), trans activists were considering what should come next. Three distinct themes emerged within Press for Change itself: the behaviour of the media, access to better health care and continued improvements in the law. These priorities were also propagated to the Parliamentary Forum.

Press, TV and film depictions of trans people remained problematic, as already described in chapters 9 and 10. The problems seemed more pressing when the government itself had already conceded that trans people deserved better rights.

The British tabloid press was full of *Big Brother* contestant Nadia Almada in the summer of 2004. Her story coincided with the passage of the Gender Recognition Act in Parliament. The public's support for her made it really feel as though a watershed had been crossed. The euphoria wasn't to last, however. Very soon the press would be dogging the lives of trans people even more than before.

In chapter 17 Helen Belcher describes how a new generation of trans activists began making real inroads into that problem at last.

With the NHS, in spite of a key legal case being won against a recalcitrant health authority in 1999, there were problems across the board – not just with obtaining referrals to gender identity clinics but in dealing with the country's hundreds of thousands of general practitioners and hospital doctors. Research by Press for Change showed that at least a fifth of doctors had no idea how to help trans patients even if they were disposed to do so. The ways that gender identity clinics worked were also increasingly under scrutiny, as Stuart Lorimer described in chapter 2 and Lynne Jones in chapter 8.

The Gender Recognition Act (2004) was an empowering force. Previously activism had been limited by the reluctance of many trans people in Britain to stand up and complain about the status quo. Afterwards people seemed to feel more confident – as though they were at last entitled to complain more vocally when things were wrong.

That feeling of legitimacy found an outlet with a big change that was happening online. From around 2004, anybody could set up a blog and become a pundit. It wasn't long before YouTube arrived, and then social media. The previous generation had needed to rely upon information services created and managed top-down by trans organisations, usually based on email news servers and conventional websites. That monopoly on access to an audience was about to be smashed. With it went the authority of the old-guard organisations. New stars were about to emerge, with an ability to grow an audience governed by the persuasiveness of their writing and oratory. Their followers were largely made up of a new generation of young trans people with fresh ideas and less of the emotional baggage acquired by the previous generation.

Work leading up to the Gender Recognition Act (2004) had also inspired interest in a range of other bodies. In chapter 13 Carola Towle explains how trans inclusivity came to British trade unions. Suddenly there was more work for trans activists, asked to undertake training and help in devising equality policies for groups such as Britain's fifty regional police forces and the regulatory bodies in fields such as nursing. The demand soon completely outstripped the capacity of the old guard, whose organisations weren't funded to support permanent staff for outreach and education. Press for Change was essentially half a dozen volunteers working in their own time from spare bedrooms without any substantial funding or resources.

These changes weren't all simply the result of the Gender Recognition Act (2004) post-legislative bonanza. Things were coming to the boil for gay, lesbian and bisexual campaigners too. The noughties were very much the equality decade...

The Labour government finally repealed Section 28 in 2003. The Civil Partnership Act was passed in 2004 – six months after the Gender Recognition Act. Moves were afoot to replace Britain's three statutory equality regulators – the Equal Opportunities Commission, the Commission for Racial Equality and the Disability Rights Commission – with a new single body. This finally came into operation in 2007 as the Equality and Human Rights Commission (EHRC). Gaps in equalities law were being plugged: LGB discrimination was to be outlawed just as trans employment prejudice had been. A new single equality act was being planned. Public sector bodies also had new statutory duties to consider proactively how their operations might adversely impact women and minorities. The entire public sector was suddenly expecting expert activists from across the board to help them sort out what they needed to do – usually for free. The irony was that the demand, by pulling activists away from their own priorities, was sometimes causing more problems than public bodies naively imagined.

The existing trans organisations, such as the Gender Trust, Gender Identity Research and Education Society (GIRES) and Press for Change attempted to meet the initial demand. They were the ones with the most expertise at the time and they had developed reputations and contacts dealing already with officials in government and regulatory bodies. They were, if you like, the 'consultancy division' of the trans community. In retrospect, this focus on engagement with officials only served to leave the field more open for a new generation to emerge and fill gaps in community self-help and political leadership. A small group of volunteers couldn't be everywhere at once and the entry of newcomers to take part of the load was to be welcomed. The Press for Change ethos had always been about encouraging people to get involved.

Press for Change and the Parliamentary Forum majored on trying to get the Press Complaints Commission (PCC) to in some way deal with negative newspaper coverage. Several years of work there resulted in no more than a tiny change to the PCC's rulebook, the Editors' Code. In practice it was totally ineffective, leaving it to the new generation to devise a different kind of approach. This became the domain for the charity Trans Media Watch on the one hand and the educational All About Trans project on the other. In chapter 17 Helen Belcher explains how all that happened.

Press for Change also had to fight for trans people to be included in the remit of the new Equality and Human Rights Commission when it launched. During the preparations the man tipped as the likely chair for the new body, Trevor Phillips, toured the country running public consultations. In each location Press for Change had encouraged trans people to stand up and challenge where they stood in the new one-stop-shop for equalities. By the time the roadshow reached Press for Change's home turf in Manchester the officials realised activists weren't going to let it go. Trevor Phillips was hamstrung by a near total lack of official evidence regarding the discrimination faced by trans people. There was an implicit assumption that changes to the Sex Discrimination Act (1975) and the passage of the Gender Recognition Act (2004) had sorted everything out. On that day in Manchester the activists pitched for and achieved the first official funding for an academic study to document the problems. The resulting report, *Engendered Penalties*, published with the rest of the

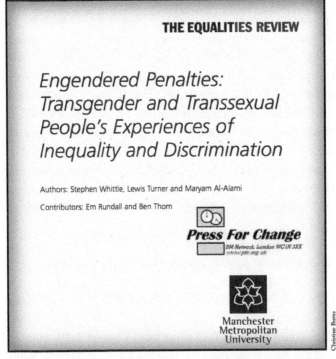

Engendered Penalties – the results of an academic research project led by Stephen Whittle – was the first officially funded systematic research in Britain to document the discrimination experienced by trans people.

official findings of the Equalities Review in 2007, was a landmark – the first proper study into trans marginalisation in Britain and also the largest ever survey of trans people at that time (almost 900 participants). A similar Europe-wide Press for Change study the following year, funded by ILGA-Europe, was conducted in twelve separate languages and took information from several thousand people. The findings were much the same across Europe.

Yet even this wasn't enough! When the EHRC launched with a bright new website in 2007 it was noticed that there was no provision addressing trans discrimination. In spite of the research findings, officials had assumed that trans people and gender identity didn't need to be featured as an explicit area of interest – they thought it was in some way covered either by 'gender' (as in the discrimination encountered by non-trans men and women) or 'sexual orientation'. The oversight meant it was impossible to search the EHRC's brand new database for transgender-specific discrimination, policies or knowledge. When the EHRC leadership were shamed into acknowledging the oversight, a bodged attempt to retrofit 'gender identity' as a category into the website resulted in a catastrophic failure – taking the Commission off the World Wide Web for weeks until a temporary substitute site could be installed. It seemed like karma.

The Department of Health, meanwhile, had its own programme of equalities work spurred by the new public sector equality duties and the arrival of legal protections for LGB people in the Equality Act (2006). Moves to set up a consultation framework – originally dubbed the Sexual Orientation Advisory Group (SOAG) – began in the autumn of 2005. As was the norm in those days, officials initially didn't seem to think they needed to do anything in parallel regarding trans experiences of the NHS. NHS commissioning bodies

(Primary Care Trusts in those days) were supposedly by then referring trans people to gender identity clinics for treatment – there was, in reality, a postcode lottery – and it didn't seem to enter anyone's head that trans people might have other dealings with the health service during the rest of their life: as patients, relatives or indeed doctors, nurses and administrators. We made our displeasure known to Department of Health officials – discreetly but firmly. So much of trans activism in those days seemed to involve hammering on doors, figuratively speaking. The body was hastily rechristened as the Sexual Orientation and Gender Identity Advisory Group (SOGIAG) and, over the ensuing two to three years, some really useful work was achieved by commissioning research and the writing and publication of the NHS's first formal guidance.

The work of SOGIAG's transgender workstream was a start on a very complex and deeply ingrained problem. Changing

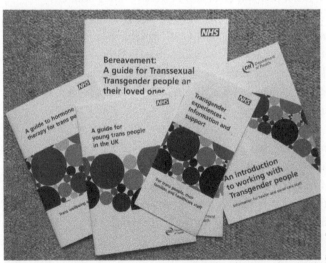

A selection of the wide range of trans-themed informational booklets and leaflets produced under the Department of Health and NHS logos, aimed at patients, parents and doctors.

attitudes, beliefs and behaviours in an organisation involving 1.4 million staff and hundreds of separate bodies has no easy fix. In any case, as with the legislation from Parliament, rules and penalties are not the full solution. Britain's complicated health service was built on a federal structure, devolving responsibilities widely. It also employs people who, in the absence of more explicit training, generally get their ideas regarding patients and co-workers from the world they inhabit. An NHS made up of people who got their ideas about trans people from warped newspaper reporting and distorted film and television portrayals wasn't going to change from within all that easily. Change the world outside, however, and it would all get a lot more straightforward.

These were the preoccupations of the trans activism old guard – the people who finally had acquired the credibility and means to push their way into dealings with officials. But in parallel a new wave had also been developing online...

In chapter 14 the chief executive of one of those new wave organisations, Gendered Intelligence, paints a picture of how he came to set it up. Sarah Brown, in chapter 16, also describes how a more general movement of young people came together and rejected the ways that the older organisations did things.

The old order of how people might identify and describe themselves was on the move too. Throughout most of the period covered by this book the lexicon involved just the idea of transvestites (people who cross-dress) and transsexuals (those who transition permanently). During the nineties the first activist wave had led to a preference for umbrella terms which didn't come from clinical classification – words like transgender and its baggage-free contraction 'trans'. But, still, folks only thought of themselves for decades as being one thing or the other. People might have had differing ideas for how to be transsexual – to what extent one accepted the conventional idea of moving between one of two binary options of man and woman, and how important 'passing' (or not) might be – but most didn't challenge the menu of options.

It wasn't until the noughties that the rather more radical idea of non-binary identity began to appear. It came with all these young voices forming the new wave. In chapter 15 Meg-John Barker, Ben Vincent and Jos Twist chart its origins and development. They note – as at the very beginning of this book – how the cultural roots of such identity go back far in human history. In reality it is only in the West that we think the idea of other genders is something strange and new. The fact that some trans people are beginning to get away from the narrow binary options imposed by Western culture suggests that we are perhaps belatedly moving towards our more natural state: as a very diverse group of people representing every alternative way to be a gendered or non-gendered person. How far that expansion of possibilities spreads into the options for *everyone* will be something to watch out for in the decades ahead.

Of course, non-binary identification is not compulsory. Trans people can still be binary-identified, just as non-trans people can be. But the opening of options is for everyone. Some second-wave feminists have said for over forty years that they want to do away with gender as a way of breaking the grip of patriarchy – well, here's a group of people showing how it is done.

So much else has happened in the last ten years or so. There are more trans groups than ever before and more people standing up to be counted. Trans activism in the nineties was about a small number of volunteers who could be counted on the fingers of one or two hands. Now it is impossible to count. Some specialise in activism, as Trans Media Watch has done.

Trans volunteers with the All About Trans project talk one-on-one with BBC executives during a day's 'interaction' with BBC Scotland in February 2017. These events, organised by On Road, are a non-confrontational way for media executives to meet and learn about trans people first hand. On Road is a charity that tackles social problems by improving media coverage of misrepresented groups and issues.

Some, like the All About Trans project and video filmmakers like Fox Fisher (chapter 18), reach out to educate. Some inhabit social media. And some individuals make change just by advocating for the things that affect themselves personally.

Work with allies has mushroomed too. In February 2015, after an extensive consultation with over 700 trans people, the prominent British LGB lobby group Stonewall announced that it would henceforth be an LGBT organisation and would bring its resources and expertise to bear on the political and social issues that needed to be tackled. The trans community had punched above its own weight for years. It is remarkable what was achieved by committed volunteers on a shoestring. However, the scale of the challenge remaining was too big for that approach to continue. With Stonewall behind them, trans people are able to get more done.

Prominent figures from the new generation of trans people, as featured in
the *Independent on Sunday*'s 'Rainbow List' in 2015.

These are the factors that collectively led to the non-trans
world thinking in 2015 that trans people had suddenly appeared
as if from nowhere. But, as this book shows, the emergence you
see now has a very long history, stretching back decades. The
question shouldn't be 'where have trans people suddenly come
from' but 'how come we were blind to their efforts before?'

In chapter 1 we began the contributions to this anthology
of trans people in Britain with the story of Adrienne Nash and
her struggle to obtain treatment to live her life to the full in
the 1960s. It's fitting, therefore, that we end the book with the
story of a modern transition by a public figure, Stephanie Hirst
(chapter 19), taking a break from her career and being able to
return to the work she loves. If you wanted to find a picture to
encapsulate how much British trans people's lives have changed
in fifty years, then look no further.

13

The Trade Unions

CAROLA TOWLE
Carola Towle is UNISON's national officer
for LGBT equality. She has worked for the
union in this area since 1990. UNISON's
1.3 million members work in public services,
in the community and voluntary sector, for
private contractors providing public services
and in the essential utilities. UNISON
has a long-standing commitment to
LGBT equality at work and in how public
services are delivered. Its trans network
has gone from strength to strength over
the past two decades. Carola previously worked for community projects and
in international solidarity. She lives in south-east London with some of her
rainbow blended family.

This chapter looks back at how trans workers have influenced
trade unions and how those unions have taken up work for trans
equality. It's the story from one trade union – indeed the story
from one person in one trade union, aided by the memories
and words of others. There will be many other versions of this
history. This is why it is so important to get these stories down.
So here is UNISON's story.

UNISON is a merged union, formed in 1993 from three
public service unions: COHSE (Confederation of Health
Service Employees), NALGO (National and Local Government
Officers Association) and NUPE (National Union of Public
Employees). NALGO was the first UK union to have a lesbian

and gay group. I joined the union's staff, working on lesbian and gay equality, in 1990. During the 1990s, the dominant view was that trans issues were gender issues and so not something the lesbian and gay group had to think about. Looking back, this was never going to work. Gender issues were effectively women's issues, focusing on sex discrimination, equal pay, childcare. There was little room for trans women and no acknowledgement of trans men.

I had thought our chapter was going to start around the early 2000s. So it was with great pleasure and a wry smile that I recently read the very first NALGO lesbian and gay newsletter. Dated October 1974, this unofficial bulletin invited 'all homosexuals, bisexuals, transvestites and transsexuals' to get in touch. The record doesn't show active involvement of trans members at that point. But it's pleasing that there was initial recognition of the historic alliance – a recognition that fell out of view for the best part of two decades.

The other lesson from those first days is the way the actions of one individual, at the right time and with the right message, made such an impact. NALGO member Howard Hyman wrote to the union's magazine asking if there were other gay members out there. Not all responses were positive but this sowed the seeds for what is now our lesbian, gay, bisexual and trans group.

This theme recurs through our history. The strength of trade unions is in our collective voice. Alone, a worker is vulnerable and isolated. But the collective voice builds from individuals speaking out.

NALGO may have had the first lesbian and gay group, but (as UNISON) we were not the first to consider reframing it to cover sexual orientation and gender identity equality. During the nineties, there was growing recognition of the need for action on trans workers' rights. Case law was building, leading to the Sex Discrimination (Gender Reassignment) Regulations (1999) (chapter 7). In some unions, such as MSF, the Manufacturing, Science and Finance union (now part of Unite), trans activists became involved in lesbian and gay networks, without a formal decision in those unions to change the name and remit of their groups. In other unions, like UNISON, responsibility for advice on trans workers' rights went to gender equality leads.

In 1998, the Trades Union Congress (TUC) held its first policy-making lesbian and gay conference. Previously, there had been annual seminars, which were of an advisory rather than decision-making nature. Now, individual unions were invited to submit motions, which were open to amendments from other unions, before being debated and voted on by delegates at the annual conference.

In 2000, MSF moved an amendment on trans inclusion to a UNISON motion on involving black and disabled lesbian and gay members. It was the first time trans inclusion had been debated in this forum and few unions had a policy on it. Opinions in the room were strong and divided. UNISON argued that this controversy distracted from the much-needed focus on black and disabled lesbian and gay workers, which was also lacking in a lot of union organising. The MSF amendment was defeated, but trans inclusion was now on the agenda.

Indeed the following year MSF, seconded by the First Division Association (FDA), and the National Union of Teachers (NUT), seconded by Equity, the actors' union, submitted standalone motions on the principle and practicalities of trans inclusion to the 2001 conference. Both were carried.

Those outside the union movement need to know that changing union and TUC rules takes time. Lesbian and gay organising was set out in rules that could only be changed by two-thirds majority votes at delegate conferences of the whole union or TUC. But work could start on preparing the ground for more formal trans inclusion and the TUC lesbian and gay committee invited an observer from Press for Change to attend its meetings. This was taken up by Claire McNab, who expertly guided the early steps.

In UNISON, we recognised how much we had to learn and there was a nervousness about getting it wrong. We owe an enormous debt to Claire, Christine Burns and Stephen Whittle, all of whom advised us privately and spoke at our more public events, helping us to advance understanding of trans issues amongst lesbian and gay members. We were also influenced by our participation in ILGA, the international LGBTI association, which began to include trans issues in its work programme from the early noughties. Ailsa Spindler, then executive director of ILGA-Europe, was one of the first out trans activists to address our annual conference.

Another milestone in our journey was when probation officer Eleanor Levy met one of UNISON's lesbian and gay co-chairs at the annual conference of the Lesbians and Gay Men in Probation (LAGIP) group. Eleanor was a UNISON member but had been unaware of our lesbian and gay group. She subsequently attended UNISON's lesbian and gay conference and later became the first out trans member elected to the lesbian and gay committee. This could not have been better for the group. Eleanor's humour, resilience and willingness to be a patient educator were just what was needed. Under her leadership, the informal network of trans members began to grow.

It was time to move towards replacing the lesbian and gay group with a group for lesbian, gay, bisexual and trans members. There was resistance from some lesbian and gay members, for a range of different reasons. There were pockets of transphobia and biphobia within our community. For others, it was something new, that they needed time to understand. It may seem surprising now, but many lesbian and gay members had never met anyone they knew to be trans. Others simply liked things as they were and didn't want them to change.

We knew we needed to bring as many members with us as possible. So throughout 2003, we facilitated discussions with our regional lesbian and gay groups. This paved the way for lesbian and gay conference agreeing to submit a rule change to the 2004 UNISON national delegate conference to replace the lesbian and gay (L&G) group with an LGBT group. In anticipation of this, we called the first national meeting of trans members, with Eleanor as convenor, and a similar meeting for bi members. Eleanor writes of her own memories of that time:

> Speaking at my first conference, I felt I was a lone voice and did not fit in, both regarding my job in criminal justice (a minority group in UNISON) and my trans identity. But there was a wave of positive support. My involvement at local, regional and national levels in proposals to reform L&G into LGBT led me to shop steward accreditation and delivering LGBT training.
>
> Other strong memories are of the national lesbian and gay committee meeting in Belfast and a visit to a local swimming pool with my partner Jenni. We got a barracking from locals on the street where we walked hand in hand. I felt a growing sense of responsibility and anxiety that I could not represent the range of trans views ably enough. This was soon followed by relief as other trans members started to join in, along with other bisexual members. Finding the common ground in a diverse group was just as much about the warmth and fun we had, and the empowerment we enjoyed, as about the business formalities. One thing was certain: I was no longer a lone voice.

Eleanor Levy was not alone in her feelings about stepping forward among her peers. A contemporary of hers, Anna May Booth, writes: '[I] attended my first Trade Union conference at Harrogate in 1989. While there I heard of an LGB group within the union called Lesbians and Gays in MSF (LAGIM) – the trade union was now called the Manufacturing, Science and Finance union following the merger of ASTMS with TASS. Anyway, I found someone who was a part of LAGIM and I asked him if I could join. He replied that he didn't know: there were no members at that time who identified as trans. However he said he would ask. He was true to his word, and returned next day to say I was in! I spent the following decade attending local, regional and national meetings including national meetings of LAGIM until, in 1998, I attended the MSF annual conference in Bournemouth where I 'came out' to the whole union before around 700 mainly male delegates. There was a motion on the agenda concerning discrimination and harassment which I made it known I would like to speak to, as Anna. Afterwards someone said I had made union history in the UK, possibly Europe.

Call us naive, but we thought that as this was a rule change about the lesbian and gay group, from the lesbian and gay group, delegates would simply vote it through. But in rule change debates, if anyone raises a dissenting voice, you are unlikely to secure your two-thirds majority. A delegate took to the rostrum and said that as a straight trans person, they did not want to be associated with the lesbian and gay group. A seed of doubt was sown and, although we won a simple majority of votes, it was not enough.

I can still feel the crushing disappointment of that moment. It's still etched in branch secretary Jenny Harvey's memory too: 'I was sitting in the visitors' balcony during the debate. At the time I was not out to anybody and I recall the feeling in the room shifting dramatically when the trans delegate spoke against the change. I also remember looking down as the delegation from my branch voted against. It was heartbreaking and so frustrating. I could have cried (and probably did later on).'

But I guess this setback did us good in the end. We had brought the lesbian and gay group with us but not involved the wider union in the conversation. UNISON agreed to change my job title immediately from lesbian and gay equality to LGBT equality. We had a year to do better and that time was used to reach out to the wider membership and strengthen our case.

We articulated clearly why this was the right thing, mentioning how widely we had consulted, and we took the points out to branches and regions. The chairs of the lesbian and gay committee went to meet with the activist who had spoken against the rule change. They were clear that they would not be interested in joining an LGBT group but agreed not to oppose its creation.

When it came to the 2005 conference, we had leaflets and T-shirts with our slogan 'LGBT – stronger together'. We even had a campaign song 'Is This the Way to LGBT' to the tune of '(Is This the Way to) Amarillo'. (And, yes, it was pretty bad!)

We asked other self-organised groups, branches, regions and the union's national executive committee to submit the same rule amendment as the lesbian and gay group. UNISON's president chairs the annual conference. They call each debate by announcing the title of the business under discussion followed by the name of the submitting body. On that historic day in June, the roll-call of submitters went on and on – and on. Those of us in our campaign T-shirts had to reach for the tissues. We knew it was OK.

Eleanor was the first out trans activist on the national stage, but of course there were many others in UNISON membership. For some, their trans history was not something they wanted to focus on in their union activism. For others, this high-profile campaign on trans inclusion was a turning point. Several UNISON members who had regularly represented their branches at national delegate conference over the years felt able to attend in their true gender for the first time.

Jenny Harvey recalls 'the dizzying blend of excitement, fear and exhilaration, as conference drew near':

> Those fears necessitated a plan. Should plan A not work, I had a plan B escape kit. I had stowed some other gender clothes at the bottom of my case and arranged for dual gendered, double sided credentials, with my new 'improved' name and photo on one side and my old name and picture on the other. But at my eve of conference regional meeting, I was given the warmest and most heartfelt welcome from all my regional friends. That night I taped over the 'chicken out' side of my ID.
>
> An introvert at heart, I hoped to get through conference unnoticed, hiding behind my heavily fringed wig. However that reserve was blown away on the first day when I spied a huge throng of LGBT activists in T-shirts, with balloons and campaign leaflets, calling for an inclusive new LGBT group. That letter T stood out to me as if highlighted and in bold type. At that time there were so relatively few out trans members in our union (and indeed society) that I had never met another similar soul. My coming out coincided with UNISON's LGBT members being front and centre in our union as never before. I've learned that when you're a six-foot-two (plus heels) trans woman, you may well stick out above the crowd, but the view is damn well worth it.

For Phillippa Scrafton, who went on to become the national LGBT committee's first out trans chairperson, the LGBT rule-change debate was hugely significant. She had been a UNISON rep for over fifteen years in her male gender role. Having only told around a dozen people about her planned transition, she took to the stage and told 3,000 UNISON members that she was transgender. Her speech in favour of the rule change was decisive for UNISON and marked a watershed in her own life. She said: 'For me, its impact resonated for more than a decade. It allowed me to find my voice to challenge transphobia and biphobia in the workplace and to develop as an equalities campaigner and as a person. I credit my career in Darlington Borough Council to the support I received from members of UNISON's LGBT self-

Phillippa Scrafton on the front cover of *U* magazine in 2015.

organised group and staff during my transition. The impact of that decision is the reason I'm here today!'

Given the years of preparation, our LGBT group was soon fully functioning. Our new mantra was 'no silent Ts (or Bs) in LGBT'. The trans network elected its reps to the two seats reserved for trans members on the first national LGBT committee. From the start, and ever since, there have also been trans members elected to seats for regional reps, bi reps and black and disabled LGBT reps on the committee. We are a diverse union and we are proud that our trans network has always reflected this.

Jaden Biggs was involved before UNISON's transition (as we like to think of it) and remains involved today. He says, 'LGBT UNISON has been inclusive in representing black voices and has contributed to defining me as the trans man I am today, giving me the tools to navigate within the workplace and black community. Our Black LGBT caucus has highlighted black trans issues within UNISON. Within this political movement, my UNISON colleagues have become like family. I think many members would say the same.'

Trans members have not only been active within the LGBT group. Increasing numbers have held other mainstream roles in the union, including the most senior elected position in their region and membership of key negotiating and policy-making bodies. For example, Jenny Harvey is a senior member of UNISON's National Health Service group executive. Jaden is a long-time member of our national nursing committee. Suzanna-Yong Lee played a key role on the national Black Members committee. Emma Procter has been regional convenor and a member of the body that negotiates local government pay in England, Wales and Northern Ireland.

Alongside these examples of involving trans members in our membership democracy, we were developing negotiating advice and training for reps and examining UNISON's own practices and facilities to make sure they met the needs of trans members. All of these things are an ongoing process rather than a single task to be done once and then ticked off the list.

Our most ordered and quoted publication ever is the guide for reps on supporting trans members, written by James Morton and published jointly with the Scottish Trans Alliance. James was another highly influential member of the national committee. We benefited so much from his razor-sharp mind and ability to express things in a way that even the most resistant person could not fail to respond to.

There have been so many actors in our brief history and the naming of some rather than others is uncomfortable, if not unfair. But another who made a big impact in those early days was national committee member Lucy Persechino. Lucy's directness and irrepressible likeability made her an ideal trainer for union reps and managers who often came with no knowledge at all of trans workers' issues, and sometimes had some rather odd misconceptions.

Looking back, Lucy reflected:

This came at one of the most important times in my life as a transgender woman. I was forty-four and in my 'Real Life Test'. I felt very self-conscious of my appearance, whether my voice sounded masculine, and was I being stared at. UNISON made me feel very comfortable.

At this time, the average age for a transgender person to start treatment was their late thirties to early forties. Before the Internet, information and research were very hard to access and many transgender people were living lonely and isolated lives. For me the biggest factor was the workplace becoming a safer environment for people to transition.

Ten years on, it gives me so much pleasure to see people starting transition at an earlier age and education about trans issues reaching into schools and the public domain.

This was the main inspiration for me to run training on trans awareness. I did not want to see future 'Lucys' living so much of their life unhappy, feeling uncomfortable in their skin and possibly self-harming as a coping mechanism. UNISON gave the underdog a voice and protection.

Much of this phase focused on UNISON's own members and organisation. But alongside this, there was also our outward-facing work. We lent UNISON's weight to calls for legal improvements, properly funded, accessible and inclusive public services and changing attitudes across society. As a public service union, we have a particular interest in how those services are delivered, as well as the rights of the workers that provide them. We welcomed the chance to publish guidance for health staff on providing care for people who are trans, jointly with GIRES, under the title *It's Just Good Care*.

We have tracked the impact of public spending cuts on trans people and services in comparative research carried out in 2013 and 2016 for UNISON by NatCen Social Research. The findings, needless to say, are not a pretty read. They inform our campaigns for more and better.

We have used our influence in the TUC, with other unions, through LGBT Labour and in the Labour Party to push trans equality up the agenda. For all the progress made, too many trans people remain isolated in the workplace or when seeking work. We welcomed the establishment of the TUC trans workers' group – Trans Workers UK. This was set up by Megan Key, Juno Roche and Michelle Winstanley to support and share positive workplace practice. It promotes positive stories of trans employment across all sectors – private, public, union and non-union.

The positive stories have so much power. At one trans network meeting, we stuck a camera and microphone in a side room and asked if anyone wanted to put their experiences on record. After a light edit, we had a short YouTube film on UNISON's work for trans equality, which we have used extensively in union meetings and workplaces. Frances Shiels talking about starting a new job, Jaden on his positive experiences of transitioning at work, Natalie Roberts on managing service user attitudes in her outward facing role, Phillippa Scrafton on the support offered by UNISON... all powerful messages.

And of course nothing stands still. Our bargaining advice on trans workers' equality has had so many revisions, it's lucky it's a Word document that we print in short runs and can update at will! When we started out, the dominant discourse was still very much based on a medical model of trans identities and a binary understanding of gender. There was enormous emphasis on privacy. Workplace issues focused on how much time a member might need off for medical treatment.

Now an increasing number of our members – and people across society – identify outside the gender binary. We have re-examined our internal policies and procedures for unnecessary gendering and to see if they are inclusive of non-binary people. UNISON's clerical teams have been great allies as they are the ones who administer the systems and have tracked down the myriad forms and systems that record members' gender, including how the question is asked, how information is stored and when this is really necessary. Sometimes the computer says no, but so far we have always found a workaround.

This has fed into our bargaining advice and negotiations with employers. Yes, we still focus on the importance of confidentiality and regularly provide advice on best practice regarding workplace transition. But now we also negotiate on dress codes that work for gender fluid members, give advice on inclusive language and campaign for the recognition of non-binary people in official documentation.

Dave Merchant, one of the two trans reps on the current national LGBT committee, and the committee's co-chair, commented: 'As trade union activists, we recognise the importance of ensuring that everyone is able to work in an environment that is safe and comfortable. Non-binary people often face many hurdles to being able to come out in the workplace – including a lack of understanding from colleagues and managers, no formal protection under existing workplace policies and a lack of legal recognition. It is therefore vital that we work towards the full inclusion of non-binary people within

2015 UNISON Trans Caucus participants. L-R Front: Phillippa Scrafton, Sophie Whitehead, Janet Royston, Jaden Biggs, Victoria Benjamin, Alexandra Myers, Ben Turnbull, Sue Pincombe and Sally Jacques. L-R Back: Natalie Roberts, Dave Merchant, Emma Procter and Diane Howard.

the workplace, making sure that policies and practice reflect this, and educating managers and colleagues as to the relevant issues. Trade unions have an important role to play in this, both in liaising with the relevant departments to produce and update policies, and through the work of activists and reps within the workplace.'

There is no doubt that we still have far to go. But on any journey, it's good to stop and enjoy the scenery from time to time. One sight we savour is UNISON being featured in Transgender Europe's best practice guide, published early in 2017, illustrated by our favourite trans network photo (to date!). Another is this book.

And so to the next chapter...

14

Gendered Intelligence

DR JAY STEWART MBE
CEO / Co-founder of Gendered Intelligence
Jay co-founded Gendered Intelligence alongside Dr Catherine McNamara in 2008. Gendered Intelligence is a community interest company aiming to increase understandings of gender diversity and improving the quality of lives of trans people. He has been involved in the trans community since 2002 and continues to be passionate about making the world more intelligent about gender. As Gendered Intelligence has grown, Jay has moved into a chief executive role and oversees a growing team. In 2013 he gained his doctorate in the visual cultures department at Goldsmiths, University of London with his thesis 'Trans on Telly: Popular Documentary and the Production of Transgender Knowledge'.

In 1997 I graduated with a first-class fine art degree from the University of East London. The moment I stepped out of the scruffy ex-YMCA building in Plaistow there was a gaping black hole ahead of me and an existential meltdown in the pipeline. I had no real job prospects and very little understanding of how to 'make it' as an artist, even if that was what I wanted to do. As a student, feminism, lesbian and gay studies and postcolonial studies provided me with rich and exciting ways for me to explore the questions I had about gender, identity and selfhood

– not least my own. It would not be until eight years later that I would find myself discussing my own gender identity with doctors at gender identity clinics and journeying towards living as a man. This chapter seeks to weave my own lived history with that of the political and cultural landscape of transgender equality as we entered a new millennium – the noughties.

With no clear idea of what to do with my life, in 2001 I began studying for an MA in visual cultures at Goldsmiths College. It was here that I became interested in theories of gender politics. Visual cultures was then rather a new discipline in the academic world, drawing on an array of artefacts and concepts from other fields such as film studies, TV studies, art history, theatre and performing arts. However, what makes visual cultures distinct is, in part, the way it looks to flatten out hierarchies attached to cultural objects. It challenges the snobbery attached to the pursuit of what constitutes 'good' or 'bad' art. Being in the visual cultures department allowed me to think about the politics of taste, value and identity as well as to think about the realm of the public sphere and the importance of discourse.

Queer theory was the roadmap to my own self-understanding. 'Queer' in a broad sense is articulated as a political movement, working to deconstruct or undo 'compulsory heterosexuality' and homosexual prohibition. It was vastly popular in the late nineties and early noughties across the academic world. Importantly for me, queer projects revisit and revise how the categories of 'man' and 'woman' are understood as some sort of fixed set of essentialised single identities. Thinking queerly was to expose the system of gender norms in which we are all often unthinkingly immersed. Seeing the system for what it was obliged us to challenge the ways in which certain aspects of gender become 'normalised' and dominant – starting straight away with the idea that being exclusively either a 'man' or a 'woman' is somehow natural and/or inherent. Consequently, at this time, the trans figure emerged as a queer emblem which, through its challenge to the very language of difference, exposes the various constructs of gender, demonstrates an opposition to the dominant forces of strict gender codes and practices and reveals gender construction through the work of the law.

Judith Butler had become an instrumental figure in queer theory and feminism, in part because of her focus on transgender identities. Another academic, Jay Prosser, expressed his own troubled sense of transgender bodies being used to further queer theory, but criticised that practice as it didn't place enough emphasis on the material everyday lives of transgender people.

In the early part of the noughties I found myself looking for support around my gender identity. I found FTM London – a grass roots support group in London for trans masculine people. Like many trans people entering a support group for the first time, I was nervous and apprehensive, but I was greeted with warmth and kindness. It was so wonderful to see thirty to forty trans men and trans masculine people in one room and to see the diversity of how these individuals were expressing their own gender and also talking about it. This was my light bulb moment. If I was to transition then I could do it in a way that suited me, not how I thought I was supposed to. I wouldn't need to fulfil someone else's idea of what it means to be a man. I realised that it was possible to live an authentic life.

At FTM London I not only found 'my people' but I also found my cause. In what felt like no time at all I was volunteering to get involved in a whole array of activities, from contributing to the newsletter to setting the chairs out and making cups of tea. Later, I joined the management committee and attended meetings at the London Mayor's office for LGBT communities. Eventually I took the role of chair and I started facilitating the groups themselves. It was all completely grass roots – everyone mucking in. There was very little money in the organisation but we didn't need any. The venue was donated and everyone was a volunteer. We marched at London Pride, printed postcards and invited guests in to speak to the group. Around this time, I noticed some trans people as young as sixteen attending. Their presence highlighted to me that FTM London members consisted mainly of people in their thirties and forties, but these young people needed a space too.

One of the speakers who came to visit the group from time to time was Stephen Whittle of Press for Change – the organisation spearheading work on legal recognition for trans people. Between 2002 and 2004 there was a fair bit of debate about whether the Gender Recognition Bill was going to be a good thing for trans people. Some of us viewed the proposed legislation as a reinforcement of our entrenched gender binary system, with heteronormative assimilationist undertones. The process of gaining legal recognition was to involve applying to the Gender Recognition Panel for a gender recognition certificate (GRC). A GRC, if issued, enabled the applicant to receive a birth certificate in their 'acquired gender'. Only trans people who had received a clinical diagnosis as having gender identity disorder (or gender dysphoria, as it is termed now) could be successful with their application, and would need to supply evidence from at least two 'medical experts'. The process was in effect saying that doctors – not trans people ourselves – validated our identities. It didn't feel very empowering. In addition, you could only be recognised as male or female and your identity had to be demonstrably 'permanent'. I was quite new to the realm of legislative processes but what I was quickly learning was that the law doesn't like fluidity, uncertainty or flexibility and certainly didn't reflect any of the queer thinking that I was being exposed to at Goldsmiths through my postgraduate education at the time.

So was the trans community expected to be happy with such an important piece of legislation that was going to give some trans people more human rights but leave others out? Stephen Whittle, Claire McNab, Christine Burns and other members of Press for Change had their work cut out in brokering some of the sentiments from the trans community and trying to work with the government and the law. Compromise was inevitable. In the end, the Gender Recognition Act (GRA) that was passed in 2004 exposed more of the fragmented and multitudinous dimensions of the community. Indeed there was no *one* trans community – only trans *communities*.

On 10 September 2004 I attended the sixth International Congress on Sex and Gender Diversity, which was hosted at Manchester Metropolitan University and organised by Press for Change. These periodic conferences were community-organised and operated on an international basis. Trans people had for years been inviting serious academic discourse. Whilst I was new to this world, the tradition went back to the origins of trans activism, starting with the Gendys conferences from 1990 in the UK. Certainly, trans activism in the US had a long history, but it was interesting to note that these conferences in the UK – and not least the achievement of the Gender Recognition Act (2004), which had raised the legislative bar internationally – attracted trans activists from the US and around the world. On a personal note, I have absolutely no doubt that this conference changed my life. Not only was I to be introduced to the world of transgender

The audience at the 2004 International Conference on Sex and Gender at the Manchester Metropolitan University, organised by Press for Change.

studies and to identify the niche of my Ph.D. project, but I also was to meet my future life partner, co-parent and fellow co-founder of Gendered Intelligence, Catherine McNamara.

With the Gender Recognition Act (2004) so recently passed, it was understandable that much of the content of the conference was reflective of that. At the conference, the founder of FTM International and author of the 2004 book *Becoming a Visible Man*, Jamison Green, gave a keynote that made a distinction between privacy and secrecy, which I found really useful. A key idea behind the Gender Recognition Act (2004) was the human rights principle of privacy and the right to a private life. Indeed, it was the judgment delivered at Strasbourg on 11 July 2002 in the case of *Christine Goodwin (and 'I') v United Kingdom*, where the European Court of Human Rights held unanimously that UK legislation was now violating human rights under ECHR Article 8 (respect for private life) and Article 12 (right to marry). The government's response to these decisions of the European Court of Human Rights led to the Gender Recognition Act (2004). Issuing a new birth certificate did not only recognise the trans person's gender identity in legal terms, it also offered privacy – the principle being that knowledge about a person's trans history is entirely confidential and it is for the trans person to share that information as they see fit. The Gender Recognition Act legislation was so clear on this that in fact, if a person were to share this information in an official capacity without consent, then that would constitute a criminal act. However, Jamison Green argued that secrecy is another matter. Feeling as though you are living with a deep dark secret that you are afraid to share is to live potentially a rather stressful life.

What's more, we cannot consider such rights to privacy outside of a context of prohibition and violence. We must understand these moments of disclosures, or 'coming out', as acts carried out within a culture of hetero- and gender-normative dominance. After all, no one comes out as a heterosexual or as a cisgender person (at least not quite in the same way). Trans people choose not to disclose in part for their fear of safety. It left me thinking about the fact that not everyone feels safe to share their sex/gender identity and history. If everyone did feel safe to express their gender, I wondered, what kind of world would we live in, and how would gender be manifested in society? For me, my project was not so much seeking legislative change, but instead seeking to shift culture, to change the environments that trans people find themselves in so that they can feel safe to come out, safe to be themselves.

Another important debate at the conference centred around the causality of trans. This was to become a central aspect of my Ph.D. project. At this time, there were divisions between those who felt scientific explanation would aid understanding and acceptance and others, such as Claire McNab, who delivered a paper called 'The Life and Times of the Sliced Transsexual Brain'. In light of the 1995 publication of 'A Sex Difference in the Human Brain and its Relation to Transsexuality' by Zhou et al, which looked at post-mortem slices of brains, including those of trans people, McNab issued a warning about research that reinforced the idea that being a transsexual was inherent and essentialised. An essentialist reading of gender identity (that people were just 'born that way') conflicted directly with the queer theory described earlier in this chapter.

The conference discourse was rich and complex. It struck me that whilst strong feelings were at play, there was absolute respect for diverse opinions and viewpoints. If we were to celebrate diversity in the trans community, it seemed to me that these diverse viewpoints were an important part of that.

During the breakout sessions and while networking in the corridors, I met Catherine McNamara, who was writing her Ph.D. thesis around trans masculinity and performance. She had

Research on the physical brain structure of transsexual people, whilst obviously well-intentioned, became a point of contention among trans activists in the UK in the mid 1990s. The work – mainly by a Dutch team (Zhou, Hofman, Gooren and Swaab) – was driven by the expectation that, if science could show there was a physical reason or diagnostic marker to explain why transsexual people were the way they said, then official and social acceptance would follow. The rationale was similar to that of researchers elsewhere who had hunted for evidence of a so-called 'gay gene' to prove being gay was not a 'lifestyle choice'. Press for Change activists like Claire McNab thought this was dangerous. There were several reasons. First, just supposing such a diagnostic marker were found then it might indeed help trans people who had a positive test result, but it could further marginalise people whose trans condition didn't pass the litmus test. Second, such research might lead to calls for potentially trans foetuses to be aborted. Third, if trans people were to stake their futures on a scientific test then where would that lead if the next set of researchers disproved the first? Premature claims of finding a 'gay gene' had immediately led to just these kinds of outcomes before other researchers failed to replicate the initial findings. McNab and her colleagues argued instead that trans people should persist with their strategy of arguing for trans rights simply on the basis that trans people self-evidently existed. You didn't need to know *why* a trans person was trans to argue for the same human rights as everyone else. In 2002 the European Court of Human Rights, after waiting over fifteen years for a scientific explanation of transsexuality, came to the same conclusion.

delivered a paper sharing some findings about the relationship between applied theatre practices and the everyday lives of trans masculine people. This included voice work practices that took account of the ways in which gender is located in the voice, including tone, register and range. Catherine worked at the Royal Central School of Speech and Drama and, following the conference, I was invited to attend voice workshops. I also made connections with other trans masculine people and voice practitioners.

In 2005 Catherine sent me and a few colleagues an email forwarded from the Wellcome Trust, a funder that supports projects aimed at building public engagement about topics in the medical world through the arts. I recalled how some of the young people at FTM London were talking about their own needs, which were not the same as those of trans adults. They were negotiating and navigating a world that was different. They were at school or college and being trans was tough.

Over a period of about six months, we developed an idea for a £50,000 project that would explore the science of sex and gender through arts-based workshops for young trans people. It was so exciting to hear that we had been successful obtaining the funding. This would be the first time we would bring a group of young trans people together from across the UK and it was so beneficial to have the budget to pay for their travel. At that time we did not know if we could reach a group of twenty young trans people. This had never been done before. However, trans youth came from far afield and from very diverse backgrounds to attend four weekend workshops. Despite a growing online community, for me coming together in a live setting felt so special and so important to this cohort. Friendships were emerging and nuanced discussions were had about people's understanding of the relationships between sex, gender and science.

From our experience working with young trans and gender questioning people for the first time through what we called the Sci:dentity project, it was extremely noteworthy how, on the whole, the young trans people we worked with each had an extraordinarily high level of intelligence when it came to thinking about gender. The eighteen young participants between the ages of fourteen to twenty-one had the opportunity to interview various 'experts' in the field of medical science, within sex and gender specialisms. These were Dr Andrew Levy, an endocrinologist; Dr Richard Curtis, a specialist in gender identity disorder; and Terry Reed, co-founder of the Gender Identity Research and Education Society (GIRES). In many ways, the questions and responses from our young trans people gave these 'experts' a run for their money. Furthermore, what became clear to the young people searching for knowledge around what it meant to be trans was that, as endocrinologist Dr Andrew Levy put it, 'there isn't any' and the answer to their questions, more often than not, was 'no one really knows'. It was not so much, then, that we sought to equip young people to pursue the knowledge that is *out there*, but more to create a project that placed at its centre an *application of intelligence* when it came to thinking about gender and to produce knowledge of our own. What's more, the knowledge generated from young trans people was equally instructive to medical professionals. I truly believed that, and I still do. The workshops culminated in a multi-media exhibition at the Royal Central School of Speech and Drama in London in June 2006; a short documentary film of the project was also made to platform the voices of young trans people.

The second phase of Sci:dentity involved members of the team delivering workshops to Year 10–13 students in secondary schools (ages fifteen to seventeen). Here, some students admitted that they had 'never thought about this kind of thing before'. Questions around what it means to be a gendered being or to have a gender or even further to challenge gender norms (specifically through a trans identity) were found to be rather complicated. This was also felt by the various teachers, youth workers and professional staff that we came across, confirming for me how unconfident they felt, not only in thinking about the lives of trans people, but also in becoming mindful of how their own behaviours worked to regulate other people's gender identities as normative.

In 2007, we delivered our first Trans Community Conference in collaboration with the arts organisation Transfabulous, who programmed arts festivals, workshops, performances and club nights for trans and queer communities. Transfabulous was co-founded by Jason Barker and Serge Nicholson, who were interested in the idea of building and celebrating trans culture through the arts. The conference was billed the day before the Transfabulous festival and we used it to welcome invited guests including Kate Bornstein, Jamison Green, Ignacio Rivera and Christine Burns. One hundred and fifty members of the trans community and our allies from across London, the UK and beyond gathered at Oxford House in Bethnal Green. The conference set out to tackle some of the key issues in the areas of the workplace, trans health, visibility and private spaces. The focus was on the ways in which trans people accessed services, spaces and relationships. It gave us an opportunity to think collectively about driving social changes, identifying the barriers and experiences of discrimination and creating trans inclusive environments.

Key speakers at the Transfabulous conference in Bethnal Green in 2007. L-R Kate Bornstein, Jamison Green, Christine Burns, Jay Stewart and Catherine McNamara.

Gendered Intelligence was set up by Catherine McNamara and myself and constituted in 2008 as a not-for-profit community interest company (CIC). At that time CICs were not that common but, after some exploration, we decided this would be the best legal structure for us in order to hit the ground running and drive the organisation from the offset without immediately having to build a board of trustees, as a charity would require. CICs are designed for social enterprises that want to use their profits and assets for the public good – that was certainly us – they are easy to set up, and have in-built features to help ensure they stay focused on benefiting the community. The structure also gave us the flexibility to be innovative and to act quickly when responding to the various opportunities that came our way, including generating income through running educative workshops.

Our key concept – making the world more intelligent about gender – drew on pedagogist Howard Gardner's idea of multiple intelligences, which argues that intelligence is not linear or monolithic, but rather that people can be intelligent in multiple ways. (He specifically argues *seven* different ways.) Intelligence is about an aptitude; it demands application and therefore labour around processing and thinking. Intelligence can be a process of learning, but it can also be an un-learning of the social norms that are so deeply embedded in our mindsets and in our behaviour. We have come to know the expression 'unconscious bias' to reflect this.

We committed ourselves to the idea that a person could become more intelligent about gender. Fundamental to improving the lives of trans people, and young trans people in particular, was to educate the people around us. So we developed a range of workshops, presentations and training sessions aimed at different audiences that worked to increase understandings of gender diversity, and we were devoted to placing trans voices at the centre of everything we did.

As Gendered Intelligence began to grow, it became a priority for me to gain funds to pay for resources, to value people's time and their skills. There had been (and continues to be) so much goodwill and donated time from within the community and from others who also feel passionate about equality for trans people. My commitment as a co-founder of a growing organisation is to start to carve out paid roles for people who were tasked with carrying out projects and activities in a professional manner. In 2009, we received funding from the Equality and Human Rights Commission (EHRC) to deliver more youth work and we employed one of our former young people, Finn Greig, to deliver the project. In 2010 Finn wanted to take his young members on a residential. I recall him convincing me that it would be incredibly valuable, so we scraped together enough to take eight young people camping. He was right. Our camping trips have gone on to be a flagship project and stand testimony to the power of these kinds of projects to change young trans people's lives. By the end of our grant from the EHRC in 2011, austerity and a shrinking public purse were on their way and, due to limited access to statutory support and ever-increasing competition for grants through trusts and foundations, we knew we had to think about where our income was going to come from. We had always delivered trans awareness training, school assemblies and workshops for students, but now it was time to step this up to generate a surplus so that we could invest that back into the organisation and use it to support our work with young trans people.

Around this time, Simon Croft, another trans man who had roots at FTM London, got more involved with Gendered Intelligence. Drawing on his expertise in the voluntary and community sector, he came up with our corporate vision: 'Our vision is of a world where people are no longer constrained by narrow perceptions and expectations of gender, and where diverse gender expressions are visible and valued.'

Together we set a scene where we could sell training and educational products to the wider community and gain funding to deliver our youth work. As for so many others who were setting up projects, campaigns and organisations within and for the trans communities, it was often a case of learning on the job. Throughout my time at Gendered Intelligence I have often felt that I am entering into uncharted territory and that there is a need to respond quickly and learn fast. I have been driven by passion and desire to make things happen. And so too have my team members. I have also recognised the importance and productivity of being kind – both with young people and with professionals, who can feel nervous talking about trans identities, wanting to get it right and not offend anyone.

Agreeing conduct within our group settings is what has made the difference in terms of people having a positive experience. It's about making people feel safe. And if we can do that in our youth settings, then *any* provision can. All of our youth groups have working agreements and we talk at length about how we want to work together, how we want to be in the space, and what to do if we are feeling upset or if someone has had a negative impact on another member of the group.

It was not until February 2015, though, that I took the decision to become an employee and work full time at GI, moving into a chief executive role. There is still so much to do. Across the country young trans and gender-nonconforming people continue to be very isolated. Schools, colleges and universities are experiencing more and more students coming out as trans and are looking for support themselves. The public, private and voluntary sectors are all placing a more central emphasis on trans inclusion in their services for customers, students, service users and staff. We have done some amazing projects and worked with some very prestigious organisations. We have developed a reputation for delivering a professional service, but people tell us that we're not scary or off-putting to clients who are new to trans issues and worried about saying the wrong thing. Our modus operandi is to be positive. Our history of grass-roots community work and arts-inspired social action is core to how we approach things. The fact that we are a trans-led organisation is also something that other organisations really value when working with us.

We continue to support and platform the emergent voices of young trans and gender-questioning people. Young people in our community continue to have so much to say and the trans community more broadly have so much to gain from listening to them. Currently we are working with about 500 young people each year in the regions of London, Bristol and Leeds. We now take seventy-five young people camping annually. We support parents and carers too, and we deliver a range of support provision in educational settings. We continue to be approached by organisations across all sectors to work with them through training, consultancy and other professional services to ensure their provision is inclusive of trans people.

Gendered Intelligence operates in a complex landscape, and we know that if we want to fulfil our mission then we need to work at all levels: from supporting young trans people to increase their confidence and reducing their sense of isolation to influencing government policy, via improvements in our learning, social and work environments. It's certainly not all plain sailing – as a glance at our UK and worldwide media coverage will reveal. Whilst we see an increasing number of balanced, informative articles about trans people reaching wide readerships, there are still a substantial number of polemic and negative pieces appearing, both in print and online. It is for this reason that, going forward, we are committed to influencing policy, working with central and local government to ensure that a trans person can feel safe, thrive and have access to a high quality of life alongside everyone else.

15

Non-Binary Identity

Meg-John Barker is a writer, therapist and activist-academic specialising in sex, gender and relationships. Meg-John is a senior lecturer in psychology at the Open University and a UKCP accredited psychotherapist, and has over a decade of experience researching and publishing on these topics, including the popular books *Rewriting the Rules*, *The Secrets of Enduring Love*, *Queer: A Graphic History* and *Enjoy Sex*. Website: www.rewriting-the-rules.com Twitter: @megjohnbarker

Ben Vincent is a sociologist specialising in gender studies and health. Their Ph.D., 'Non-Binary Gender Identity Negotiations – Interactions with Queer Communities and Medical Practice', was awarded in December 2016. Their forthcoming publications include a chapter on historical and cultural diversity in the book *Genderqueer and Non-Binary Genders*, and a book on best practice in binary and non-binary trans health care. Website: www.genderben.com Twitter: @genderben

Jos Twist is a clinical psychologist working at the under-eighteens Gender Identity Development Service at the Tavistock. Their doctoral research explored sexualities of partners of trans and non-binary people, with a paper from this research winning the 2016 postgraduate award from the Psychology of Sexualities Section of the British Psychological Society. They are a regular contributor to and a sub-editor for the online magazine *Beyond the Binary*.

Perhaps the most notable trans development in recent history has been the emergence of a clear and vocal non-binary movement. We (Meg-John, Ben and Jos) are all non-binary ourselves, as well as being engaged in the non-binary movement as activists, as researchers, and – in the case of Meg-John and Jos – as practising psychologists working with non-binary clients in the voluntary sector (Meg-John) and the gender identity clinic (Jos). In this chapter we introduce non-binary genders for unfamiliar readers, and chart the history of this movement from its roots in various strands of feminist, queer and trans activism, to its current place as a key branch of the wider trans movement.

'Non-binary' is the most common British umbrella term for people who experience their gender as neither male nor female. Non-binary people can have a fluid experience of gender, experiencing themselves as more male, more female, both, or neither, at different times. Other non-binary people experience themselves in a more static way as somewhere between male and female, or as a separate third gender category, for example. Some experience their gender as neutral, or do not have a gender. Others experience a partial or a muted sense of gender. There are also many conceptions of gender around the world that do not easily fit with the Western binary gender system, which traditionally only recognises men and women. Any experience of gender identity that is not exclusively male or female can be understood as falling under the non-binary umbrella.

Given the definition of trans as not identifying with the gender assigned at birth, non-binary people can be viewed as trans, because – with the exception of some intersex infants – babies are exclusively assigned either male or female at birth. This means that, like trans men and trans women, non-binary people don't identify with their birth-assigned gender. However, it's important to be aware that not all non-binary people identify as trans, as, for example, some associate a trans identity with social or medical transitions which they do not necessarily seek. As with trans men and women, some non-binary people seek gender-affirming hormones and/or surgeries and some do not. Intersex people may have binary or non-binary gender identities as genitals, chromosomes and other biological factors do not dictate identification. Also, it's important to be mindful that many people and groups prefer other terms, such as non-gendered, genderqueer or androgynous as the umbrella term, or would prefer specific non-binary experiences and identities to be treated separately. If in doubt, it's always worth asking what term people prefer where this is relevant.

It's difficult to estimate the proportion of people who are non-binary because few national surveys offer gender options beyond male and female and because, until the non-binary movement came into being, very few people would consider identifying in non-binary ways even if this resonated with them. As non-binary people become more visible in popular culture, it is likely that larger numbers of people will identify in this way. From the data collected so far, it appears that around one in 250 people *identify* themselves as other than male or female when given the option to do so, while over a third of people *experience* themselves as to some extent the 'other' gender, 'both genders' and/or 'neither gender' (of the two historic options recognised).

Writing this chapter in 2017, the non-binary movement is still very new – and it's developing all the time. To demonstrate just how new it is, Google's Ngram Viewer, which charts the number of mentions of phrases in published texts, provides no results for 'non-binary gender' prior to 2008, the latest year the program can currently chart. Our own experience was that we only became aware of a number of people embracing non-binary identities, names and pronouns after 2010, which was an important part of what enabled us to do so ourselves. The *Beyond the Binary* magazine – specifically aimed at UK non-binary people

– launched in 2014, as did the Nonbinary Inclusion Project, the main UK campaigning organisation that grew out of the Think Outside the Box campaign, which began in 2010.

However, this should certainly not be taken to mean that people were not experiencing themselves in non-binary ways, or fighting for non-binary rights, before 2010. For example, the Gender Identity Development Service at the Tavistock clinic, where Jos works, have always seen non-binary children – it's simply that they have only been *referring* to themselves in this way for the last five or so years. It's important here to remember that our current understandings of gender are historically and culturally specific, and people have understood and experienced gender in very different ways across time and space.

The history of the non-binary movement

In terms of deep history, non-binary experience dates back centuries. For example in Britain, we could understand as non-binary the Shakespearean boy players, or the patrons of nineteenth-century Molly-houses, where people assigned male at birth met for sex and often dressed or acted in feminine ways. However, tempting as it is to make arguments for the legitimacy of the current movement on the basis of such past examples, we must be wary of the risks of reading the present onto the past, and getting into arguments over who such historical precedents 'belong' to. Certainly it is clear that gender was not commonly understood in a binary 'opposite sexes' way, as it is now, until the late nineteenth or early twentieth century. Prior to that, in Britain, men and women were commonly regarded as two sides of the same coin – a single 'sex' (the word gender only came to be used in the twentieth century), with women being a somewhat inferior, 'inverted' version of men. Therefore we could argue that both binary and non-binary understandings of gender are relatively recent things!

It's vital to remember that many cultures around the world do not have binary gender systems. The experiences of Hijra people in India or Kathoey in Thailand, for example, cannot and should not be viewed through a Eurocentric lens as equivalent to Western non-binary or trans experiences. Such diverse understandings remind us that the current Western way of seeing things is just one way of doing so, as well as reminding us that in a multicultural society, people will experience and express their genders in diverse ways depending on their background.

Activist movements fighting for the rights and recognition of people who identify as something other than men or women also have longer histories in many countries and cultures globally. In 1990, diverse Native American and First Nation people chose the intertribal term 'Two Spirit' as an umbrella term for a culturally specific gender/sexual/spiritual experience which has always existed within these cultures. They highlighted the devastating impact of Western genocide of indigenous people on this group, and used the expression Two Spirit to replace previous offensive colonially imposed terms. Thanks to gender-related activism, several Asian and Australasian countries now offer third gender options on passports, censuses and the like.

Current Western non-binary movements also have historical precedents in the older feminist, queer and trans movements. Since the sixties and seventies some feminists, like Sandra Bem and Marge Piercy, have argued for the dismantling of the gender binary as a path towards gender equality. Queer activism and queer theory since the eighties and nineties have critiqued normative binary assumptions of gender (male/female) and sexuality (straight/gay) as key roots of oppression. There have been vocal oppositions to binary gender assumptions in trans activism and trans studies dating back to a similar period, for example in the writing of US activists like Kate Bornstein and Riki Wilchins, and in edited books such as *PoMosexuals:*

Challenging Assumptions About Gender and Sexuality, and *Genderqueer: Voices from Beyond the Sexual Binary*.

Our focus for this book is on the British context, so what were experiences like before the recent emergence of the visible non-binary movement in the UK? To answer this question we spoke with a number of UK activists whose work dates back to the nineties and noughties. Two who agreed to be quoted here are Christie Elan-Cane and Nat Titman. Like ourselves and many other non-binary people, Elan-Cane and Titman use gender-neutral pronouns – in this case 'per' and the singular 'they' – instead of 'he' or 'she'. Full lists of gender-neutral pronoun options can be found online. As with the non-binary categories mentioned earlier, it's always worth checking what pronoun people use in order to refer to them correctly.

Christie Elan-Cane stresses that it's important to remember that back then 'there was no political awareness, there was no public awareness, there were no words within most people's vocabularies (including mine) and, crucially, there was no Internet'. Being non-gendered meant that per could 'neither go back nor move on when society perceived me – and treated me – as a non-person who had no civil rights'. When Elan-Cane founded the Non-Gendered campaign, which fights for legal and social recognition outside of the gendered societal structure, per initially experienced poor media coverage, although per did have more positive experience engaging with some academics, such as Richard Ekins, and politicians, such as Simon Hughes MP. The Gender Recognition Act (2004) was a heavy blow as it meant that non-gendered people were excluded from protections and rights afforded to others. In recent years Elan-Cane has been able to move per campaign online, and has experienced more positive press in the form of 2014 *Huffington Post* and *Pink News* articles, which chart per experiences in more detail than we are able to here.

Titman reflects that the major shift they have noticed since 2000 'has been from a community that primarily talked about rejecting the mainstream's definitions and limitations to one concerned about how to exist within mainstream society'. They say that:

> Up to the turn of the century we were a primarily online community that mainly talked in terms of queer/radical self-expression or deconstruction of binary gender roles, categories and rules.
>
> Starting with our complete exclusion from the Equality Act (2010) and then highlighted with the 2011 census and again by the Marriage (Same Sex Couples) Act (2013), the discourse moved past the stage of theory, analysis and rebellion, to one that mainly involved people trying to get on with their lives, either protesting how much worse they were treated when accessing medical transition, or just existing in the world, trying to use public toilets, changing rooms and hospital wards, get ID, a driving licence or a bank card, order groceries, see their GP, or enter education or the workplace without being misgendered.

Titman reflects that there was a shift around this time from focusing on differences in identity, presentation and terminology to commonalities in experience and struggles faced. The most frequently used British unifying terminology changed from 'genderqueer' (which is still often used as an umbrella term in the US) to 'non-binary', partly to reflect this change from a radical to a more pragmatic politics. They feel that the British non-binary movement to some extent overtook the US movement at this point, due to this shift and through the coordination of activists. They discuss these recollections in more detail on their website, Practical Androgyny.

The non-binary movement today

There is a frustrating tendency of the mainstream media to report non-binary campaigns as 'new' even when they date back decades, and to report non-binary identities and experiences as only applying to young people. Elan-Cane and Titman's experiences offer a helpful counterpoint to this as, like Meg-John, they are both over thirty-five and have been working in this area for around twenty years.

Titman also charts a few early victories of the more coordinated and pragmatic non-binary movement, suggesting that 2011 could be regarded as the pivotal year. Some individuals had already managed to get the non-gendered title Mx on their bank cards, driving licences and correspondence previously. However, 2011 was the year in which campaigners such as Cassian Lodge (of Mx Activist/The Genderqueer Activist) crowdsourced evidence of these hard-fought concessions and used this to persuade the UK deed poll service to offer Mx alongside other titles on their legal change-of-name application forms. This paved the way for many banks, local councils, universities and other organisations to do the same. Also in 2011, the World Professional Association for Transgender Health's *Standards of Care* was updated to be more inclusive of non-binary genders. This meant that non-binary people and campaigners had more ammunition when fighting for appropriate services from the National Health Service – something that was further strengthened in 2013 by the American Psychiatric Association's *Diagnostic and Statistical Manual's* (DSM-5) redefinition of 'gender dysphoria', rather than 'gender identity disorder', as in the previous edition.

Gratifyingly, it would be impossible to chart all the key moments in UK non-binary activism, for there are so many. 2014 could be regarded as another key year given that, in addition to *Beyond the Binary* and the Nonbinary Inclusion

Project launching hugely successful public-facing websites that year, this was also the period in which the previously LGB charity Stonewall conducted a trans consultation prior to becoming trans-inclusive. Non-binary people were one of the groups specifically engaged in the consultation, and Stonewall now has non-binary staff, and has spoken out vociferously on the specific stigma experienced by non-binary people, and the need for a gender-neutral option on British passports.

Following the 2015 general election, during which the charity UK Trans Info requested pledges to support non-binary rights and inclusion, trans campaigner Ashley Reed launched a 30,000-signatory petition for the UK to join the growing number of countries which allow trans people (binary and non-binary) to self-define their gender, rather than having to go through a Gender Recognition Panel. The Ministry of Justice responded that it would not even consider opening up certification to non-binary people because only 'a very small number of people consider themselves to be of neither gender' and 'we are not aware that that results in any specific detriment'. Non-binary people used the social media hashtag #specificdetriment to challenge this response, and *Beyond the Binary* and the Scottish Trans Alliance both conducted surveys to chart the specific detriments experienced by non-binary people. Previous research had already documented the relatively high levels of mental health difficulties amongst non-binary people. These surveys supported those findings and also found that over three-quarters of non-binary people avoid situations for fear of being misgendered, outed, or harassed; two-thirds feel that they are never included in services; and around half feel unable to be out at work.

In 2016, the UK House of Commons Women and Equalities Select Committee published the *Trans Equality Report*. This called for more extensive investigation into the needs of non-binary people, for a 'gender X' option on passports, to move away from gender markers on passports long term, for non-binary people to be protected from discrimination under the gender equality act, and for the updating of trans medical procedures to be inclusive of non-binary people. 2016 was also the year in which the first specifically non-binary activist/academic conference (that we are aware of, internationally) took place in Leeds, and the year culminated in the first Ph.D. thesis, specifically covering non-binary genders, being awarded to one of the authors of this chapter, Ben. Finally, bisexual activist Jen Yockney became the first non-binary person to be awarded an MBE in the Queen's Birthday Honours, necessitating the first use of the title Mx on that influential list.

The future of the non-binary movement

Drawing together the material we received from Elan-Cane and Titman, along with our own research, and the various projects which we've mentioned previously, we offer the following list as a summary of the current areas of focus of the British non-binary movement. This gives some sense of where the movement is going from here. More details can be found on the Nonbinary Inclusion Project and *Beyond the Binary* websites, as well as in the other places mentioned. Many of the themes covered in this chapter are also discussed in greater depth in two recent books which Meg-John has been involved in putting together, *Genderqueer and Non-Binary Genders* (for which Ben also wrote a chapter), and *How to Understand Your Gender*, as well as in Ben's forthcoming book on trans health care.

Areas of focus:

- Campaigning for the rights of non-binary people to self-determine their gender, and to have this accurately recorded in documentation which displays gender, such as passports and organisational records, or to have gender markers removed entirely from such documents.

- Stronger data protection provisions to protect the privacy of people who don't wish to be forced to disclose assigned or legal gender when this cannot be justified to be necessary or guaranteed to be kept confidential as sensitive personal information.

- Ensuring that the gender-neutral title Mx is provided as an option by all institutions, and that gender-neutral pronouns are adopted where appropriate, and recognised as legitimate.

- Revising equality legislation to include non-binary people and/or obtaining commitment from the government and all political parties to make all future legislation gender neutral so that it can be inclusive of non-binary people.

- Providing support and resources for non-binary people themselves, for example through websites like *Beyond the Binary* and support organisations like Gendered Intelligence.

- Awareness-raising and education to improve cultural understanding and media coverage of non-binary people, such as that provided by Trans Media Watch and All About Trans.

- Providing non-binary people with access to NHS medical services in a way equivalent to that sought by (binary) trans men and women – through GPs and gender identity clinics – including recognition of the diversity of assistance they may require. People focusing on this include the Action for Trans Health group as well clinicians like Stuart Lorimer (see chapter 2) and Christina Richards, who work within gender identity clinics towards these aims. Access also needs to be fully inclusive of those whose genders intersect with other marginalised identities (for example, see Sabah Choudrey's GIRES guidance on *Inclusivity – Supporting BAME Trans People*).

- Making public spaces such as toilets and changing rooms gender neutral or non-binary inclusive.
- Conducting and reporting grass roots and academic research with non-binary people to obtain statistics regarding their prevalence and the challenges they face, so that campaigns can be grounded in persuasive evidence.
- Provision of non-binary specific and inclusive social and supportive spaces, following the example of initiatives like Bar Wotever, Be: Non-Binary, Quintasensual Festival and Open Barbers.

It is also important that the wider trans and LGBT+ movements continue to be inclusive of non-binary people. In terms of trans activism, this would mean the explicit inclusion of non-binary people in campaigns around prisons, hate crime and asylum seeking, as well as gender recognition more broadly.

It is difficult to know where we will go from here. At the time of writing, non-binary gender has been in the news for many reasons: some schools scrapping gendered uniforms, a non-binary character on mainstream TV show *Billions*, and an important book, *Trans Like Me*, being released by long-time genderqueer activist, musician and writer CN Lester. The backlash was intense during the summer of 2017, with non-binary activists Fox Fisher and Owl (Ugla Stefanía) being attacked on mainstream television and social media sites when they stood up against claims that non-binary gender didn't exist. We hope that the future will see progress towards non-binary rights and recognition, and the relaxing of rigid binary gender expectations for everyone, but that progress is unlikely to be plain sailing.

16

The Activist New Wave

SARAH BROWN
Sarah lives in Cambridge with her two partners and three stepchildren. She served as a city councillor in Cambridge and was, for a time, the UK's only serving transgender elected politician. Passionate about equality for LGBT people, Sarah is a trustee of a local charity for LGBT young people, and advises Stonewall on transgender issues. In her spare time she enjoys climbing mountains and sailing. She appeared for five consecutive years in the *Independent on Sunday*'s 'Rainbow List' of most influential LGBT people.

My name is Sarah and I am a trans woman. I grew up in an East Midlands mining community in the seventies and eighties, where I felt very isolated. I didn't know there were other people like me, apart from portrayals on TV, which were so dismally inaccurate that they threw me off the scent of who I truly was for years.

Things started to change when I went away to study at Cambridge University in 1992. I was introduced to the Internet, albeit in a form that would be unrecognisable to the generation that was to follow. Still, I discovered embryonic resources for transgender people on Usenet, a series of discussion groups which were prominent before the rise of the web. I was terrified of being outed and didn't participate, but I did watch and learn.

By the time I started formal transition in 2005, at the age of thirty-two, the world had changed. Nobody had quite started to talk about 'social media' – Facebook didn't arrive for the British public until the autumn of 2006 – but blogging had burst onto the scene and for the first time trans people could control how our own transitions were represented.

I found and read a number of transition blogs. One resonated in particular: the blog of American cardiologist Dr Becky Allison. I had never written a blog or a diary myself, but I found Dr Allison's writings extremely helpful and wanted to pay it forward. In November 2005 I started documenting my own transition on the Livejournal blogging website. I even live-blogged my sex reassignment surgery, posting an update mere minutes after I had returned from the operating theatre.

Through blogging I found myself increasingly part of a community of trans people like myself. We all blogged and we all shared our triumphs, our pain and our joy. Many of us became very good friends, not just online but in 'real life' as well.

Although estimates of prevalence vary considerably, everyone agrees that trans people are rare. LGBT people represent around 10 per cent of the population. Trans people are perhaps 10 per cent of LGBT people and, before the advent of the Internet, we faced an uphill task to overcome our isolation. Trans people would often only encounter each other at their gender clinic, with scant time to compare notes. The Internet changed this. Like-minded trans people would cluster into online communities. These would, in turn, develop into groups in the 'real world', particularly around large cities.

Around 2007, something very significant started happening in London.

A few London-based trans people started to hold monthly meetings on the evening of the third Tuesday of each month at Gay's the Word bookshop, near Russell Square. The meetings had regular speakers on topics of interest to trans people (clinicians, academics and so on). The existence of a critical mass of trans people in and near London and the ability to easily spread the word via the Internet meant that meetings were well attended from the start. Trans people, at least in the capital, were staring to meet on our own terms, and we had much to discuss and indeed become angry about.

It was in the spring of 2007 that the General Medical Council commenced fitness to practise hearings against Dr Russell Reid, a private gender practitioner who was much loved by many of his patients. Throughout the two decades prior, many desperate trans people had found his clinic in Earls Court to be the only place left for them after being unable to obtain treatment on the NHS. Complaints against him had been made by other clinicians, who claimed his treatment protocols were too lax. Many trans people saw in this a political motivation and the hearing was well attended by observers from the community, including myself. We took turns to spend days sitting in the hearings and then reporting back on each day's proceedings to each other through our blogs.

Many defence witnesses spoke of how they'd found Dr Reid was the only person who would help them when, for whatever reason, they had been refused treatment by NHS clinics. Many spoke of treatment practices in the relatively recent past that they had felt were abusive. The press, not present to hear any of these stories, ignored them and only descended en masse for the final day, to hear the verdict. Their stories presented Dr Reid as a dangerous maverick, acting recklessly with patients portrayed as not competent to know their own minds.

Lots of trans people were angry at both the circumstances under which the hearing had come about and what they saw as biased and one-sided reporting in the press. Dr Reid was criticised for poor communication with his patients' GPs, but not struck off. The result was largely moot as he had already retired from practice by that time.

The spring of 2007 turned into summer and another reason for trans people to feel aggrieved rolled round. In June of that year, the BBC recorded for Radio 4 another series of what it called *Hecklers* debates, in which a person would present their position and panellists would be invited to interrupt at various points and 'heckle'. The first such debate in the new series featured freelance journalist Julie Bindel. The position she was advocating in the debate was 'Sex Change Surgery is Unnecessary Mutilation' and she was opposed by long-time LGBT activist Peter Tatchell, Professor Stephen Whittle of Press for Change, psychotherapist Michelle Bridgman and gender clinician Dr Kevan Wylie.

The audience for the recording, at the Royal Society of Medicine, was packed with trans people. I was there and recognised many from the fledgling Trans London, as well as lots of people I hadn't met before. This was the event at which I met author and veteran trans activist Roz Kaveney, with whom I would go on to cause significant mischief over subsequent months and years.

It is a perennial irritation to trans people that media coverage of us has seldom moved on from the dismal clichés and misrepresentations that I remembered from my youth. Many present felt Bindel's argument was no exception. She concentrated on the (vanishingly small) phenomenon of 'trans regret' (those who, for whatever reason, seek to reverse their transition). She said that she thought hormone treatment and surgery should not be available. She said she thought trans people should be offered what she called 'talking cures' instead.

Bindel had already drawn the ire of many present through her previous writings, including a February 2004 piece in the *Guardian* weekend magazine headlined, 'Gender Benders

Beware'. In it, she spoke of 'Kwik-Fit sex changes' and claimed 'a world inhabited just by transsexuals ... would look like the set of *Grease*'. She later apologised for the tone of these remarks, but not their substance.

After the recording, drinks were served and the audience was encouraged to mingle with the panel. I found myself in a group speaking to Bindel, along with other Trans London regulars. Despite being charming and self-effacing, Bindel was unapologetic about the way she habitually portrayed trans people and trans issues in her articles. We told her that she was misrepresenting us. We were unhappy that she portrayed medical transition as an easy option, rather than the reality of indifference, abuse and the need to turn to grey market drugs which many of us faced. We put it to her that her inaccurate portrayals were contributing to the stigma and discrimination trans people continued to face.

Bindel denied her writings had much influence, but pledged to do better in future. The reader may draw their own conclusion about whether this has ever materialised in evidence. My view is that it has not.

Summer wore on and in September I found myself with a whole gaggle of trans people in Kensington Gardens at the 'Picnic for Change', held in order to raise funds for the trans activism group Press for Change. I had attended the same event in 2006 and it was a small affair; 2007 was very different: the event was much larger and, while the 2006 picnic looked like a nondescript bunch of people having, well, a picnic, this was a bold affair advertised with bunting and a big rainbow flag.

Once again Roz Kaveney was there. We got talking about the rise of a new breed of trans women: largely lesbian trans women who were out and proud not just as lesbians, but also as trans. US trans activist Julia Serano had just published her book, *Whipping Girl*, which was very much a manifesto for trans women. Many of us saw it as our call to arms. We were here, we were queer, and by gosh, we had grievances we wanted to air. The mood wasn't ugly; we were going to build a better world.

A few weeks later, we succeeded in changing a BBC news headline which referred to trans women as 'male patients'. This was small beans but, long before the fledgling Twitter had gained the popularity to mobilise consumer power, it showed us that a small number of people could, if we made a noise in the right way, effect change. The year 2008 would prove to demonstrate that in spades.

For years there had been a music festival in the US state of Michigan: the Michigan Womyn's (sic) Music Festival (MWMF). It was a long-standing open sore in the feminist movement that the organisers of the festival had an entry policy that excluded trans women. In reality, the situation was akin to a 'don't ask, don't tell' policy and lots of trans women attended anyway, but each year the festival was a flashpoint.

In May 2008, Manchester's Queer Up North festival invited MWMF performer Bitch to play a gig. Bitch reportedly supported MWMF's transphobic exclusion policy. Her stated position on activism to end the discriminatory policy was that it was 'making men comfortable and satisfying men'. Trans people in Manchester were angry that an ostensibly LGBT festival was seen to be endorsing transphobia and exclusion of trans people.

Attempts at dialogue with the organisers were met largely with indifference. Anger and frustration was expressed in our online communities, and a few of us resolved to hold a protest outside the event. I travelled to Manchester with some friends and a hundred flyers run off on an inkjet printer. We met up with local activists and assembled outside the venue. By the time the festival-goers started to arrive for the gig, there were a dozen of us with flyers and banners. We handed the flyers to the attendees, explaining that they contained 'information about the artist', and our message was generally well received, with some attendees even walking out in support of us.

Lots of people asked us if we wanted them to boycott the performance, but we encouraged them to go in and enjoy the music, having paid for their tickets. However, we asked them to just be aware of the context of trans exclusion.

It became apparent that we had hit a raw nerve when the director of Queer Up North came out to meet with us. Our presence there appeared to be causing him some embarrassment. It seemed that we had hit upon a winning formula for protesting against transphobic discrimination. Event organisers would cosy up to transphobes, tacitly giving approval for their behaviour, as long as they weren't publicly embarrassed by it.

We resolved to cause that embarrassment. In 2017, as I write this, those on the receiving end of these protests counter them by mischaracterising them as 'attacks on free speech', usually with the help of a large print or broadcast media organisation. This serves to centre the issue on the subject of the protest, portraying them as a victim and denying the protesters a fair hearing. However in 2008, when Twitter and Facebook were barely known, this method of protest proved difficult to counter.

The UK's trans population was about to be given a lesson in just how powerless we actually were, though. At the end of the LGBT Pride parade in London that July, stewards had taken to policing the entrances of the public toilets in Trafalgar Square. Foreshadowing the 'bathroom bans' that have become prevalent in US politics, the stewards refused to allow anyone they suspected of being a trans woman, including one cis butch lesbian, into the female toilet. The result of this was an impromptu protest outside the loos and the intervention of an off-duty LGBT liaison officer with the Metropolitan Police. Anger escalated when the police officer sided with the stewards, wrongly asserting that a gender recognition certificate was needed to use the correct toilet. By the end of the day one trans woman, desperate to use the lavatory, went into the male facilities where a man then sexually assaulted her. The perpetrator was never found.

As with Queer Up North before, we felt badly let down by our cisgender 'friends' in the LGBT community. This time a woman had been hurt.

A few weeks later, our anger was further stoked by the Royal Society of Medicine, which was hosting a conference on the use of puberty-blocking drugs in adolescent trans people. While we regarded these drugs as a good thing, the Society had invited American-Canadian psychologist Kenneth Zucker to give the opening address. Zucker had gained some notoriety amongst trans people for the use of what we considered to be 'conversion therapy' in his Toronto clinic, a claim he has denied. Similar to so-called 'ex-gay' or 'reparative' therapy, his approach sought to make young trans people accept the gender they were assigned at birth, seemed to often exacerbate their distress. Years later his clinic would be shut down by the Canadian authorities, but at the time we were appalled by the possibility that clinics in the UK could embrace these practices.

As with Queer Up North, I joined a number of other trans people and held a protest outside the event. We had pooled our resources, producing a flyer that we each printed in quantity, to spread the cost around. Embracing the power of the Internet, the flyer contained an explanation of our grievances and links to more information online.

People took our flyers in such large numbers that, some time before the opening address was due, we had run out. Embracing guerrilla activism, I was dispatched to a nearby copy shop, clutching one of our last remaining leaflets to procure another hundred. We also arranged to have some members of our team infiltrate the conference and leave copies of the leaflet around inside for attendees to read. Years later the tide would turn against the sort of therapy practised by Zucker, but this didn't feel like a quick win in the way the Queer Up North protest had.

It had been a year since my friends and I had picnicked under the shade of a tree in Kensington Gardens, excited by the prospect that we could change the world. Despite her promises to be more considered in future, Julie Bindel seemed increasingly to be strident about trans people in the press. It felt as though our own LGBT community had turned against us through embracing transphobia in the arts and enforcing the kind of toilet access for which the US Republican Party would later become infamous. The same medical bodies which were shunning 'ex-gay' therapy seemed ambivalent about similar practices used on trans people. As time passed, optimism turned to disappointment and disappointment, in turn, to righteous anger.

And then, a week after the Zucker protest, LGB charity Stonewall announced that it was shortlisting the very same Julie Bindel for its Journalist of the Year award.

Our righteous anger turned to pure rage.

At the time, Stonewall regarded itself as an LGB organisation (without the 'T'). It had been formed, originally, to combat the 1988 Section 28 legislation which forbade 'promotion of homosexuality' in schools. That battle had been won and Stonewall had morphed into a more general gay rights organisation. Completely separate, but operating in parallel, was Press for Change, which had been formed in 1992 to campaign for equality for trans people and what became the Gender Recognition Act (2004).

It was widely believed within our circle that there had been some sort of 'back room' agreement between Stonewall and Press for Change to divide the LGBT 'turf' between them. Leaders of both organisations were cagey about what form the agreement took, or even if it existed, but that was the perception.

Despite the belief that had arisen in some quarters, Stonewall and Press for Change had very little to do with each other, apart from polite and distant mutual acknowledgement, for many years. As other contributors to this book have remarked, there was, throughout the seventies, eighties and early nineties, a gulf between lesbian and gay groups on the one hand, and trans groups on the other. Some lesbians, gays and bisexuals were dismissive of trans people and some trans people were regrettably quite homophobic. Groups like Press for Change were keen to bridge that gap and warmly supported the idea of L&G or LGB becoming LGBT but, as far as campaign objectives were concerned, Press for Change was better equipped to pursue legal advances for trans people and Stonewall's clear mandate was LGB. In 2003, however, Press for Change and Stonewall recognised that as they were both pursuing new legislation in Parliament (the Gender Recognition Bill and the Civil Partnership Bill, both to be debated in 2004) they had better discuss how to avoid anything that might unintentionally conflict with the work of the other. A meeting was convened, where leaders of the two discussed their lobbying plans and objectives. There was agreement on how to avoid commenting on the other's subject area, particularly in terms of marriage, but that was as far as any division of 'turf' went. There was no need to divide anything else as it had always been neatly separated and neither organisation saw any need to change that. They were both good at their own specialities. Later, when Press for Change faded from the scene, the former PFC leaders warmly welcomed the idea, advocated by a new generation of trans activists, that Stonewall, under its new chief executive, Ruth Hunt (2014–), should embrace trans campaigning too. After extensive consultation, Stonewall made this their policy in 2015.

A lot – perhaps as many as half – of trans people are also lesbian, gay or bisexual. This division of responsibilities did not fit with the newly emergent queer-focused trans activism.

Paradoxically, many who fell into both the LGB and T camps felt that *neither* organisation represented their interests. When I and other activists tried to engage Stonewall and Press for Change we were given what felt like a brush-off. Stonewall sent out form letters to dozens of trans protesters saying that Ms Bindel was nominated for 'bringing a lesbian perspective to journalism', seemingly oblivious to the fact that many of the recipients of the letters were lesbian trans women.

By late 2008, the ad hoc communities we had built on blogging sites were starting to coalesce around the popular and increasingly mainstream Facebook. A number of trans activists had grouped together there to discuss taking things further. A desire to discuss these things in public led to various supporters of Ms Bindel joining in, followed ultimately by Julie Bindel herself. She complained that the protesters were 'bullying' her and suggested she was considering legal action.

In hindsight, the short period of Internet-based activism prior to this point had been an age of innocence. Many trans women are IT-savvy and, as such, we were early adopters. But

A new wave of trans activists protest outside the V&A in November 2008 on the occasion of Stonewall's annual awards ceremony.

things were starting to change, with those we were protesting against increasingly working online too. The two groups would clash more and more, both online and off. This served only to pour petrol on the flames.

Into all of this came some of the 'trans elders' who had been involved in Press for Change, with pleas for moderation and compromise. Perhaps this was ill-judged, as we certainly felt we had a genuine grievance and did not take kindly to what we saw as the old guard trying to assert their authority and maintain the status quo.

Stonewall stuck to its guns. Bindel and her followers stuck to their guns. We stuck to our guns, and on the evening of 7 November 2008 the largest trans rights demonstration the UK had yet seen – about 150 people – assembled outside the Victoria and Albert Museum to protest Stonewall's awards ceremony.

The protest was loud, colourful and good-natured. It featured the by now customary leaflets which were handed out to the great and the good attending the event. For the first time we encountered a counter-demonstration by way of the self-proclaimed 'Julie Bindel fan club'. This consisted of a handful of women facing us on the other side of the red carpet. After Ms Bindel herself arrived they upped and left as we sang after them, inviting them to come and join us at the pub after the demonstration.

The significance of this counter-demonstration was missed, probably by everyone, and certainly by me at the time. It heralded what would grow to become the 'TERF wars'. TERF is an acronym for Trans Exclusionary Radical Feminist; it was coined by radical feminists who wished to distance themselves from increasingly vocal transphobes, whose goal was to prevent the participation and inclusion of trans women within feminist movements and spaces.

2008 was a pivotal year in the struggle for trans acceptance and equality in the UK. It saw the rise of Internet-based activism led by people who had the confidence, thanks to advances in acceptance and visibility won by trans pioneers, to publicly identify as openly trans and queer. It saw the coming of age of a generation of trans people who, perhaps ironically, refused to conform to the world bequeathed by those same pioneers, and led us into direct conflict with them.

The consequences of what we did would not become apparent for some time, but eventually:

- The Michigan Womyn's Music Festival would close its doors for good rather than openly accept trans women through its gates. The last event was in 2015.
- Dr Kenneth Zucker saw his clinic closed by Ontario health officials after an independent investigation raised questions over his clinical practice.
- Stonewall reinvented itself as a comprehensive LGBT charity, placing equality for trans people at the heart of its work.

In 2014 I delivered one of the opening speeches at the London Dyke March, a gay pride event specifically for lesbians and bisexual women. Ironically I was subject to a protest by 'TERFs', who picketed the event, waved placards and tried to embarrass the organisers by handing out leaflets. They had organised their protest on Facebook. Several of the people who protested outside its awards in 2008, myself included, now work inside Stonewall to develop its trans workstream.

There is still much work to do, but progress has been made on building that better world we envisaged while eating picnic food on a lazy summer day in Kensington Gardens ten years ago.

17

Better Press and TV

HELEN BELCHER

Helen is one of the founders of Trans Media Watch, and has been campaigning on trans rights, including trans health care, gender recognition and same-sex marriage, since 2008. She gave the charity's evidence to the Leveson Inquiry in 2012 and to a parliamentary inquiry in 2015. She was named as one of the most influential British LGBT people for three years running. In 2017 she stood for Parliament in Chippenham as a Liberal Democrat. She is happily married, has two adult children, misses singing in a choral society, sits as a school governor and, in her spare time, runs a growing software company that she started when she transitioned in 2004.

My first encounter with 'trans on the telly' was the 1980 BBC mini-series *A Change of Sex*. Watching Julia Grant go through various assessments and tasks was fascinating but, being in a room full of teenage boys at boarding school at the time, I slowly realised I couldn't show anything other than disgust to be sure of not standing out too much from my peers.

The series was what I would now call 'zoo television' – treating trans people as exhibits, objects of fascination. This is a mechanism that persists to the current day, needing a narrator to intone and explain. The narrator explained that Julia 'felt like a woman' – something that was challenged by psychiatrist John Randell. While educational, to a point, what this did to the teenage me was to make me decide I couldn't be a woman because I didn't know what one felt like.

Throughout the nineties, trans people were a staple of programmes like Channel 4's *Eurotrash*, or as a target of comedy. A number of worthy documentaries were also broadcast. But authentic trans voices were few and far between.

The situation in the press wasn't any better. The factual reporting of the rare trans stories in the fifties quickly moved to a sensational approach when covering the stories of Christine Jorgensen, April Ashley, Caroline Cossey (aka 'Tula') and American ophthalmologist and tennis pro Renée Richards. And there it got stuck. In the mid-2000s a friend of mine found herself the subject of a spread in one of the tabloids – an approach that hadn't changed for thirty years. By 2009 the misreporting, objectification and lack of authentic trans voices was endemic. Trans men and non-binary people were pretty much invisible. But a number of trans and intersex people were already starting to use the new social media platforms on the Internet to discuss how to challenge the traditional media coverage.

In March 2009, ITV was broadcasting a comedy series called *Moving Wallpaper*. One episode introduced a trans character, seemingly for the sole purpose of being the target of relentless transphobic jokes. This was the push to action. Over a hundred people complained to Ofcom, the regulatory body for the broadcasters. Ofcom rejected the complaint. An appeal was then launched, which Ofcom also rejected. A further approach met with the request to stop badgering them if we agreed to meet them and discuss the situation.

A presentation was put together, starting with around four minutes of non-stop transphobic clips from programmes broadcast on British television the previous year. We explained how the language used in the programmes transferred to the streets, often with horrendous results. We went through the

Broadcasting Code and pointed out where we felt Ofcom were failing. We presented the various statistics of abuse and mental health issues encountered by trans people. Trans Media Watch (TMW) was born. Brokered by marketeer Jo Shaw, journalist Jennie Kermode and activist Jenny-Anne Bishop, the Ofcom meeting included myself, writer Sarah Lennox and fledgling journalist and commentator Paris Lees.

The outcome of the meeting with Ofcom? To be honest, not a lot. But Jo managed to get an invite to a swanky Channel 4 event, where she met with Stuart Cosgrove, the channel's director of diversity and the then head of the Creative Diversity Network – a group used by broadcasters to look at their coverage of diversity and, yes, pat themselves on the back for it. She asked him in public session what the channel was doing for trans people. Stuart, a man not normally lost for words, didn't have an answer. Thus, another meeting with the emergent TMW team followed.

It was in meeting with Channel 4 that we realised that the media wasn't always malicious, but that there was a severe lack of knowledge. Some of Stuart's questions were about where the boundary for 'trans' was. What was the difference between trans people and, say, pantomime dames? We determined that we would primarily be an educational group, challenging where necessary but with a focus on explaining the effects of getting things wrong. Getting into organisations was more important than shouting outside them.

Stuart was gold dust. He introduced us to Amanda Rice, head of diversity at the BBC, but more importantly he resolved to take steps to change the channel's approach. He explained that the charter which governed Channel 4 mandated it to increase the positive representation of minorities, and started to look for methods to embed a change of culture in the organisation. He worked with us to arrange training for the channel's commissioning editors. He encouraged creative ideas for programming and suggested the creation of a memorandum of understanding (MoU), of which Channel 4 was the initial signatory. Stuart also brokered a March 2011 launch event for the MoU in the channel's London headquarters.

The launch party was an historic event. We decided we would aim high, so invited a number of activists, as well as media personalities and politicians who we thought we would be sympathetic or interested. Amongst the people we reached out to was the new government Minister for Equalities, Lynne Featherstone MP. To our surprise, she accepted. The event became the first one organised by trans people at which a serving UK government minister spoke.

Also at that event was a production company, Twenty Twenty TV, who came up with the idea for a series which followed seven trans people at different stages of transition through events in their lives. The series became *My Transsexual Summer* (MTS – see chapter 18). It was notable at the time because it largely permitted trans people to speak for themselves, even if the first episode was a stereotypical focus on surgery. MTS became the third most-watched factual programme series on Channel 4 in 2012 and was regarded within the industry as groundbreaking. Out of the many storylines covered involving the seven, two specifically threw into sharp relief the discrimination that trans people faced. The first was when trans woman Drew was turned down for a job at a bridal wear shop because of the manager's fears of what the customers might think. The second was when another trans woman, Sarah, struggled to find rental accommodation in Brighton – largely thought of as a supportive city.

But MTS was still a rarity and the press persisted in portraying trans people as deviants, undeserving frauds or simply comedic. In May 2005 the Press Complaints Commission

(PCC) had issued a press release clarifying that trans people were protected under the Editors' Code – protection that was observed more by exception than anything else.

When the TMW team met early on with the PCC their secretariat seemed sympathetic but powerless to effect any change. Journalist Jane Fae, a member of our team, asked whether a headline which claimed 'outrage' about something could be justified if only one person out of thousands actually expressed outrage. The PCC's response was, simply, 'yes'.

In July 2011, public concern with press behaviour was sparked into life by revelations that the voicemail of murdered teenager Milly Dowler's mobile phone had been 'hacked' by journalists, adversely affecting police investigations. The Prime Minister ordered a public inquiry to be led by Lord Justice Leveson, the first stage of which was to investigate the ethics, standards and practice of the press. We had incorporated Trans Media Watch as a charity by this stage and recognised the inquiry as an opportunity to show how trans people had been treated.

I attended a meeting held by the Labour media spokesperson Helen Goodman MP towards the end of November 2011, where I was told that the deadline for submissions to the inquiry was only a few days away – something we had hitherto been blissfully unaware of. I wrote to the inquiry team and requested an extension. They granted us an additional month.

The press weren't aware at the time that we were doing this. During the two months that public submissions were being accepted, transphobic pieces were very thin on the ground. However, they emerged with a vengeance on 1 December, the day after the public submission deadline. The timing (with us still drafting our report) enabled us to capture these articles and add them to our submission – written largely by Jennie and Jo and edited and formatted by me. A number of victims of press harassment, including parents of trans children, came forward to give us their stories on the condition that they weren't in the publicly available documents.

The inquiry team came back to us shortly afterwards and asked us to give oral evidence. Because of others' personal circumstances, I was the person in the frame and spent an hour talking to Robert Jay QC (counsel to the inquiry) and Lord Justice Leveson (the chair) about our submission. The anticipated press harassment to come from this emerged in two further widely featured tabloid stories: one about a pregnant trans man, and another about a five-year-old trans child. We rushed a second submission to the inquiry, acknowledged by the inquiry team within the hour, and the negative press halted – at least until Lord Justice Leveson published his report.

In the same month, February 2012, the bookmakers Paddy Power released the latest in a series of controversial adverts, this one based on being able to 'spot the trans woman'. Within twenty-four hours we had uncovered a real life trans woman who had been asked by a complete stranger in a public space whether she was trans, because of the advert. We were able to talk with Clearcast, the agency that pre-approves all broadcast advertising in the UK, and explain the danger that such an ad created. The advertisement was pulled. As a result, we were able to do training sessions with both Clearcast and the Advertising Standards Authority.

In 2012, with BBC and Channel 4 funding, TMW started a project initially called Trans Media Action. The aim of the project was to introduce media executives and editors to trans people in a non-threatening manner. A social action group, On Road, led by Nathalie McDermott, helped drive the project forwards. Following a successful series of meetings, Paris Lees and Sarah Lennox decided to give their time to this project, renamed All About Trans, and withdrew from the TMW team.

In November 2012 the Leveson report was published. The TMW evidence was given a section in its own right and our evidence was quoted in a number of other places throughout the report. Leveson added a condemnation of unnecessary outings of trans people. He compared the situation with the coverage of gay people, and noted that the press needed to raise its game considerably. In judge-speak, this was strong stuff.

But, just three weeks later, a local paper published a story about a Lancashire primary school teacher who had started to transition. This rapidly hit the national press, with the *Jeremy Vine* phone-in programme on BBC Radio 2 having a half-hour to discuss it. About twenty minutes into this segment Jeremy appeared to realise that this type of coverage might actually be a problem – something I had warned the BBC diversity team about a couple of hours earlier. A particularly nasty opinion piece by regular columnist Richard Littlejohn was printed by the *Daily Mail* under the headline, 'He's not only in the wrong body... he's in the wrong job'. Littlejohn asked whether anyone had thought of the 'devastating effect' on Meadows's pupils of her change of gender.

The press camped outside Lucy Meadows's front door for two weeks over the Christmas and New Year period, even though no new coverage was printed. We advised Lucy to get in touch with the PCC to call the journalists and photographers off, and also to discuss making a complaint.

Also, at the start of 2013, news broke that private doctor Richard Curtis was being investigated by the General Medical Council (GMC) about the treatment of some of his trans patients. This appeared to be a repeat of an earlier GMC case, against another trans-friendly doctor, Dr Russell Reid – news of which had been broken in 2004 by the same journalist. As a result, trans people quickly expressed outrage on social media – the common complaint being that the GMC were investigating the wrong doctors. This led to the #TransDocFail hashtag on Twitter, via which ordinary trans people recorded their personal experience of being treated or maltreated by doctors. The campaign received over a thousand allegations of medical malpractice via the hashtag within twenty-four hours.

The media started to take notice, but this interest was suddenly derailed when *Guardian* columnist Suzanne Moore wrote an ostensibly unrelated opinion piece about women's bodies stating that women were angry with themselves for 'not having the ideal body shape – that of a Brazilian transsexual'. Trans people, already angry about #TransDocFail, swarmed to social media again, expressing outrage at the insensitivity of Moore's comments, referencing the very high murder rates that Brazilian trans women suffered. With that, the impetus behind media scrutiny of the medical treatment was dissipated.

Contrarian columnist Julie Burchill followed up Moore's line with a whole piece in that Sunday's *Observer* attacking trans women, calling us (amongst other things) 'screaming mimis' and 'bed-wetters in bad wigs'. Several hundred people launched complaints with the PCC. Those were dismissed by the PCC in March, the day before Lucy Meadows's death was announced. Following this, nearly a quarter of a million people signed an online petition calling for Richard Littlejohn to be sacked from the *Daily Mail*.

The net effect, however, seemed to be that the press did actually pause. The Lancashire coroner investigating Lucy Meadows's death condemned the press coverage as a factor. The *Observer* took down the Burchill piece – only for the *Telegraph* to republish it in a column by Toby Young. Transphobic coverage pretty much ceased for over a year. So, it seemed, did all other coverage of trans people.

One notable exception was a Cambridge academic who made the press after being gored by a stag in the Scottish

Highlands. Some tabloids made unnecessary reference to the unfortunate academic's trans history. Following her complaint (which was upheld) the press apologised for their coverage, and the PCC – shortly to become the new Independent Press Standards Organisation (IPSO) – announced new guidance on the reporting of trans issues.

In August 2014 high-profile boxing promoter Kellie Maloney published details of her recent transition in a Sunday paper. It turned out that she had taken out an injunction six months earlier preventing another paper from outing her. This prompted a series of trans outings. The press insisted that each one was positive, setting a role model. Affairs reached fever pitch in March 2015, when American former Olympian Caitlyn Jenner announced her transition – a truly global news event. The saturated media coverage of Caitlyn Jenner drew to an end this phase of press coverage, but other, more sinister, themes were already emerging...

A number of student unions had either adopted or were discussing adopting measures that would deny some personalities the opportunity to speak on certain contentious issues, generally to do with Islam or holocaust denial, at campus events. Julie Bindel was excluded from one university on the grounds that she was thought to hold transphobic views. Branded 'no-platforming', the actual instances of this were rare, but the media leapt on them and suddenly, despite not being the initiators of these policies, trans people found themselves in the middle of a debate about freedom of speech. The growing fury of the media coverage meant that even things which weren't no-platforming were considered as the same.

The second theme to emerge concerned the treatment of trans children. Historically, treatment of trans people required getting past what was perceived as a gatekeeping system fronted by a number of doctors (usually psychiatrists). There was a fairly close-knit group of medics working in this area, amongst whom were Dr Randell and Professor Richard Green in London (see chapters 1 and 2), and Drs Blanchard and Zucker in Toronto. It's only relatively recently that more enlightened views of treating gender identity have come to the fore.

Treatment of trans children in reality simply means letting them express their gender without medical intervention until puberty, or surgical intervention much later as young adults. The topic has been a controversial issue until recently, when the emotional damage caused by suppressing someone's self when young was recognised. In 2016 the BBC broadcast a sensitive documentary fronted by Louis Theroux that followed some trans children in the USA, and highlighted the struggles they faced in either seeking treatment or making decisions with their parents about what treatment would be appropriate. This was largely welcomed by most trans people, who talked about it through social media and blogs. However, a separate BBC documentary (*Transgender Kids: Who Knows Best*) at the start of 2017 focused on the Canadian clinic, now closed down by health authorities, where Drs Blanchard and Zucker worked and had run a process that some described as being close to reparative therapy. The documentary positioned the debate as being between world-renowned experts and trans activists who had taken their jobs away. A complaint was made to the BBC, led by TMW and co-signed by many other organisations. However that was rejected a couple of months later. The effect of this has been to cast doubt over the effectiveness of the BBC complaints process.

The third theme was linked to the first, and that was the supposed freedom to publish pieces that alleged that trans women were not 'real' women. For the first three months of 2017 this felt relentless, as one piece after another emerged in the press. Attempts by trans people to respond were generally batted down with demands to not 'silence' the debate. The upshot of this was that, until the general election was called in April 2017, trans people found ourselves at the centre of a debate about what responsible journalism and reporting actually means. It has been pointed out that it's an odd kind of debate where you only ever hear from one side.

However, there were some other more promising developments.

Non-binary people were not really visible, let alone understood, when TMW emerged into the world. Now a relatively large percentage of youngsters identify as gender-fluid – far more than identify as trans – and this is starting to make some people think about gender in a different way. Medical processes in the UK have adapted to make space for treatment of non-binary people and a parliamentary select committee inquiry, chaired by Maria Miller MP, also heard about the problems non-binary people face.

The growing level of parliamentary interest in this area is also very welcome, as part of an increasing focus from a wider set of bodies. As an example, England's largest LGB charity, Stonewall, announced the intention to work closely with the trans communities in early 2015. Having made that key strategic decision after careful consultation, they have moved to create a Trans Advisory Group (which I'm part of) and ensure that their practices are inclusive of trans people. The parliamentary inquiry already mentioned received some generally favourable media coverage in January 2016, as did Stonewall's April 2017 *Vision for Change* policy document, outlining campaigning priorities for the next five years.

One product of the original Trans Media Action project was the Trans Comedy Award, which led to the successful BBC sitcom *Boy Meets Girl*. Rebecca Root was the first trans actor to play a trans character in a mainstream series on British television, following Laverne Cox's role in the US Netflix series *Orange Is the New Black*.

The overall analysis is that some progress has been made, although there are still some areas of concern with how trans people are now positioned in the media. Media portrayals, when they happen at all, still usually concentrate on a transition narrative, where a person is moving from one gender expression to another. Otherwise they are commonly looking to validate – or, possibly more often, invalidate – the trans experience in some poorly defined way.

While the occasional trans person does appear in front of a television camera, sometimes without being associated with the trans label, there still seems to be a dearth of trans people behind the scenes – at the editorial desk or as scriptwriters.

As indicated above, regulatory bodies still also have some improving to do. TMW's 2010 survey showed that a large number of trans people felt it was pointless complaining about media coverage as complaints were usually rejected. While projects, such as the All About Trans interactions with media professionals, attempt to change media attitudes from within, occasionally a firmer stick is required. But engagement with complaints processes is still cumbersome and, often, you are left with the impression of engaging a corporate defence procedure rather than an opportunity to learn.

In summary, there has been some welcome and much-needed progress in trans representation but, to quote Lord Justice Leveson from his section on the representation of trans people in the press, 'the game needs to be raised significantly higher'. Only when this happens will trans people feel included in our society rather than simply tolerated or observed as some kind of freak show.

18

Making History Today

FOX FISHER

Fox Fisher is an award-winning artist, filmmaker and human rights campaigner. After contributing to Channel 4's *My Transsexual Summer*, Fox set up the production company My Genderation, making over sixty short films which have been endorsed by the BBC, Channel 4 and the NHS. Fox has created films for cliniQ, TGEU, IGLYO and Trans Iceland and is advisor to All About Trans, facilitating interactions with the BBC, the *Daily Mail*,
the *Sun* and the *Observer* to discuss trans representation. Fox promoted trans matters on ITV's *Good Morning Britain* (with Piers Morgan) and *This Morning*, the BBC's *Victoria Derbyshire* and *Inside Out* and *Arte Europa*. Fox is a patron for LGBT Switchboard, co-creator of Trans Pride Brighton, co-founded a trans acting course at Royal Central School of Speech and Drama with Gendered Intelligence and plays Jake in Radio 4's *Tales of the City*.

In the summer of 2011 the first major British reality TV series about trans people aired on Channel 4. Although the show had the now outdated name *My Transsexual Summer*, it started an important conversation with the nation about trans issues. Up until that point, the discussion within the media can only be described as having been generally prejudiced, harmful and full of tropes – and it still is in many ways. The documentary itself had a very cis-centric view and focused on the people involved from an over-saturated, binary, medical perspective. Many contributors felt exploited – none were paid, and a few were told to 'keep it simple' for the cameras.

I was one of the seven people on the show. When I wanted to talk about my identity and what I described as 'genderqueer' at the time, I was told that the audience just wouldn't understand anything beyond the binary and I had to simplify my story and say that I was a trans man. After the show aired, I felt very upset with the final edit and how the whole thing had panned out. I felt frustrated, cheated and my mental health suffered as a result. This confirmed that if there was to be content made about trans people – and if it wasn't to be from a cisgender, voyeuristic perspective – it had to be done by transgender people themselves.

The majority of production companies creating trans content are run and staffed by cisgender people and, no matter how much they may seem like your best friend while filming, their main interest is making money, at the expense of trans people and their actual realities. So myself and Lewis Hancox, who is a trans man and appeared alongside me in *My Transsexual Summer*, picked up a digital camera and started making our own documentaries about the trans people around us. Thus My Genderation, an ongoing film project celebrating trans lives and trans experiences, was created.

Lewis and I started from scratch and we didn't have the same equipment as the major production companies, but we had something they didn't have. We had the experience and the understanding of what it was like to be trans in a society where we are grossly misunderstood. We had integrity. We had connections through individuals reaching out after watching *My Transsexual Summer*, or through media interactions arranged through All About Trans. Now Lewis has moved on to a successful comedy career, and the project is run by myself and my partner Owl. We have created over sixty short films about trans people, with endorsements for our productions coming from the BBC, Channel 4 and the NHS. What we do with our films is to reflect a trans person back to themselves, so they can see themselves in a new light. For a shy person like Alice (the second person we ever filmed), who I would often see alone at events in the poetry and queer scene, the film we made about her gave her confidence. After her film was released, people would approach her more and start conversations and compliment her for who she was. I realised then the power that film has: to connect.

This is something I feel the major production companies and TV channels haven't yet grasped: that trans people are one of the most vulnerable groups in society, and making content on the issues they encounter is a very delicate matter. It is so easy for someone who isn't trans to fall into tired tropes of trans storytelling and misconceptions that fuel stigma and hate. Even trans people struggle not to fall into those tropes. Often we tell our stories in the media in such a way that makes the majority comfortable with us, in hopes that they'll understand. Trans people aren't given a manual about how to explain their identities, and they don't necessarily know all the right vocabulary. We offer tired stories of how we played with certain types of toys or how we always knew we were 'born in the wrong body' and we always wanted to be who we are. For some people this reflects the truth of their experience, but for others it doesn't: it just seems like what people want to hear. Toys don't make anyone's gender identity, nor are they a reliable indicator of what drives us. These are just stereotypes we've all heard – language that we are all taught – whether we are trans or cis. And the reason why we perpetuate it is because that's what everyone wants to hear in order to be comfortable around us. And we're inevitably affected by that.

With the emerging and expanding trans community we are constantly finding new ways to describe our experiences.

Initiatives like the trans acting course I helped set up at the Royal Central School of Speech and Drama with Gendered Intelligence are examples of assisting trans people to succeed in the media and arts world. We did this because of the daily barrage of negative trans press. It's more important than ever to help and enable trans people to speak up for themselves and hone their acting skills. Our opportunities are often severely lacking and roles with trans characters are still mainly given to cisgender actors.

Another event with a mission of 'putting the T first' is one I helped co-found in 2013. Trans Pride Brighton, now in its fifth year, was started out of the need to celebrate trans lives and raise awareness of our issues. It was also started to give us a chance to meet up on another day other than Trans Day of Remembrance (TDOR). TDOR is an event held on 20 November each year all around the world to remember those who have been killed or committed suicide due to discrimination and violence. We

Trans people have an extended history of studying and critiquing film and video. An annual film festival focused on transgender themes began as long ago as the mid-nineties.

therefore wanted another event where we could celebrate and remember the good things. At Trans Pride, trans people and our allies can celebrate all our wonderful diversity, meet in the flesh after connecting online, and keep in touch online afterwards.

By the power of social media

Social media has played a huge role in raising awareness about trans issues. The Internet is the biggest medium that has helped move trans issues into another realm of public focus and understanding. And there's no denying that it's a massive platform for trans people to find each other and seek support. Platforms such as YouTube, Tumblr, Facebook and Reddit have enabled trans people, including myself, to connect and share information. And, by sculpting our profile or character through video games, trans people have been given the power and safety to explore a representation of themselves. This gives us a better quality of life much earlier than was possible before. The Internet is also where hormones are bought without a prescription, where an isolated trans guy can buy a used binder to flatten their chest before 'top surgery', petitions can be created, and where 7,000 comments of hate can be written in twenty-four hours about your latest vlog on being non-binary. Indeed, sadly, the Internet is also a place where cyber-bullying is rife. I know this as a fact, because all of those things happened to me.

Twenty years ago, you could not find the same amount of resources on trans issues and you could often only find help and advice if you knew where to look. It was rare to see a trans person speak in a video, on public media or on TV. The only representation we had of trans people for many decades was through films where they were depicted as the butt of the joke, the psychotic killer, the freak, mentally ill, a person who deceives and tricks people, or an object not to be desired. Today, you can find so many videos, articles and materials that are challenging these ideas and fighting for trans people to be respected for who they are. Because essentially it doesn't cost people anything to respect our identities, but the lack of respect costs many of us our lives.

For the last few decades we have also seen a group of feminists advocate against trans people, and in particular against trans women. In their view, trans women are not 'real' women, but men who are appropriating womanhood in order to enter feminist spaces and disrupt them. They believe trans people are enforcing rigid gender roles that continue to oppress women. The argument is that trans women can never truly be women because they were not born with the same types of sex characteristics as cis women are typically born with. There is a consensus within most of the feminist movement that gender is a social construct and that women are oppressed and diminished down to their genitals, reproductive organs and bodies. It is hypocritical to reduce trans women to their bodies and claim that their sex characteristics govern who they are or can be. It is highly un-feminist – indeed, it's a tactic used by the patriarchy and oppressors of women.

In 2016, Germaine Greer was invited to speak in Brighton for International Women's Day. Greer is infamous for her transphobic and harmful views towards trans women dating back to the seventies and eighties, but she was invited to Brighton – the home of Trans Pride. I started a petition where I demanded that the organisers of the event dis-invite Greer, as it seemed to me a huge insult to the trans community in Brighton and beyond. Despite a petition with just shy of 20,000 signatures, and some pretty hateful comments directed at me online, the organisers didn't back down. International Women's Day at the Brighton Dome became a space that wasn't safe for all women. The organisers were not willing to take a stand with trans people, leaving us yet again disappointed by those who claim to be our allies. Greer's views do not exist in a vacuum – they contribute to a matrix of hate that fuels stigma, discrimination and violence against trans people. Just as harmful views against women contribute to their oppression, harmful views against trans people contribute towards theirs. The fact that we don't stand up against hate and condemn it only allows it to continue. By not saying anything, you are siding with the oppressor and saying it is okay for them to continue what they are doing.

The petition I started and the discussion that arose isn't one of a kind. This kind of protest has been happening ever since social media became a prominent tool for marginalised groups to use. Before that time, those who had hateful views about trans people or other minorities had free rein to exercise them and we on the receiving end had no voice. It was only once the voices of trans people and their allies broke through on social media that the issue of 'free speech' suddenly came into play. People who had been expressing their derogatory views, often for many decades, now react to criticism from targeted minorities by saying their free speech is being limited or jeopardised. The ironic part is that when trans people couldn't manage to have their objections and arguments heard, no one ever wondered about how it was affecting *their* freedom of speech. And let's be clear: Germaine Greer not being allowed to speak at one event at the Brighton Dome is in no way affecting her freedom of speech. She has one of the biggest profiles within the feminist movement and she can exercise her views freely on various public platforms without hindrance. She gets paid to speak at events all over the world. The fact that we didn't want Greer to speak in Brighton was a stand against hate. It was a group of marginalised people who had been silenced for many decades standing up for themselves and demanding to be respected. It was a group of people sick of their lives being constantly up for debate. Because trans lives should never be – and *are* never – up for debate.

The Internet is everyone's playground

But the fact that anybody can access the Internet also means that people who are against trans people and their rights can speak out and gather followers. And they are doing so, with entire threads on websites, videos on YouTube and other material being put out there. There is a group of people I've encountered who are dedicated to advocating against trans issues; they can be found commenting below the line on almost any video, news article or other kind of material shared on the Internet about trans people. With the rise of awareness, we often see a rise in hate. With the current political situation in the world, minorities are finding themselves being more discriminated against and are facing more violence than ever before, and the foundation for this discrimination and hate often comes from social media. People who are capable of exercising their hateful views from a safe distance find others online with the same views and take action.

With increased communication opportunities for trans people, many of us are speaking out and sharing our thoughts and views. This has created an array of trans people with different ideas, thoughts and ideologies. There is certainly no single way to be trans, and no single right way to understand being so. But with that diversity comes conflict from within the community itself. Differences can be good – they stimulate thinking – but negative examples of this are the kind of trans people who represent a very conservative, cisnormative, binary view that is heavily under the influence of outdated gender stereotypes. They are often binary trans people who directly advocate against trans people who don't fit into a cis-centric, passing stereotype of a binary trans person. These people sometimes have a huge online audience and speak out against non-binary people and the introduction of gender-neutral pronouns. Some of them even go so far as to advocate against trans youth gaining access to hormone blockers and treatment. Whilst the majority of trans activists are pushing for change and recognition of all trans people and their identities, there are others who seem to think that conforming is the only acceptable solution and that we should all try our best to fit within these rigid categories of gender, otherwise we are not trans at all.

Trans people are therefore not only under attack from society and a certain group of feminists, but also from within our own community. One of the reasons why there might be a reluctance to accept trans people in all of our diversity is because we inherently challenge the notions of gender and norms created in society. This suggests that gender isn't a fixed thing, which, for someone who's never had to question the sex they were assigned at birth, can feel like a threatening idea. It forces people to think that perhaps their own identities aren't 'real' or 'authentic', which is why they often violently lash out. That push back takes the form of discrimination, stigma and violence and contributes to the tired discussion of trans people being 'real' or not. Because 'real' to such people doesn't actually mean *real* – it means people who fall neatly into the social norms we've created around gender; those pure enough not to challenge the system.

New genderation

On a more positive note, with the rise of awareness of trans issues, people now have the opportunity to be themselves at a younger age. This creates a whole new perspective and conversation about gender and gender identity, and we are now seeing a new group of trans people with very specific needs socially, medically and legally. Access to hormone blockers for trans youth has been much discussed, and recently we have seen articles, documentaries and other material that tries to use fear-mongering tactics to make us believe that trans kids cannot know their identity for themselves. People question the fact that they are given hormone blockers to safely pause puberty. Flawed research statistics and the voices of disqualified doctors claim that about 80 per cent of all trans kids desist being trans. This idea of the 'desistance myth' has been debunked by many already. Anyone with knowledge of research methods and people who read into the actual data will soon realise huge flaws in the numbers of people counted and the premise behind these numbers.

The fact is that trans kids have always existed. Many trans people can confirm this as most of us (but not all) have felt that they were trans from a very early age. Many of us tell stories about how we would've loved to have access to medical care and social support as kids. Many of the simple medical interventions now being offered to young trans people could have saved us years of agony, as we felt our bodies betray us through puberty and develop in an alien-feeling way that was beyond our control. The fact that trans youth today has access to hormone blockers that can prevent all of this happening is something so valuable and something so important to a trans person's quality of life.

There is an interesting paradox around age when it comes to trans people, which reveals a lack of understanding and willingness to actually support youngsters on their terms. Within the clinical protocols for evaluating adult trans people there is an emphasis on looking for evidence that we have experienced being trans from a very young age. Those who do are often viewed by society and the medical establishment as more 'authentic' trans people. We've all heard the story of a trans person who knew all along but didn't have the opportunity, or people to look up to, or simply didn't have the knowledge that being trans was an actual possibility. In many cases that's true, but certainly not exclusively. But this idea is enforced by the medical establishment throughout their diagnosis processes, where this becomes an essential part of their evaluation. Now, finally, young kids are coming out, saying: 'I'm trans and I need support.' But, all of a sudden, society has become very hesitant to give them the services that they need, even when there are so many trans people who are living proof that they would have had a much better life if they had had access to hormone blockers – being able to buy time by deferring puberty long enough to be sure that transition is right for them and they are old enough to give their own consent.

There is a disconnect between the narratives that society has built around trans people and their lived realities. Perhaps people are only willing to hear the narratives of people experiencing this from a young age and they feel as if this is a comfortable confirmation of our identities, but when it comes down to it they are still not willing to give young trans people the support they need. This, to me, is a clear example of how trans people aren't truly respected for their identities and how we are almost always only granted acceptance through a heterosexual and cisgender lens.

The future is trans

As the cracks in the binary system of gender start to form and break, the idea of gender and sex expands. We move beyond the binary of sex and gender and start to realise that the reality isn't as simple as people liked to believe. And it's not as though ideas of the diversity of gender have not existed throughout time. In many societies and cultures we have various examples of different genders and expressions. But most of those cultures were crushed under the foot of Western colonialism, which stigmatised and practically erased the idea of gender diversity, resulting in horrific consequences for groups of people who could be considered a part of what we call the trans umbrella today.

In the case of non-binary people, they challenge the duality of gender. Being non-binary means that your gender identity is not explicitly nor exclusively 'man' or 'woman'. Non-binary people can be both, move smoothly between the two, experience no specific gender, or exist completely outside of this binary. Non-binary offers an alternative to the gender order, where people question and interrogate the notion of gender and the destiny society assigns to those categories. It challenges the very core of gender and sheds light on just how fragile these categories are. And this provokes different kinds of reactions, both within and outside of the trans community. Many non-binary people don't feel as if they can be or are a part of the trans community because of the focus on medical transition. Many choose to define themselves outside of the transgender umbrella. But the idea of challenging the sex you were assigned at birth inevitably ties both binary trans people and non-binary people together. It is a shared notion and an experience we all have, regardless of how we might then identify differently from what we were assigned at birth. In my mind it is therefore important that we all come together and realise that we are stronger together than apart. For me, non-binary people are a firm and important part of the trans community.

For non-binary trans people who want to have a medical transition of some sort, meanwhile, the access at present is often little to none. The medical establishment and society as a whole isn't yet willing to accept that anyone who doesn't identify as either strictly a man or a woman would want access to hormones or surgery. Most people who even have a basic awareness of non-binary as a concept are still under the popular but erroneous belief that all non-binary people are androgynous, preferring to live somewhere in between the two gender binaries when it comes to expression and identity. But this is where people confuse identity with expression. Expression refers to how you express your gender outwards – feminine, masculine or androgynous – whereas identity refers to your own sense of self. Non-binary people, and anyone for that matter, can have any gender expression. For some people a medical transition becomes a necessity to achieve a gender expression that they need in order to feel comfortable in their own skin. For others, different ways of playing with appearance is what they need. The notion of expression is so neatly tied to the binary of 'man' and 'woman', where men are expected to conform to the masculine and women the feminine, so it becomes a given that non-binary people should express themselves as somewhere in between or as a mix of both. But in reality expression isn't so neatly tied to these categories and people within all categories have all sorts of expressions, whether they're trans or cis.

The younger generation is already more aware of all of this. They are defining outside the binaries of sexuality and gender and are actively denouncing outdated gender stereotypes. Social media remains one of the most powerful tools to raise awareness on a global level and bring social change. With more access to social media than ever before, we need to start using those tools and not be afraid to come out and be proud of being trans. We need to stand up and show the world that we are here and we exist. In order to make progress, we need to become the gatekeepers, the creators of content. In many parts of the world people still cannot come out, and it is up to all of us to change that and fight for a better future.

I would never have guessed I was going to dedicate so much of my life to fighting for human rights. But one person can make a massive difference and there are different ways of fighting for our rights. No rights were ever gained through conforming to oppressive norms. The fight for equality is a long history of radical and brave people not being afraid to step up and demand change.

19

A Very Modern Transition

STEPHANIE HIRST
With over fourteen awards and eleven years hosting Capital FM's *Breakfast Show*, Stephanie is one of the UK's biggest radio stars. In 2014 she took a planned break from broadcasting and, in October of that year, revealed that she was transgender. Having taken a sabbatical from the airwaves, Stephanie returned to radio and moved to the BBC where she hosts a *Vinyl Revival* show every Saturday night on BBC Manchester. Expanding into TV, she is part of the extended family on ITV's *Lorraine*, where she has also been a mentor for their Change One Thing campaign. She has also recently presented for BBC *Breakfast*, BBC *Inside Out* and written for the *Independent*, the *Telegraph* and the *Huffington Post*.

Recently I sat on a sofa that was no ordinary sofa – this one had millions of viewers each morning as it was situated on the set of ITV's *Good Morning Britain*. As I sat there chatting to the hosts of the show, I became acutely aware of how far we have come in recent times. Here I was about to comment on a story which had broken about a ninety-year-old who was finally transitioning from male to female after a life of constantly questioning their gender.

Ninety years! I managed thirty-seven.

She finally felt it was time to become her true, authentic self after years of worry, denial and anxiety, saying that her whole life had been a lie. Instantly, I was in awe of this woman Patricia Davies.

I can almost imagine the relief she must have felt, because the moment I announced *my* decision to transition – live on BBC's 5 Live in October 2014 – it was as if my whole world was suddenly 'in colour'. Before then, I was trapped in a perpetual cycle of self-hate and denial.

You could say I had it all: a £200,000-a-year salary, an Aston Martin on the drive and a broadcasting career some people could only dream of. Yet I knew that, the more successful I became, the more imprisoned I was within my success and body, which was male.

Speaking to many trans people over the years, I've found that, no matter how different our backgrounds were, we all shared one thing in common: gender dysphoria. And, however how hard we tried to brush our feelings under the carpet to try and live our lives without disrupting the status quo, it would not go away. People have told me they made lists of pros and cons for transitioning, to which I always respond with a resounding 'YES! I did that too!'

I genuinely thought I would lose absolutely everything I had ever worked for – and I must stress I'm not a materialistic person. Yes, Molton Brown hand wash is lovely in the bathroom, but £1.50 antibacterial stuff from Asda does the same job.

Due to the messages that society had projected onto me and millions of others, I had always worked on the assumption that to transition would mean losing loved ones, friends and my career. And yet now, in 2017, that is simply not the case for an increasing number of people who transition. Yes, it's still sadly true for some, but it's no longer the given that it once was.

For most of my life, the fire of hatred for anyone on the trans spectrum was fuelled by the media. I would sit in a radio studio, where I presented my daily breakfast show, surrounded by the day's newspapers. Every few weeks one or other of those papers would have a negative story with a horrific pun-bashing headline: 'GENDER BENDING BIKER' ... 'SEX CHANGE CHARLIE' ... these stories did nothing but make me want to take my own life. Because that was starting to look like the only option, based on the vitriol that was projected onto me.

Ever since I can remember, I've felt different. I 'knew' I was a girl, but I didn't have a word for how I felt until I saw Caroline Cossey being interviewed (or should I say patronised) by Gloria

My Story by Caroline Cossey.

Hunniford on television one day in 1991, whilst I was off school sick. I'd fallen asleep on the sofa and awoke to see a beautiful lady describing exactly how I felt. I sat up, stunned at what I was seeing before my very eyes. I dived off the sofa, grabbed the nearest videocassette and slammed it in the recorder, managing to catch the last ten minutes of her interview, in which she was promoting her new book.

I promptly hid the tape under my bed. My parents could never quite work out what happened to 'Tape 7' of our video collection.

That television interview was my information. Up until that point I had no answers for why and how I felt the way I did.

Getting a copy of Cossey's book became almost an obsession. Not being able to pay the £12.99 for the book from WHSmith, I visited my local library, asking almost weekly whether *My Story* by Caroline Cossey had arrived yet. Eventually, after six months, it came. I'm sure that for a good year no one else got the chance to borrow it. To me back then it was my equivalent of Google, and the start of my journey to womanhood.

I would read the book every night before sleep, then hide it under my bed with 'Tape 7' – it made me feel less alone. That's something which ninety-year-old Patricia must have felt in recent times, due to the conversation which is finally being had by the general public.

As a mid-seventies baby, growing up during the eighties, surrounded by picket lines of miners on strike, survival was something that was deeply ingrained within me. I shudder to think what would have happened had I got caught on the odd Saturday night, when I would walk around our block on the council estate where I grew up, fully dressed in my mother's clothes. But I didn't care. It wasn't enough just parading up and down my parents' bedroom – I had to be 'outside', free of the constraints of our house.

These were the first tentative steps towards the emergence of my true self. Looking back now, as I write, it seems on one hand a lifetime ago but, on the other, only yesterday.

When I announced my transition, I was asked by many of my friends if I would be moving from my home town of Barnsley in Yorkshire.

'Whatever for?' I would say.

'Because, well... you know... people won't accept you there. You need to move back to London, where it's more cosmopolitan.'

There was no way I was leaving home – not yet anyway. I knew by being a public figure I could help start a conversation, which in turn would help educate people once they heard or read my story. People underestimate Barnsley folk as small-minded and bigoted. They couldn't be more wrong. One month after I'd transitioned the local council honoured my engagement to switch on the town's Christmas lights for an audience of 15,000 people. By doing so they helped draw a line in the sand to the people of the town, saying, 'Steph is one of us and we accept her for who she really is.'

Things had changed. I was hugged in the street. Flowers arrived at my house. Builders in the street would shout 'We're proud of you, Steph.' This was acceptance.

You see, we all feel the need to be accepted, loved and cherished.

Every single day we compare how others behave, judging them good or bad, right or wrong. Those who fit our personal ideology are accepted, while those who seem not to fit in are shunned, bullied, and in certain areas of the world maimed – even killed – for not conforming to society's 'normal' box.

But what is 'normal'?

All of us are different. It is the one thing that makes each and every one of us unique, no matter what our culture, sexuality or gender.

For the majority of us, when we are born we are cherished by our parents and families. We spend those first few formative years being unconditionally accepted. It is often not until school that we find our first experience of non-acceptance. Here is where we forge friendships and form our social skills, learning to find our level in life, which will go on to either help or hinder us during our time on earth. I most certainly wasn't accepted by everyone during my schooling. Seen as effeminate and attention-seeking, I was pretty much doomed during my time in the tough Barnsley schools I attended.

At home though, I felt warmth and love, away from the outside world's preconceptions and judgements.

Every night, just praying that the boy's body I was born with would one day develop into a woman's gave me naive hope as a child. But once reality hit, the years of inner torment and denial followed. At least I was blessed with a distraction…

From the moment my father sat me down in front of our seventies Fidelity radio (which at that very point was playing Queen's 'Bohemian Rhapsody'), I was instantly captivated by this thing called 'radio' – and, of course, the groundbreaking song it was playing.

Radio was different. It was like a club where everyone was welcome, no matter where you were from or who you were. I needed to be in that club, inside that radio, the voice that people heard.

My parents believed in their heart of hearts that if their only child was happy creating their own radio shows in their bedroom, who were they to argue? It was the escapism I needed to get away from the gender dysphoria, along with the continuing bullying and beatings I got at school.

But clearly I needed to be heard. Maybe that's why I love the medium of radio so much: it creates a one-to-one connection. Just you and me.

Joining my local radio station as a 'general dogsbody' – otherwise known as 'helper' – the acceptance I got from my childhood radio heroes was unbelievable to me. On the one hand I'd got my peer group at school, who clearly were judging the book by its cover. On the other hand there was this group of professional broadcasters who saw a glimmer of talent in me, and wanted to nurture and grow it. I'd been accepted somewhere at last, and it felt amazing.

Acceptance is an emotion that I wish could be used more, but I believe we are on the right track.

Years before I changed my gender, people who had the strength to transition were shunned, 'outed' by the press, deemed unemployable and were pretty much the bottom rung of the ladder for acceptance on the LGBT spectrum.

I, on the other hand, to the outside world, had male privilege – I was at the top of my chosen field in radio and had been accepted within the circle of my generation's well-respected broadcasters. I wasn't aware of this at the time, of course. It was pointed out to me by many people after I (as I like to put it) 'blew my life up' – because it had got to a point where suicide was an option.

It literally was death or transition.

So I made one of those 'pros and cons' lists.

To possibly lose:

My life, or my relationship, my career, my friends, my bank balance, my home, pretty much everything I'd ever worked for.

To gain:

Authenticity – I was willing to let go of who I thought I should be, in order to be who I truly was.

Imagine having to be the opposite gender for the rest of your life from now on. It would feel wrong to you, wouldn't it?

Well, that's how I felt every single day of my life until I transitioned to my natural state of comfortableness. As a woman.

Although the journey was long and arduous, the thing that changed it all for me was having the Internet at home. Connecting that 56k modem into the phone socket on the wall in 1998... hearing the sound of the dialling tone... then to be greeted by Netscape Navigator, which took me to the search engine Ask Jeeves (long before I discovered Google!), where I typed the now dated word 'transsexual'.

I was presented with varying degrees of information. The first links from search engines in those days were to adult-themed pages, but then I would go on to discover a number of sites over the years like urnotalone.com. Information and support sites like these opened up a new world to me. I felt safe and secure in the knowledge that I was most certainly not alone. Once my bedroom door was closed, late at night, I spent hours searching the net for information.

Late one night I found a site called Kim Angel, run by a trans woman who was in the early stages of self-discovery. Looking at her page and clicking through the photo galleries shown on my large cream fifteen-inch LCD monitor, I felt a connection with this person.

I saw a 'contact' tab, so I sent a message to her. This felt scary.

I remember the next day, pressing the F5 button on my keyboard to keep checking my Freeserve email account. After a couple of days, she replied.

This turned out to be a connection of a lifetime. Although she was much further ahead in her transition than I was at that point, she was one of the key people who helped me find my true self. In part, that's thanks to the Internet.

The Internet has made us feel less alone. Yes, it can also be blamed for lots of bad in this world, but the amount of good it's given us is unreal – connecting those who feel alone, both young and old, and giving them someone to talk to.

A quick search on the social media photo site Instagram and you'll find thousands and thousands of people who identify on the trans spectrum. I can't imagine how much that would have helped me. I guess I might have had the strength to transition many years earlier, as so many more young people are doing now.

It really is so wonderful to see how far we have come. Writing these words in mid-2017, I feel like the landscape is finally changing. Yes, there is still a way to go, but I believe there has been a genuine societal shift in understanding the fluidity of gender and the complexity of how brains form in the womb.

This is because a conversation has been started – be it by the openly trans person in a community, or people like Caitlyn Jenner, Kellie Maloney and myself, who were and still are professionally in the public eye. This causes the media to report these stories and request interviews. They know that, whether it's print or broadcast, the public will (for now) show interest and fascination. But they also know now that we, the interviewees, will hold them accountable, for instance by requesting to proofread an item before it goes out. This makes sure no shifty business is undertaken, and ensures that a piece won't be an anti-trans stitch-up.

I also find that society is more open to speaking about feelings than previous generations. My grandparents would never talk of any such thing. Even my parents – born in the late forties and early fifties in the baby boom generation – weren't totally comfortable speaking about their feelings.

As I grew up in the nineties, however, we started to share our feelings more. That has led us to 'Generation Z', who are growing up with the normality of people of all genders, sexuality and ethnic backgrounds. This new generation will see fluidity in all people, and look back in total horror at how trans people were discriminated against during the late twentieth and early twenty-first century.

This fills me with absolute joy. Twenty years from now will be a completely different landscape and, by the way things are shifting, it will be much easier for those who question their gender identity.

So my message to them, and to everyone, is this: always have the courage to be yourself.

I love the person I've become, because I fought to be her.

FURTHER READING

Biography and Autobiography

Addams, Calpernia, *Mark 947: A Life Shaped by God, Gender and Force of Will*, Writers Club Press, 2003

Ashley, April and Fallowell, Duncan, *April Ashley's Odyssey*, Jonathan Cape, 1982

Baker, Sarah Jane, *Transgender Behind Prison Walls*, Waterside, 2017

Bertie, Alex, *Trans Mission: My Quest to a Beard*, Wren and Rook, 2017

Boylan, Jennifer Finney, *She's Not There: A Life in Two Genders*, Broadway, 2004

Cossey, Caroline, *My Story*, Faber & Faber, 1992

Grant, Julia, *George & Julia*, New English Library / Times Mirror, 1980

Green, Jamison, *Becoming a Visible Man*, Vanderbilt University Press, 2004

Hewitt, Paul, *A Self-Made Man*, Trafalgar Square, 1997

Hodgkinson, Liz, *From a Girl to a Man*, Quartet, 2015

Jacques, Juliet, Trans: *A Memoir*, Verso, 2015

Kiss, Charlie, *A New Man*, Matador, 2017

Mock, Janet, *Redefining Realness: My Path to Womanhood, Identity, Love & So Much More*, Atria, 2014

Morris, Jan, *Conundrum*, Faber & Faber (Hardback), 1974

Nelson, Maggie, *The Argonauts*, Graywolf, 2015

O'Keefe, Tracie and Fox, Katrina, *Finding the Real Me: True Tales of Sex and Gender Diversity*, Jossey Bass, 2003

Paige, Caroline, *True Colours: My Life as the First Openly Transgender Officer in the British Armed Forces*, Biteback, 2017

Rees, Mark, *Dear Sir or Madam*, Cassell, 1996 (revised 2009)

Styles, Rhyannon, *The New Girl*, Headline, 2017

Thompson, Raymond and Sewell, Kitty, *What Took You So Long?*, Penguin, 1995

Social and Activist History

Ackroyd, Peter, *Dressing Up*, Thames and Hudson, 1979

Baker, Roger, Drag: *A History of Female Impersonation in the Performing Arts*, New York University Press, 1995

Burns, Christine, *Pressing Matters: A Trans Activism Memoir*, Self published (Kindle and ePub), 2013 (Vol 1) and 2014 (Vol 2)

Feinberg, Leslie, Transgender *Warriors : Making History from Joan of Arc to Dennis Rodman*, Beacon, 1996

Kirk, Kris and Heath, Ed, *Men in Frocks*, Gay Men's Press, 1984

Stryker, Susan, *Transgender History*, Seal, 2008

Gender in Theory and Practice

Bornstein, Kate, *Gender Outlaw: On Men, Women and the Rest of Us*, Vintage, 1994

Califia, Patrick, *Sex Changes: The Politics of Transgenderism*, Cleis, 1997

Dawson, Juno, *The Gender Games: The Problem With Men and Women... From Someone Who Has Been Both*, Two Roads (John Murray), 2017

Erickson-Schroth, Laura; Jacobs, Laura, *You're In The Wrong Bathroom: And 20 Other Myths and Misconceptions About*

Transgender and Gender-Nonconforming People, Beacon, 2017

Iantaffi, Alex; Barker, Meg-John, *How to Understand Your Gender: A Practical Guide For Exploring Who You Are*, Jessica Kingsley, 2017

Lester, CN, *Trans Like Me: A Journey for All of Us*, Virago, 2017

Nestle, Joan et al, *GenderQueer: Voices From Beyond the Sexual Binary*, Alyson, 2002

Queen, Carol and Schimel, Lawrence, PoMoSexuals: *Challenging Assumptions About Gender and Sexuality*, Cleis, 1997

Richards, Christina; Boumann, Walter; and Barker, Meg-John (eds), *Genderqueer and Non-Binary Genders*, Palgrave MacMillan, 2017

Serano, Julia, *Whipping Girl: A Transsexual Woman on Sexism and the Scapegoating of Femininity*, Seal, 2007

Serano, Julia, *Excluded*, Seal, 2013

Stryker, Susan, *The Transgender Studies Reader*, Routledge, 2003

Whittle, Stephen, *Respect and Equality: Transsexual and Transgender Rights*, Routledge, 2002

Anti-Trans Polemic

Greer, Germaine, *The Whole Woman*, Doubleday, 1999

Jeffreys, Sheila, *Gender Hurts: A Feminist Analysis of the Politics of Transgenderism*, Rutledge, 2013

Raymond, Janice, *The Transsexual Empire: The Making of the She-Male*, Beacon, 1979

Fiction

Brown, Geoff, *I Want What I Want*, Panther, 1966

Feinberg, Leslie, *Stone Butch Blues*, Alyson, 1993

Education and Guidance

Beardsley, Christina and O'Brien, Michelle, *This Is My Body: Hearing the Theology of Transgender Christians*, Darton, Longman & Todd, 2016

Bridgman, Shelley, *Stand-Up for Yourself: and become the hero or shero you were born to be*, Stand-Up Publishing, 2014

Craggs, Charlie, *To My Trans Sisters*, Jessica Kingsley, 2018

Dowd, Chris and Beardsley, Christina, *Transfaith: A Transgender Pastoral Resource*, Darton, Longman & Todd, 2017

Fine, Cordelia, *Testosterone Rex: Myths of Sex, Science, and Society*, W. W. Norton & Co., 2017

Green, Jo, *The Trans Partner Handbook*, Jessica Kingsley, 2017

Henry, Declan, *Trans Voices: Becoming Who You Are*, Jessica Kingsley, 2017

Herthel, Jessica and Jennings, *Jazz, I am Jazz*, Dial, 2014

Hines, Sally, *TransForming gender: Transgender practices of identity, intimacy and care*, Policy Press, 2007

Iantaffi, Alex and Barker, Meg-John, *How to Understand Your Gender: A Practical Guide for Exploring Who You Are*, Jessica Kingsley, 2017

Kermode, Jennie, *Transgender Employees in the Workplace: A Guide for Employers*, Jessica Kingsley, 2018

Mills, Matthew and Stoneham, Gillie, *The Voice Book for Trans and Non-Binary People: A Practical Guide to Creating and Sustaining Authentic Voice and Communication*, Jessica Kingsley, 2017

Savage, Sarah and Fisher, Fox, *Are You a Boy or Are You a Girl?*, TQUAL, 2015

ACKNOWLEDGEMENTS

Trans Britain began life in a series of instant messenger exchanges in September 2016, between myself and former *Independent on Sunday* Literary Editor and 'Rainbow List' project manager, Katy Guest, who was about to join Unbound as their New Projects Editor. Katy already knew the *Pressing Matters* books I had self-published, charting the insider history of the trans rights campaign Press for Change, and it was she who suggested that there was a genuine need for something to address the mistaken idea that 'trans' was something new and faddish. Over the months that followed the idea took shape, as I sketched the structure and considered possible ways to tell such a big story, crossing several generations and with so few documentary sources. A curated series of eye-witness recollections was the natural solution in the end and the three part structure emerged from the material. Katy was there at every step, as a sounding board, mentor and cheerleader, encouraging me to persist with the idea. It was through these discussions that we decided to approach the project as an edited anthology, and it was with Katy's help that I gradually put together the proposal for what we would go on to pitch to everyone. Throughout the process – even after her colleagues at Unbound took over the successfully funded project to see it through writing, editing, and production – Katy has been there to encourage me. This is the first new book among her first commissions to reach publication, so I think it's as special to her as it is to me and all the contributors.

Anna Simpson, Unbound's Head of Editorial, also deserves an honorary mention, taking me under her expert wing even as I was still piecing the manuscript together, and guiding me through the complicated process of turning a manuscript into a book that is a true thing of beauty. As an author who has

357

self-published several titles on her own before, and written material for others to publish, I had never appreciated the order of magnitude of difference in quality control and attention to detail. If you enjoy the look and feel of this book and its quality then Anna is the expert craftswoman to thank.

Next, it would be remiss if I didn't mention the contributors, all of whom displayed remarkable patience and enthusiasm through the process of drafting and editing. Thanks also to those who helped some of our contributors with their fact checking and words – some chapters were very much team efforts, I know.

Long before any words were written it was apparent how many trans people and their allies wanted to help. The hundreds of people who pledged support during the heady six weeks of crowdfunding the publishing costs have their own roll of honour – for ever included in these pages – but I would like to give special mention to the many enthusiasts who volunteered to provide photos, scanned images, recordings and documents from their personal collections: Dawn Wyvern, Jed Bland, Tania Jane Taylor, Simon Croft, Lee Gale, Gloria Mardi Gras, Sally Payne and David Willis. If I've omitted anyone from that list then my apologies.

Thanks are also due to many who, even if they didn't end up in the manuscript, contributed useful ideas and discussions on topics I could maybe consider. They include Jay Hayes-Light, Michael Hydes, Claire McNab and Louis Bailey. Thanks to Tracie O'Keefe and Anna May Booth for quotable recollections, plus Jenny Anne Bishop, Alice Purnell, Linda Bellos and Susie Green for conversations and written material that all helped greatly.

Last but not least, a special thank you to my daughter Ellie, who has seen far less of me than usual this year, especially as the pace hotted up, and my grandchildren Harvey, Daisy and Arthur, who will now be getting their Granny back.

Christine Burns
Manchester, October 2017

INDEX

Abbott, Diane, 183
About Ray, 212, 215
Ace Ventura, 207–8
Ackroyd, Peter, 8
Action for Biblical Witness to Our
    Nation, 107
Action for Trans Health, 302
Adeyeye, Modupe, 213
Against Me!, 101
Albany Trust, 54
All About Trans, 92, 202, 213, 254, 260,
    302, 322, 328, 330
Allison, Becky, 305
Almada, Nadia, 251
American Psychiatric Association,
    *Diagnostic and Statistical Manual of
    Mental Disorders* (DSM), 59, 299
Anderson, Adele, 208
Anderton, James, 25
Anohni, 101
aristocracy, trans people and, 15–16
Arran, Lord, 218
artificial insemination, 148
Ashley, April, 2–3, 16–17, 23, 25, 36, 52,
    54, 59, 103, 206, 318
    see also Corbett v Corbett
Aston, Laura, 235–7
Atkin, Victoria, 213
aversion therapy, 46
    see also 'conversion therapy'

Baker, Roger, 106
Banana, 213
Banks, Tony, 224
Barker, Jason, 287
Barker, Meg-John, 259, 292–303
Barker, Colonel Sir Victor, 13
Barnsley, 346–7
Barrett, James, 55–6, 58, 63, 66, 185
Barry, James, 11
'bathroom bills', 4, 215, 310
Bauhaus, 98
Baxter, Stanley, 38
Beardsley, Rev. Christina, 38, 102–15
Beaumont, Lord, 169
Beaumont Society, 11, 29–32, 35, 72–3,
    91, 119, 122, 249

Beaumont Trust, 31, 37, 122
Belcher, Helen, 6, 133, 141, 201, 252,
    254, 317–28
Bellinger, Liz, 178
Bem, Sandra, 296
Benjamin, Harry, 47, 54, 56, 58
Benjamin, Victoria, 275
Beyer, Georgina, 3, 7
Beyond the Binary magazine, 292, 294,
    299–302
Bible, the, 44, 113
Biggs, Jaden, 271, 274–5
Billions, 303
Bindel, Julie, 200–1, 307–8, 312, 314–16,
    325
birth certificates, 15–16, 18, 81, 135, 139,
    159, 178–9, 200, 280
Bishop, Jenny-Anne, 319
Bitch, 309
Black, Bethany, 213
Blair, Cherie, 131
Blair, Tony, 152, 173, 183–4
Blake, Nick, 140–2
Blanchard, Dr, 326
Bland, Jed, 122
Bogoraz, Vladimir, 9
Bornstein, Kate, 287, 296
Bowie, David, 96–8, 189
Boy George, 95, 97
Boy Meets Girl, 6, 213, 215, 327
Boys Don't Cry, 211
brain research, and gender, 172, 283–4
Branch, Margaret, 54
Bray, Alberta, 14
Bridgman, Michelle, 307
British Association of Gender Identity
    Specialists (BAGIS), 66
British Monomarks, 31
British Psychological Society, 292
Broadmoor, 66
Brooker, Will, 105
Brothers, Emily, 6
Brown, Geoff, 103
Brown, Gordon, 173
Brown, Sarah, 258, 304–16
Burchill, Julie, 201, 324
Burgess, David, 140–3, 159

Unbound is the world's first crowdfunding publisher, established in 2011.

We believe that wonderful things can happen when you clear a path for people who share a passion. That's why we've built a platform that brings together readers and authors to crowdfund books they believe in – and give fresh ideas that don't fit the traditional mould the chance they deserve.

This book is in your hands because readers made it possible. Everyone who pledged their support is listed below. Join them by visiting unbound.com and supporting a book today.

Super friend
Lynn Conway

Supporters
Tabitha Adams
Shahnaz Ali
Robert Allfree
Adele Anderson
andykisaragi
Y. Gavriel Ansara
Martin Archer
Tony Arnold
Amy Ash
Richard Ashcroft
Claire Askew
Laurie Atkinson
Alana Avery
Jorge Azevedo
Carina Badger
A C Baker
Catherine Baker
Daf Baker
Léne Ballantyne

Alex Barasch
Stuart Barette
Sophie Barker
Addison Barnett
James Barrett
Barrow Cadbury Trust
Louise Barry
Theresa (Tree) Bartram
Val Bayliss-Brideaux
Richard Beard
Chritsina Beardsley
James Bellringer
Alison Bender
Laura Beynon
Kimberley Bird
Juliet Birkbeck
Katie Birkwood
Rachel Bishop-Firth
Kris Black
Sue Black
Jed Bland
Chip Blank
Susan Bloomfield

Tim Boden
Judith Bolton
Stephen Bonnlander
Charles Boot
Anna May Booth
Kate Bornstein
Walter Pierre Bouman
Sarah Bourke
Claire Bow
Stephanie Boyd
Julie Bozza
Thea Bradbury
Bridget Bradshaw
Robin Bray
Becky Brookes
Theresa Brooks
Hannah Brooks-Lane
Alexandria Brown
Jennifer Brown
Mark Brown
Sarah Brown
John Browne & Dr J E Goldring
Matt Buck
Evan Buckley
Gareth Burgess
Nicky Burr
Paul Burston
Cat Burton
Kim Burton
Chris Busby
Virginie Busette
Olivia Butterworth
Al Byrne
Naomi Byrne
Conor Byworth
Alex C
Clare Cahill
Serena Calderisi
Michael Cashman
Elaine Chambers
Liz Chapman
KJ Charles
Laura Charlton
Anna Chivers
Alex Clare
Charlotte Clark

Ken Clarke
Helz Clavering
Daniel Clayton
Laura Clements
Christine Clifford
Gemma Clutterham
Thea Cochrane
Alex Coles
Elizabeth Cook
Trevor Cook
Ali Cooley - Transography
Kai Craven
Simon Croft
Sheila Crosby
Pam Crossland
Tamsin Crossland
Helen Dale
Sue Daniels
Ingrid Davidson
Beth Davies
Dominic Davies
Theresa Davis
Liz Day
Paulette de Coriolis
Stephanie De la Haye
Sara de Virion
Donna Dee
Trisha Dee
Judith Elizabeth Dene
Grant Denkinson
Alison Devlin
Paul Devlin
Aaron Devor
Willow Digweed
Sarah Ditum
Sam Dodsworth
Claire Baker Donnelly
John Donnelly
Karen Duffin
Martha Dunkley
Charles Dunne
Graham and Chris Dyson
Alys Earl
Elisabeth Ek
Amy Elgar
Chris Elliott

Michele Farmer
Finbarr Farragher
Sam Feeney
Arlene Finnigan
Beck Firth
Jamie Fletcher
Molly Fletcher
Kim Foale
Alex Forshaw
Teresa Fowler
Rebecca Fox
Ashley Francis-Roy
D Franklin
Natasha Franklin
Jerilyn Franz
Lin Fraser
Ian Fryer
Jana Funke
Amy Gadd
Lee Gale
Abigail Gallagher
Lyman Gamberton
James Gardiner
Pamela Gawler-Wright
Gendered Intelligence
Jan Gerhards
Andrea Gertig-Hadaschik
Susan Gilchrist
Andrew Gilliver
Helen Gilroy
Tania Glyde
Nick Golding
Chloe Goodchild
Vicky-Jane Gooding
Chad Gowler
Rachael Sarah Graham
Sarah Graham
Theo Graham
Elizabeth Grant-Stone
David Gray
DK Green
Jamison Green
Sophie Green
Beverley Grover
Dani Grover
Pete Grys

Katy Guest
Kevin Gumienny
Keegan Hall-Browne
Rory Harden
Clay Harris
Dominic Harrison
Dr J Harrison
Joanne Elizabeth Harrison
Toni Harrison
Christie Havers
Georgiah Havers
Krystyna Haywood
Paul Head
Andrew Heining
Bethan Henshaw
Kevin Henson
Thomas Hescott
Julie Hesmondhalgh
Philip Hewitt
Kit Heyam
Ford Hickson
Claire Higgins
Clive Hills
Charlie Hindley
Robert Hoare
Ellayn Hodgson
Matthew Hodson
Rupert Holderness
Ayla Holdom
James Holland
Max Hopkinson
H Howitt
Ashes Howson
Nick Hubble
Deborah Hudson
Doug Hudson
Joanna Hughes
Kim Hulme
Rhi Humphrey
Suzanna-Claire Hunter
Ash Hutchison
Sara Huws
Chris Inglefield
Robert Ingram
Jo Inkpin
Jay Jackson

Sarah Jackson
Emma Jacobs
Kim James
E Jaszczak
Jamie Jaxon
Siân Jay
Mike Jempson
Marjorie Johns
Lynne Jones
Mike Jones
Jay Keeler
Cas Kemp
Natacha Kennedy
Nick Kerigan
Matthew Keyes
Ash Khan
Dan Kieran
Heather Kincaid
Patrick Kincaid
Zoe Kirk-Robinson
Charlie Kiss
Surat-Shaan Knan
Lotta Knutar
Anja Komatar
Pierre L'Allier
Rowan Langley
S. Langsdale
Jessica Lauren
Clair Le Couteur
Paris Lees
Jessica Lempp
CN Lester
Louise Lever
Helen Lewis
Susan Lewis
Sandra Lezinsky
LGBT Foundation
Isla Lim
Jessica Litherland
Dee Livesey
LJ
George Lockley
Cassian Lodge
Neil Loffhagen
Sarennah Longworth-Cook
Edward Lord OBE

Dr Stuart Lorimer
Kelly Luck
Samuel Ludford
David Ludlow
Lucas Lundgren
Ciaran Lucas MacDonald
Shona MacKinnon
Catrinoa Siobhan Mackley
Tara MacLachlan
Catherine Makin
Rachel Mann
Dru Marland
Emma Marlow
Evelyn Marr
Rebecca Marsh
Laura Marshall
Robert Marshall
Paul Martin
Mel Mason
Brian Matthews
Elizabeth Matthews
Kathryn Maude
Louise McCudden
Jane McKay
Helen McKenna-Aspell
Ian McNally
Jay McNeil
Ellen Mellor
Carolyn Mercer
Dave Merchant
Alex Merry
Veronica Merryfield
Anna-Jayne Metcalfe
Andy Midwinter
Margo Milne
Rosalind Mitchell
John Mitchinson
Lucy Moffatt
Adam Moliver
Monty Moncrieff
Harriet Monkhouse
Claire Mooney
Christy Moore
Cheryl Morgan
Jakki Morgan
Evan Mortimer

James Morton
Ada Mournian
Bryn Musson
Anwen Muston
Michael Nastari
Chandra Nauth-Misir
Carlo Navato
Kate Newsome
Carol Nixon
Sharon Nolan
Robyn Norfolk
Una Nowling
Lynette Nusbacher
Katherine O'Donnell
Aisling O'Neill
Rachel Oakes
Moose D Ofdensen
Stephen Ogden
Aimee Oliver
Laura Orchard
Fiz Osborne
Florence Oulds
Ember Overal
Kerry Pace
Zoe Palmer
George Parapadakis
Steph Parker
Andie Pas de Deux
Robert Patterson
Sally Payne
Mike Pennell
Laurie Penny
penwing
Inclusive Peterborough
Trevor Phillips
Alex Pilcher
Lisa Pinney
Julia Platt
Justin Pollard
Eleanor Pool
Lucy Porter
Dan Poxton
Mat Price
Philippa Punchard
Glenn Rainey
Clavain Ramsden

Sophie Rebecca
Rachel Reese
Paige Reeves
Remembering O
Adele Retter
Gabrielle Basso Ricci
Jennifer Richardson
Jo Richardson
Elizabeth Rimmington
Robert Rinder
Tom Rini
Samuel Harry Benjamin Roberts
Victoria Roberts
AJ Robinson
Charlotte Robinson
John Robinson
Marc Robinson
Brandon Robshaw
Juno Roche
Gary Rolfe
Kate Rose
Quentin Rothammer
Jessica Rowbottom
Joanna Rowland-Stuart
Dean Royles
Joanna Russell
Sue Sanders
Alex Sanderson-Shortt
Ranjit Sanghera
Michalis Sanidas
Lucy Schaufer
Caroline Scott
E-J Scott
Stephanie Scott
Jo Seabrook
Lynsey Searle
Seren
Lisa Severn
Charlie Sharp
Josephine Shaw
Sean Sheehy
Karen Shiels
Matilda Simon
Carla Skinner
Caroline Smale
Gerard Smith

Balbir K Sohal
Claire Solanki
Andrew Stanley
Carol Steele
Kat Steiner
Sue Stelfox
Kirsty Stevenson
Dr Kayte Stokoe
Lois Stone
Vivienne Stone
Diane Strickland
Kate Sutton
Anne Sweeney
Jean T
Jonathan Tait
Ashleigh Talbot
Phil Taprogge
Alex Taylor
Sahra Taylor
The Lipstick Thespians (Hayley
    & Alexis)
Mary Thewlis
Sue Thirsk
Beth-Jane Thomas
Ben Thwaite
Tibs
Toni Tingle
Nat Titman
Kai Pragnell Toal
Annie Tomkins
Michael Toze
Caroline Tresman
Jacqui Trowsdale
Lewis Turner

Tom Turner & Avery Delany
Wendy Tuxworth
Jos Twist
Delphine Undercover
Chris Vardy
Elizabeth Veldon
Emma Vickers
Oliver Waite
Julie Wall
Annie Wallace
Charlie Wand
Jessica Wardman
Laura Waters
Andy Watson
Wellcome Collection
Hannah Whelan
Francis Ray White
Margaret White
Andrew Whiteoak
Amanda Whittington
Ashley Williams
Jenny Williams
Jodi Winters
Gretchen Woelfle
Kim Wombles
Yvonne Wood
Robin Wren
Jackie Wright
Dawn Wyvern
Brandy Ybarra
Andrew Yelland
Eris Young
Jolene Young